PRISONGATE

PRISONGATE

THE SHOCKING STATE OF BRITAIN'S PRISONS
AND THE NEED FOR VISIONARY CHANGE

DAVID RAMSBOTHAM

Mark and Latricia,

with love and in admiration
of all that you do

David

October 2003.

FREE PRESS

First published in Great Britain by The Free Press, 2003
An imprint of Simon & Schuster UK Ltd
A Viacom Company

1 3 5 7 9 10 8 6 4 2

Simon & Schuster UK Ltd
Africa House
64–78 Kingsway
London WC2B 6AH

www.simonsays.co.uk

Simon & Schuster Australia
Sydney

A CIP catalogue record for this book is available from the British Library

ISBN 0-7432-3884-2

For my grandchildren, Charlotte, Sophie,
Matthew and Christopher

ACKNOWLEDGEMENTS

Why does anyone try to write a book in the first place, particularly one about prisons? In my case there were two main reasons. Firstly a number of people, particularly Lord Hurd of Westwell, formerly a distinguished Home Secretary, encouraged me to put down my thoughts on the future conduct of imprisonment at the end of my five and a half years as Her Majesty's Chief Inspector of Prisons.

While thinking about how to do this, never before having set out to write a book, I had the first of a number of strokes of good fortune that have surrounded the venture. Out of the blue I received a letter from Caroline Dawnay of PFD offering to be my agent if I ever thought of writing. From our first meeting I could not have asked for more interest, understanding or encouragement.

Caroline then made two other crucial introductions. Firstly Lisanne Radice, whose robust, clear and good-humoured comments were quite invaluable. Secondly Simon and Schuster UK, whose every member could not have been more welcoming or helpful to a newcomer to the publishing world. In particular I am grateful to Helen Gummer,

non-fiction publisher; Cassandra Campbell, non-fiction junior editor; Robyn Karney, copy editor; Hannah Corbett and Andrew Gordon.

Without their help I could not have satisfied my second reason. When I first entered the world of prisons and imprisonment I was struck immediately by a contradiction. On the one hand, prisons were serviced by a vast number of splendid people, whose amazing commitment to the cause of protecting the public, by helping prisoners to leave prison as more law abiding citizens than when they went in, I continue to admire. On the other, prisons, taken collectively, were failing to protect the public because too many prisoners re-offended after their release. The reason was immediately obvious. There was no penal strategy.

Throughout my time as Chief Inspector I tried to get this message across, basing it entirely on first-hand evidence gathered during prison inspections. I freely admit to feeling frustrated on my retirement that, despite all that we had demonstrated, I was joining the ranks of my predecessors – and many interested and concerned experts and analysts – whose similar efforts had also been ignored.

I therefore felt that, while my experience was still relevant, I owed two groups of people, who had helped me throughout my time, one last attempt to impress on the authorities the vital importance of a coherent strategy. Firstly, my marvellous team of inspectors who had gathered all the evidence, all of whom, if space allowed, I would like to have mentioned by name. If I single out my deputy, Colin Allen, it is because I believe that had his methods been adopted I would not be writing this book.

Secondly, all those who gave me so freely and generously of their expertise, advice and support. Again space only allows me to mention Lord Baker, Lord Bingham, Mary Blackburn, Professor Keith Bottomley, Sylvia Casale, Paul Cavadino, Paddy Costall, Dr Andrew Coyle, Frances Crook, Helen Edwards, Lord Elton, David Faulkner, Roger Graef, Dr Robert Hale, John Harding, Professor Richard Harding, Bishop Bob Hardy, Sir James Hennessy, Professor Roger Hood, Lord Hurd, Rob Hutchinson, Doctor Alison Liebling, Sir

ACKNOWLEDGEMENTS

Peter Lloyd, the late Lord Longford, Lord Marlesford, Peter Martin, Professor Sean McConville, Professor Rod Morgan, Tim Newell, Dr Sir Dennis Pereira-Gray, Colonel Trevor Philpott, Lord Justice Rose, Stephen Shaw, the late Sir Graham Smith, Baroness Stern, Sir Stephen Tumim, David Waplington, Lord Warner, Lord Windlesham, Vice Admiral Sir Peter Woodhead, Lord Woolf. There are countless others.

Which brings me to the person to whom I remain more grateful than to any other – my wife Sue. Throughout the time I have spent on the book she has been my sternest critic, tirelessly and ruthlessly eliminating anything that read like an inspection report. As I have done throughout 45 years of married life, I owe her more than words can say. I hope that 'thank you' says it all to her and the many others with whom I shared such an unforgettable period in my life.

CONTENTS

1

HMP HOLLOWAY,
13–14 DECEMBER 1995

'I have never seen anything so inhuman and disgusting as the way they treat women in Holloway.'

Holloway midwife, 14 December 1995

I WONDER HOW MANY PEOPLE, driving north up the Camden Road in London, have either thought about or know what goes on behind the high, windowless, red brick walls of Her Majesty's Prison Holloway that they pass on the left-hand side. I had not noticed, let alone been behind them, until just before 8 a.m. on the cold and frosty morning of Wednesday, 13 December 1995 when, as Her Majesty's newly appointed Chief Inspector of Prisons, I was driven to join my team of inspectors, who had begun their task at the prison two days before.

All I knew about Holloway was that it was the largest women's prison in the country where, it was said, the treatment of and conditions for prisoners had deteriorated sharply over the past nine months; so much so that the chairman of the prison's independent watchdog committee, its Board of Visitors, had taken the most unusual step of writing to express her concerns to the Home Secretary, Michael Howard. In particular she had drawn attention to the fact that the prison, forced to hold many more prisoners than its intended capacity,

was seriously overcrowded. Consequently, with insufficient staff to look after them, too many prisoners spent all day locked up in their cells, doing nothing. In short, all the symptoms that had lain behind the serious riots in Strangeways prison some five years before, when the nation had been transfixed for days by television pictures of prisoners shouting from the roof that they were steadily dismantling, were present. The chairman had pleaded, throughout those nine months, for urgent remedial action, but none had been taken.

I was told about this on my first day in office, thirteen days previously, by my admirable deputy, Colin Allen, himself a former governor of Holloway, who was to be a close friend and trusted mentor throughout the next five and a half years. I frequently blessed the day that he decided to marry a Hebridean and join the Prison Service rather than becoming a Roman Catholic priest. I did not know it then, but Colin had beaten a strike by prison staff, who disagreed with his proactive approach to the treatment of prisoners while he was governor. Now he brought his wisdom, experience, energy and, above all, humanity to his current role. His understanding of prisoners was widely known and deeply respected throughout the penal world and many members of the Prison Service sought his advice and guidance.

Almost the first thing Colin Allen said to me that first day was that I had to make an immediate decision about when we should carry out an unannounced inspection of Holloway. The situation that the Board of Visitors had disclosed to the Home Secretary had been confirmed by a number of other reliable witnesses who worked in, or had reason to visit, the prison. I suggested a week's delay so that I could at least meet the members of my Inspectorate and learn a little about the demands of the job to which I, an ex-soldier with no previous knowledge of prisons, had been appointed. The inspection would begin on Monday, 11 December.

As the car turned left off the Camden Road into the short access road to the prison, I noticed a considerable amount of rubbish in the

roadway and on the pavement. This immediately confirmed what the inspectors had reported, namely that the prison was very dirty. I wondered why prisoners could not be made to keep it clean.

The entrance road ended at two large, wooden, vehicle access doors. To their left was a large window, and a glass door through which I entered a reception area. Inside, and behind a glass screen that separated them from visitors, I could see a number of people in dark blue Prison Service jerseys. One was sitting at a desk beside a window under which I slid my brand new Home Office identity card, announcing myself as the Chief Inspector of Prisons. I said that I had come to join my inspection team and asked to be taken to them. Having entered my name in a large register, she asked if I wanted to draw a set of prison keys. I said that I didn't because I hoped to be taken round the prison, not have to make my own way.

I had no idea what I would find. I had been into two prisons during the previous week and found them to be utterly different in design. However, in each of them, having passed through the reception procedures, I had been taken into the prison compound, consisting of a number of different buildings including one called 'administration' in which the governor had his office.

Holloway had been rebuilt in the 1980s on the site of an old prison that had been there since 1852. Colin had warned me that it was like no other and how right he was. Instead of going into the prison I was led to an electrically operated glass door-lock through which all entry and exit was controlled. Once through, I was ushered into a lift that took me to the top floor of what I was told was the administrative area. So far, other than uniformed officers, there was nothing to suggest that I was in a prison – no gates or bars to unlock and what appeared to be a perfectly normal office environment. The only exception was the Statement of Purpose of the Prison Service, prominently displayed amongst the many notices on the walls near the lift. This declared that it was its duty to keep prisoners secure and treat them with humanity during the time that they had been committed

by the courts. In addition, prisoners were to be helped to live useful and law-abiding lives in prison and on release.

From the lift I was shown into what was called the Board Room, where I found inspection team Omega, led by Tony Wood, a small, bearded, wiry and alert Yorkshireman who appeared to choose every word he used with some care. I had met him briefly during the previous week when discussing my part in the inspection and liked his approach, realising that he was a terrier for detail. Before joining the Inspectorate a few months earlier, he had governed Camp Hill prison on the Isle of Wight. Because Holloway was such a large and complicated prison, Rod Jacques, the leader of the other inspection team, Alpha, had joined Tony Wood. Rod, a tall, angular, bespectacled son of a clergyman, had also only recently joined the Inspectorate after governing Liverpool, the largest prison in the country. Over the months and years ahead, I would come increasingly to appreciate the unique combination of wisdom, humour and compassion that he brought to his task. The Omega team itself consisted of two permanent inspectors, Jim Phillips – a junior Prison Service governor – and Ted Hornblow – an experienced Prison Service administrator. Friends, who liked working together, each was responsible for inspecting particular aspects of a prison such as the way accommodation wings were run, or the quality of prisoner documentation. Each had been with the Inspectorate for some time and knew what was expected of them.

The team was augmented by a number of consultants. Immediately present was John Stephenson, a large, bearded, ex-inspector of schools and an English international clay-pigeon shot, who inspected education and work training. He too had been with the Inspectorate for some time and also chose his words with care. Later, the chief medical inspector, Malcolm Faulk, a delightful, quietly spoken psychiatrist, and the nursing inspector, Maggie Lyne, a large, ebullient, theatrically dressed Irishwoman, joined us. All were united in their distress at what they had seen over the past two days.

The story that they told me during the next hour and a half was

almost unbelievable. They had investigated all the concerns expressed by the chairman of the Board of Visitors and found them to be entirely justified and extremely accurately presented. Quite reasonably, they were puzzled as to why neither ministers nor the Prison Service appeared to have investigated or responded to them. The team's immediate conclusion was that they had never seen a worse situation during their time in the Prison Service and did not know what to do about it.

Like me, the inspectors had been struck immediately by the filthy state of Holloway. Prisoners had thrown food, clothing, sanitary towels and other rubbish out of their cell windows, where they lay on the ground for days. But uncleared rubbish was not confined to the out-side – corridors, stairwells, lavatories and washing areas were all dirty. Every inspector had seen either rats or cockroaches or both. Because the prison had been told that I was joining the inspection on Wednesday, skips had been brought in the previous evening, towards which women had been seen scurrying with plastic bags full of rub-bish. This charade accentuated the folly of not allowing prisoners out of their cells to keep the prison clean. Moreover, the inspection team had photographed what they had found on arrival.

As happened at the start of every inspection, the team had been briefed by the governor. Individual inspectors then met with groups of prisoners, selected at random from different parts of the prison. All groups had had similar stories to tell.

When prisoners first arrived they were given very little information about the routine, which they had to pick up from other inmates. Little attempt was made to discover, or help given to resolve, the newcomers' immediate problems, many of which were domestic to do with their dependent children or the retention of their accommodation. Many had children who were now either in care or with relatives or friends, or, at worst, left alone. As a result of a recent government ruling, council or rent-assisted accomodation was likely to be removed from them if they were away from it for more than 13 weeks. Chaos and dysfunction characterised their past; uncertainty coloured their future.

As far as their time in prison was concerned, few had had discussions on why they had offended, nor was any attempt made to tackle problems such as improving their education skills during the period of their sentence. None knew until the last moment when or why they might be moved from Holloway to another prison. Crucially, there was absolutely no preparation for release at the end of a sentence.

In theory 140 of the 538 prisoners could attend education classes every day; in reality only 38 had done so on either of the days of the inspection. The reason given for the shortfall was a lack of sufficient staff to escort prisoners between their cells and the Education Centre. Shortage of staff was put forward by everyone in the prison – even prisoners themselves – as the main cause of prisoners spending most of every day in their cells, locked up and idle. The prison slang for this is 'banged up', a term that I was to hear over and over again from prisoners that day.

Staff shortage not only impacted on the routine of the prison but also, as the Board of Visitors reported, resulted in neglect of the normal day-to-day needs of prisoners. Meals were served at impossibly early hours – lunch between 11 and 11.15 a.m. and tea at 3.15 p.m., after which prisoners received nothing until breakfast at 7.30 the following morning. The periods of time in a day known as 'association', when they were allowed to be with other prisoners, were frequently cancelled, often at very short notice because it was said that there were not enough staff to supervise. This was a major cause of concern because association was the only opportunity for access to telephones, which allowed the women to maintain contact with their families. It was also the only time when they could have a bath or shower or otherwise attend to their personal hygiene.

The management structure of a prison is very similar to that of any other organisation. A nominated governor is in charge, assisted by a number of subordinates, each with specific responsibilities. For example, there will be a head of prisoner activities and a head of security. The inspectors felt that the Holloway management team was weak in both capability and in experience of working with women. Prison

6

officers said quite openly that they felt let down by poor management – a major contributor to low staff morale, which, in turn,
contributed to poor treatment of prisoners.

One of the most obvious indicators of the attitude and competence
of a management team is the way in which requests and complaints
are handled. Prisoners often used official laid-down procedures requiring them to submit requests and complaints in writing, to which
management was required to reply within seven days. Almost invariably, however, and in defiance of procedure, prisoners in Holloway
either received no reply at all or had to wait for far longer than seven
days. The quality of managerial response was poor – dismissive or
unhelpful, with little explanation of why a particular line had been
taken. Prisoners could not point this out to managers because, from
the governor downward, they were rarely if ever seen around the
prison. How could managers possibly know what was, or was not,
going on in the prison if they never saw what was happening for
themselves, let alone be able to brief government ministers and Prison
Service Headquarters? Inspectors confirmed that management seemed
to be conducted largely by remote control.

The women in Holloway reported that they were subjected to a
considerable amount of physical and verbal bullying, both by staff
and other prisoners, but seldom complained because they did not
believe complaints against prison officers were taken seriously. The
numbers of prisoners who 'self-harmed' were also said to be alarmingly high. This referred to those who cut themselves with various
sorts of weapon, for a variety of reasons including lack of self-esteem,
hatred of themselves, and personal distress. While such action was not
often life-threatening, it was nonetheless salutary that many staff dismissed it as 'drawing attention to themselves'. The team advised me
that the extent of self-harming was a clear indication of the level of
misery prevailing in the prison population. Illegal drugs were said to
be freely available, while, at the same time, it was virtually impossible
to get treatment for substance abuse if you wanted it, and those from
ethnic minorities were discriminated against.

Security procedures were not good, and insufficient numbers of staff had been trained to use the official procedures and equipment required whenever a prisoner had to be controlled or restrained. As personal injuries could result in such situations, this was a serious deficiency. Excessive and unjustified intimate body-strip searches were carried out without management authority. This was a highly emotive subject, not only because of the degrading methods involved, but because they could be held to constitute an assault.

In sum, overcrowded Holloway was being badly managed. Little or nothing was being done beyond containing prisoners, who were not treated in accordance with the rules. Worst of all, neither government ministers nor Prison Service Headquarters appeared to have made any plans to rectify the situation.

Holloway had been designed as both a mental hospital and a prison, and both had to be inspected. My medical inspectors described the medical centre quite simply as a disaster area, quoting over 500 complaints put in by patients about their treatment. Again, there had been a resounding lack of response; again there was no evidence of leadership by managers.

Malcolm Faulk and Maggie Lyne made me aware, for the first time, of the very serious problem posed by the large numbers of mentally disordered people in prison. Many of these were so seriously disturbed that they had been sectioned under the Mental Health Act and ought to have been transferred to one of the NHS special hospitals such as Broadmoor. In addition, there were a number of others whom psychiatrists believed should not be in prison but in NHS secure units for the mentally ill. I now learned to my surprise that, alone in the country, the Prison Service was not part of the NHS but maintained its own independent Health Care Directorate. Although the numbers of mentally disordered prisoners were so high and included some who had already been in special hospitals, prison Health Care Centres were hopelessly under-staffed and ill-equipped to look after them. But, because NHS planning excluded the numbers of mentally disordered in prisons – estimated in an admirable but unactioned report by a Dr

John Reed, published in 1993, to require 500 beds per year – transfer was all too often painfully slow. As a result many of these mentally ill people had to wait months for transfer, during which time their condition often deteriorated through lack of suitable treatment.

Holloway also had a Mother and Baby Unit, in which mothers were allowed to keep babies born while they were in prison until they were nine months old. They did not have their babies in Holloway, but in the maternity unit at the nearby Whittington NHS Hospital, where special security arrangements were made. However, the conditions in the Mother and Baby Unit left much to be desired and I was advised that it was something that I should see.

Armed with all this information but somewhat stunned by it, I wondered how I should play my day. Should I challenge the Governor with what the team had told me and ask her to explain herself? Or should I keep quiet and let her show me her prison as I had originally intended, saying that, as this was my first visit to Holloway I was anxious to learn about it from her? I decided on the latter course.

And so, at 10 a.m., as previously arranged, Tony Wood took me to the governor's office, where he introduced me to Janet King. Stockily built and studious looking, she seemed more like a schoolteacher or bureaucrat than my expectation of a prison governor. Like many others, I suspect, I had been conditioned to expect someone more obviously authoritarian and – yes – military. The amount of paperwork around her large office gave an indication of what occupied most of her time. If it all had to be dealt with, it looked as if it would keep her at her desk for several days. Previously she had been deputy governor of the adult male Manchester prison in which the 1990 riots had taken place. I would have imagined that she, of all people, would have understood the point made by the Board of Visitors: that the current situation in Holloway mirrored that in Manchester in 1990. But she made no mention of that during any of our discussions.

The only thing that distinguished Ms King from being a bureaucrat was the black leather belt around her waist, with a black leather pouch

containing a set of prison keys secured to the belt by a long loop of silver chain. I had been issued with a similar belt, pouch and chain the week before when I went to HMP Belmarsh to be taught how to use keys properly. These had to be kept out of sight for obvious reasons, particularly when opening gates. In the past, keen-eyed prisoners had made copies of those that they had been able to observe because of careless use. Keys are kept in the pouch until needed and, once the type of key needed to open a lock is identified, it is selected from the bunch, the remainder being kept hidden in the hand.

After the usual introductions, I asked the governor to tell me exactly what was Holloway's role. She said that it did not have a specific role; it was primarily a local prison, which meant that it held unsentenced prisoners until they were tried in a local court. Other than preventing them – or any sentenced prisoner – from escaping, getting them to court on time, and complying with Prison Rules and operating instructions, she had been given no specific directive as to what Holloway was expected to achieve with and for any prisoner. What went on in the prison was entirely demand led, based on the numbers and types of prisoners who were sent there. Currently the demand was to hold 538 prisoners, sentenced and unsentenced, in a prison and with a staff designed to cater for 400.

The 538 included those with life or long-term sentences, as well as those serving medium and short terms; high-security, low-risk, and foreign national prisoners were kept there, together with those awaiting sentence, the mentally disordered, and even four 15-year-olds. I asked why these last had been sent to an adult prison and where they were held. She told me that she had been told to take them, acknowledging that child protection was a major issue but admitting that she did not know exactly where they were being held. I suggested that we try to find them during our tour of the prison.

The governor explained that policy for the treatment of women in prison, drawn up by civil servants at Prison Service Headquarters, came down to her in written form. If she needed advice or guidance she asked her area manager, who was responsible for line-managing all

prisons in North London and part of East Anglia. He had never worked in a women's prison and so was not a very useful source of practical advice, but there was no one else to ask because no one at Headquarters had overall operational responsibility for the oversight of women in prison. Her area manager allocated her budget and a great deal of her time was taken up with budgetary issues. Essentially, she did not have enough money with which to run the prison, but had to make do with what she had been given. She was constantly having to decide where to make cuts which, because 80 per cent of her budget went on inadequate staff numbers, invariably impacted on activities for prisoners.

As far as Holloway was concerned, the governor regretted that her own management team lacked the experience necessary for running such a complex prison, and that the inexorable rise in the size of its prisoner population over the past eight months had altered its pace of life unstoppably. Undoubtedly staff were feeling the strain caused by overcrowding, reflected most obviously in the amount of Time Off In Lieu (TOIL) that they were owed to compensate for extra duties worked. In March they had been owed, on average, 24 days; now that figure had gone up to between 80 and 100, which faced her with an impossible situation. The only ways in which the size of this millstone could be reduced – by allowing staff to take the days off that they were owed – would be to close the prison, which was impossible, or draft in temporary staff from other prisons, which would create similar problems elsewhere. To put this figure in perspective, she said that the maximum average of TOIL days owed that a governor could afford to live with was ten.

Janet King described the attitude of the Prison Service to both women's prisons and women prisoners as 'paternalistic'. After the recent escapes from Whitemoor and Parkhurst high security prisons, the Home Secretary had ordered a deliberate concentration on 'security, security, security', which had led to the introduction of many new rules and regulations that were very difficult to implement in an institution such as Holloway. I asked her how relevant such rules –

designed to prevent high-risk and dangerous adult males, including terrorists, from escaping – were for women prisoners, many of whom had not yet been convicted. She said that the same rules applied to all, while admitting that they were very staff intensive. For example, whenever a prisoner was admitted to hospital for any reason, including giving birth, nine prison officers had to mount a 24-hour 'bedwatch'. As six prisoners were currently in hospital, this meant that 54 members of staff were unavailable for normal daily duties.

I asked the governor to show me as much as possible of what she had told me as we walked around the prison together. In particular I would like to speak to both staff and prisoners. I left where we went, and in what order, up to her to decide.

At last I began to feel that I was in a prison. I was led down some stairs, along a short passage, and through a locked door. Behind this, instead of seeing a number of buildings, I found myself in a long, wide, empty corridor, blocked at intervals by metal barriers in the middle of which were locked, barred gates. The governor explained that this internal 'road' ran the whole length of the prison forming a central axis with separate side gates allowing access to different parts of the prison.

People had told me that prisons had a quite distinctive smell, but so far I had not experienced it in any of the three I had been into including Holloway. This was due, I was told, to the ending of 'slopping out' – the emptying of chamber pots in the morning – because all cells, or nearly all cells, now had integral sanitation. The men's cells that I had seen the previous week were little more than lavatories and I wondered whether any concessions were made for women, particularly in cells where two or more spent so much of the day locked up. However, the next five hours provided me with a kaleidoscope of impressions that left me appalled that any responsible minister, or official, could have allowed such treatment and conditions to be imposed on any of their fellow human beings. To ignore them was to send a message that those in authority found such a state of affairs acceptable.

This at once undermined the efforts of anyone, such as the Board of Visitors, who tried to do anything to improve matters.

Our first stop was the kitchen, where the self-confident catering manager, his white, aertex, trilby hat stuck at a jaunty angle, asked me whether I would like to taste lunch. When I said yes, a generous plate of hot and appetising chicken, covered with gravy and accompanied by roast potatoes and vegetables, was produced. He then asked if I would like to taste the vegetarian alternative, an equally acceptable nut cutlet. The inspection team told me later that the prisoners they saw had lukewarm and unappetising stew.

Having looked around the kitchen and spoken to some of the catering staff, I noticed a group of women wearing protective clothing. These, I was told, were prisoner kitchen orderlies, who could earn up to £10 per week for working there. I went over to talk to them, remembering Colin Allen's advice that, when speaking with women prisoners, you should be prepared to discuss generalities for two or three minutes before they felt confident enough to offer up any information. How right he was. After I had asked them about their duties and whether they had received any training, one of the women suddenly said that she had to work in the kitchen because that was the only way she could earn enough money to buy phone cards so that she could speak to her three children once a week. She told me that she lived in Falmouth and that her mother could not afford to bring them to visit her. Although Holloway was a long way away, she dreaded being moved to another prison, which might be even further from home and where she might not be able to get work. This could happen to anyone in Holloway without warning.

I turned to Janet King and asked her what a prisoner from Falmouth was doing in Holloway. She replied that what she described as Holloway's 'catchment area' totalled 240 courts, and that any unsentenced woman from anywhere in England south of the Wash was bound to be sent there before trial. This meant that when called to appear in court, they had to be taken there, daily, by cellular van. If the journey there and back was too long to be completed in a day, a prisoner would

be kept overnight in a police cell. She admitted that she often had to send what she called 'overcrowding drafts' of sentenced prisoners to other prisons, at very short notice, in order to accommodate new unsentenced prisoners who had to be held in Holloway.

In reception the first person I saw was a young, pregnant woman, in tears, sitting by herself in a small, dark room. I asked why she was there and why no one was with her. I was told that, although she had not yet been 'processed', she had been brought in from the van because she was both pregnant and distressed. However, no one could be spared to sit with her because there were not enough staff. The outside temperature that day was minus four, and I asked how many other women were still sitting in the van. I learned that there were six or seven, who could only be brought in one at a time because there was nowhere else to hold them until they had been processed. No exception could be made even during extreme weather conditions.

We walked past the empty gym on our way to the area where visits took place, and then to the segregation unit. As we moved along the 'road' we saw only a few other people, some of whom were in civilian clothes. The governor told me that these were probation officers, teachers or volunteer workers, who had some particular task to perform in the prison. I also noticed that, unlike the governor and all members of the inspection team including myself, no uniformed prison officer, male or female, was wearing a name badge. The governor explained that this was because the Prison Officers Association (POA), which was to figure prominently in my life over the next five and a half years, had refused to allow its members to wear them, allegedly for security reasons. This seemed odd to me as, in the army, one reason why we wore our names was to protect us from being mistaken for someone else. I wondered if it was because they felt that they had something to hide? Prisoners knew who they were anyway, because their colleagues referred to them by name.

There was no one in the Visits Centre, so observing that important activity had to be left for later. The segregation unit is the part of a prison that is used for the punishment of those who have broken

prison rules. In some institutions it is used also to hold prisoners who, for one reason or another, ask to be separated from the others for their own protection. It was grim and dark, with six dour-looking staff presiding over six locked doors on either side of a corridor. Beside each door, in the middle of which was a metal flap that staff could lift to see inside the cell through a small, glass panel, was a card giving the name of the occupant. I asked to talk to a woman who had been sent to the segregation unit for seven days for fighting.

The door was unlocked and I entered a tiny, bare cell, hardly longer than the six-inch high concrete plinth that passed for a bed, on which the prisoner had been lying before we entered, half covered by a blanket. The only furniture was a rather battered and unstable looking cardboard table and chair. There was no window worth the name, just a small, barred grille high up on one wall. On the wall opposite the plinth was a stained – albeit stainless steel – lavatory and washbasin. Other than the crumpled blankets on the plinth, the only other possessions that I could see were a book and a plastic mug.

The prisoner, all the time looking at the staff in the doorway, told me that she knew why she was there, and was being treated 'OK'. She said that while she was in segregation she had no access to education or the gym, nor did anyone come to discuss her offending behaviour. She was meant to have one hour's exercise in the fresh air every day, but did not always get it because Holloway was so short-staffed. She was able to get a shower, and saw the chaplain and the doctor or a nurse every day. She was also visited by members of the Board of Visitors but, other than that, was left alone except for meals.

The staff told me that there were always a number of women in the segregation unit, which was unusually empty at present. However, some prisoners were waiting for their crimes to be 'adjudicated' on that afternoon and they expected to receive at least four more women as a result. They also received women who had self-harmed or tried to commit suicide, so that they could be kept under close observation. This did not seem to me to be an appropriate use of a punishment unit, particularly as such prisoners probably needed

medical help. Clearly, if the segregation unit was the barometer of the prison's attitude to its inmates, more attention needed to be paid to the word 'humanity', so prominently displayed in the Statement of Purpose.

Everywhere we went I saw cigarette ends, slices of bread, bits of paper, and other uncleared rubbish in corners and stairwells, or on the ground outside where it must have been thrown from cell windows. But there was little sign of prisoner movement.

I asked one of the male officers on duty how much training he had had for working with women in prison.

'On the job only,' he replied.

'Do you think that officers working with women should be given special training?'

'Absolutely, but then who would give it? Newbold Revel [the Prison Service training college] doesn't do courses on women.'

Janet King added that only six days a year were allocated to training, but that she was so short-staffed that even this was impossible to achieve. My team had told me of the lack of training in control and restraint procedures but, clearly, it went further than that. I realised that lack of training in general was yet another issue demanding attention. How could staff, particularly male staff, know about working with women prisoners, especially in the circumstances of an overcrowded Holloway, unless they had been trained?

On one wing I was introduced to two prisoners, one an elderly, rather grandmotherly figure and the other a younger, somewhat sinister-looking woman, her skin stretched taut over her face. I was told that they were wing cleaners, selected because of their reliability, who had been deliberately 'buddied up' so that the elder could look after the younger. Both were inside for murder. Although they might mention this, I was warned that on no account should I ask about their crime. They told me that they were among the lucky ones because they had a job that got them out of their cells. There was nothing to do in Holloway, which, because it lacked opportunities for education or work, was not really a suitable prison for life-sentenced prisoners.

Their duties were to keep the landing and the ablutions clean, but they were not responsible for any outside areas.

The elder of the two asked if I would like to see her cell, which she had decorated personally. It was quite unlike the one that I had seen in the segregation unit. Although not much bigger, the walls were decorated with family photographs and cards, and she had a number of her personal possessions on display. She had the same stainless steel washbasin and lavatory, but a metal bed and wooden table and chair. Talking to her, it was clear that she had become totally institutionalised. She accepted the daily routine, feeling safe within it, because she had a job. She was visited regularly and was happy to 'do her time' until her release. No attempt was being made to address her offending behaviour, nor was she pressing for any. Her one regret was that, due to shortage of staff, people spent far too much time 'banged up'.

As we moved away, I noticed, through the panel in her cell door, an educated looking young woman, sitting on her bed reading. I asked to speak to her and, on entering her cell, saw a pile of books on a shelf over her bed, the top one by Bertrand Russell. I asked her why she liked reading this sort of book.

'I'm a philosophy graduate,' she replied.

'You shouldn't be locked up in here all day,' I said. 'You should be working in the library.'

'I agree,' she replied, adding that she been asking for a job there for months without response.

I drew this to Janet King's attention, suggesting that such people could be very useful in a prison in which reading must be such an invaluable time-filler.

In the Education Centre I at last found something positive. Although the Centre itself was empty because education had been suspended for the day 'due to shortage of staff', I found an Afro-Caribbean woman firing a brilliantly coloured jug in the shape of a pineapple. This was part of her application for a college course after her release, which I learned later that she had been awarded. The feeling of hope that this

encouraged was reinforced when I met one of the teachers, who told me how many women prisoners had serious educational problems which could be tackled if they were able to come to classes. In addition to reading, writing and arithmetic, the Centre could provide a whole range of art and domestic skills courses that could be adapted to provide suitable day care activities for the mentally disordered. What was disheartening, though, was that teachers never knew when, or how many, prisoners would be brought to classes 'due to staff shortages', so that there could never be any continuity of instruction.

Holloway was one of the five women's prisons in the country with a Mother and Baby Unit in which, because it was a closed prison, mothers could keep babies born to them while they were in prison until they were nine months old. Different rules apply in open prisons, where they may keep their babies up to the age of 18 months. However, every case is kept closely under review by Social Services staff, and babies can be removed from their mothers at birth if felt to be at particular risk. Of the seven women currently in the unit at the time, some wanted to transfer to open prisons, some would be released before the nine months were up, and two were about to have their babies removed. All were clearly waiting for my arrival, as they and their babies were gathered together in the main activity area. Again a few generalities were exchanged about how long they had been there and whether they were visited. But nothing prepared me for what came next.

'Do you think that it was right that I was in chains?' asked one woman.

'Chains when?' I asked.

'When I was having him,' she said, pointing to her son.

'Are you telling me that you were in chains while you were in labour?' I asked.

'Yes,' she replied.

'So was I,' said one or two others.

'Am I hearing correctly?' I asked the governor.

'It's security requirements,' she replied, going on to detail under exactly what regulation.

All the mothers then joined in, competing to tell me of their own particular experiences. One described how humiliated she had felt when attending an antenatal clinic in chains. She had been trying to keep herself to herself when a small boy came up, peered at her, and shouted to his mother to come and look at this woman in chains. The whole room turned round. Another described how embarrassing it was to have to go to the lavatory on the end of a long chain, and attached to a male officer because there were not enough female officer escorts.

I can only describe my initial reaction to the Health Care Centre as one of intense disgust. As we moved down a dark corridor towards the office in which the staff were gathered, I heard shouts, sobs, sounds of people kicking or striking doors, and the dull, rhythmic thud of someone banging their head against the wall, coming from individual cells. There was nothing like the proactive atmosphere that I had come to know in the mental health unit at the Hillingdon NHS Hospital, which I had chaired until two weeks before.

Unable to encourage much response to my questioning from the nurses or Prison Service hospital officers, and in the absence of any psychiatrist to whom I could talk, I knew I could take no more and told Janet King that I had seen enough for one day. I reminded her that we had still not found any of the 15-year-olds, but said that we would find them tomorrow. Thanking her for showing me round, I asked her to take me back to the Board Room to rejoin my inspectors.

Team Omega was in no way surprised at my reactions to what I had seen.

John Stephenson, the education inspector, produced a piece of paper that a prisoner had pushed at him under a cell door listing 'Things that have changed since the Inspectorate came'. The fact that there had been some change suggested that staff knew very well what was wrong.

I expressed my overwhelming conclusion to the day's events:

something had to be done with the utmost urgency to improve the treatment and conditions for prisoners in Holloway. This continued to beg wider questions about why no one in authority had done anything about what had been so clearly pointed out by the Board of Visitors, but that could come later. I made no secret of my hatred of the 'cult of managerialism' – the fallacious belief that you can run anything on a plethora of written instructions and rules, without having to exercise 'hands on' supervision and leadership – when applied to dealing with people.

During the next somewhat depressing two hours, as individual inspectors described what they had seen, or not seen, during the day, I became aware that Tony and Rod were very worried about the publication of the inspection report. Apparently it could take up to a year before ministers released reports for publication, and then only after a long-drawn out exchange of questions and answers between civil servants in the Home Office and officials in Prison Service Headquarters, in which the Inspectorate was not involved. It had taken over two years for one particularly unfavourable report to emerge, but that was tame in comparison with what would have to be said about Holloway.

My head reeling, I left the team to join my wife and two friends at the National Theatre; I remember absolutely nothing about the play we saw because I could only think about what I had seen and heard during the day. By any normal standards of responsibility and accountability, I believed the governor and the senior medical officer should be sacked. But, in fairness, so should those in Prison Service Headquarters who not only had allowed what I had seen to take place but also to continue unchecked. Had Holloway been a bad army unit, a reinspection would have been ordered after a set period of time, which I remembered actually happening in a process that resulted in the replacement of the commanding officer. However, I was not in a position to remove anyone. I could only make recommendations to the very ministers and Prison Service senior managers who were responsible and accountable for what I

had seen. How was I to get through to them that the Holloway regime was unacceptable?

I slept on it.

The following morning, my mind made up, I returned to Holloway via the Home Office, where I picked up Colin Allen who was joining the inspection team for the day. I told him that we would not be there for very long as I was suspending the inspection, which we would resume in six months time. He startled me by shouting 'Yes' and punching the air, saying that everyone had been agonising about how to end the inspection, but no one had thought of this way of ensuring that timely and necessary action was taken.

On route we discussed tactics and, in particular, what we should do about the press. Because the inspection had not been completed no report would be published. I did not want to say anything personally to the press, but just to leave the prison once I had told the governor what I intended to do. However, it seemed sensible to prepare a statement outlining what we had done and why, leaving it for the prison to use only if and when what had happened was discovered. Having told the governor, I would then inform the Home Secretary, the Prisons Minister and the acting Director General of the Prison Service.

When I told Tony Wood and his team what I intended to do they immediately pointed out a snag. The governor was attending an Industrial Tribunal that morning and would not be back in the prison until noon. So we agreed to continue the inspection as planned until then. I would go first to the antenatal unit, and then to the Education Centre to see the co-ordinator who had not been there the previous day. In the meantime our public relations officer would prepare a press release that I could hand to the governor.

In the antenatal unit, after Maggie Lyne, the nursing inspector, and I had introduced ourselves to one of the midwives, I noticed a large board on the wall of her office on which appeared to be a number of names with ages beside them. Two of them were 15.

'Are those girls pregnant?' I asked her.

'No,' she answered.

'Then why are they down here?'

'Because they don't know where else to put them.'

'Are all these other women pregnant?'

'No, there's psychotics and psychiatrically disturbed as well.'

'What on earth is going on here?'

At that the midwife shut the office door, and, looking me straight in the eye, said: 'I'm an Ibo from Nigeria, where they are meant to be less civilised than here. But I have to tell you that I have never seen anything so inhuman and disgusting as the way they treat women in Holloway.'

I looked across at Maggie, whose eyes caught mine, saying it all.

At the Education Centre I looked quickly into the library before entering the co-ordinator's office. Who should be there but yesterday's philosophy graduate!

'That was quick!' I said.

'Yes,' she replied, 'but I wish you'd come months ago'.

The co-ordinator confirmed everything her colleague had told me the previous evening, adding one rider. She had been working at the prison since March, but the governor had never once visited her during that time.

Back in the Board Room, we discussed and agreed the prepared press statement. This confirmed that inspectors had been so appalled by what they had found that I had suspended the inspection. Inspectors would return in six months, by which time I would expect action to have been taken on a list of points handed to the governor and the Director General of the Prison Service. No report on the suspended inspection would be published. However, aspects of what we had found, as well as our recommendations and requirements, would be included in the report on our follow-up inspection. The Prison Service members of the team felt that it was essential to say all this, because the Prison Officers Association might be tempted to distance the involvement of their members once they realised that criticism was in the air.

Just before noon Janet King returned and, after Tony had warned her that I wanted to see her urgently, he, Colin, Rod and I entered her office. I began by saying that I was taking what I understood to be a most unusual step, suspending the inspection as of now for a period of six months. I told her that, individually and collectively, we had been utterly appalled by the treatment of and conditions for prisoners, highlighting the filth, the absence of activities and the wholly inadequate medical arrangements. I acknowledged the difficulties with which she and the prison were faced, particularly the overcrowding and the shortage of staff, whose owed hours of TOIL were totally beyond her ability to resolve. I said that I would be reporting all this both to ministers and Prison Service Headquarters, because both would have to be involved in any rescue plan. We would complete a detailed list of our findings as quickly as possible, which we would send to her so that she was in no doubt about what needed to be done. In the meantime Rod, who knew her personally, would stay with her for the rest of the day so that she could ask any immediate questions. (Humane and caring man that he is, he had volunteered to do this so that there was someone to whom she could turn as she appreciated what could be a devastating blow to her career.) I then handed her the press statement, which I said was not to be released unless the media began asking questions.

The governor's eyes never left mine as I spoke, and she assured me that, whether she was still in charge or not, she could promise that urgent action would be taken to put things right. I left her before thanking the inspection team in general and Tony Wood in particular. We all departed from the prison ashamed, angry and disgusted. We were most unhappy about what we now knew went on, or did not go on, behind those red brick walls beside the Camden Road.

Once back in my office I telephoned both Michael Howard and Ann Widdecombe, telling them what I had done and why and confirming that I would be seeing Richard Tilt, the acting Director General.

My meeting with Richard was my first visit to Prison Service

Headquarters in Cleland House, just off Millbank, and the first of many times I took the lift to the Director General's office on the fifth floor. I introduced myself to Richard Tilt, a gentle, grey-haired, softly spoken man who greeted me civilly, acknowledging that we had never yet met, whereupon I immediately launched into my reasons for wanting to see him so urgently. I explained why I had suspended the inspection of Holloway, confirming that I would let him have a copy of all that I had promised to send to the governor, together with what would have been our findings and recommendations, as soon as I could. I gave him a copy of the press notice and asked to see the Director of Women, only to be told that there wasn't one.

'Who lays down what is to happen to women prisoners?' I asked.

'A Grade 7 civil servant in the policy branch,' he said.

'But who ensures that it actually happens?'

'The area manager.'

'But Holloway's area manager only looks after prisons in London and part of East Anglia. Who makes sure that women in Holloway are treated in the same way as women in a prison in Lancashire?'

'No one.'

'Who on the Prisons Board has worked with women in prison?'

'No one.'

The remainder of our meeting consisted of generalities, after which I returned once again to my office to think things through. From my point of view the Holloway experience, while distressing, had been invaluable, because I had been able to see at first hand, in only my second week in office, that there were a number of very serious problems with the way that imprisonment was run. I assumed that ministers would want to know how their responsibilities were being exercised and would welcome independent and objective quality assurance, based on fact and not on theory. But therein lay the rub.

The same ministers to whom I was required to report had already rejected or ignored evidence given to them by people with first-hand knowledge. What I had seen in Holloway was an affront to human decency that was wholly unworthy of a civilised society. If my

experienced professional inspectors were as shocked as I, a complete outsider to prisons, who had seen a number of appalling sights in my military career, what did this say about the standards of those in the Prison Service who were responsible for the situation? I had never before encountered so many deeply unhappy or emotionally damaged people for whom so little was being done. Heaven knew what their lives outside Holloway were like if they did not find its conditions a deterrent. The word 'inertia' naturally came to mind as I reflected that Colin Allen had had to fight against exactly the same conditions ten years before. This posed a number of questions. How had Holloway been allowed to degenerate into such a state? Who was responsible for women prisoners? Why had Michael Howard done nothing? What could we do about it?

Life was clearly difficult for the overstretched and insufficient prison staff, many of whom appeared to dislike the women prisoners as much as the women disliked them. The prison was overcrowded and underfunded. The governor and her managers lacked any direction as to what they were expected to do with and for prisoners, while being subjected to an endless barrage of paper work. As well as convincing ministers and the Prison Service that what we had seen in Holloway was totally unacceptable, I would have to try to convince the public that what had so disgusted their independent inspection team, should so disgust them that they would not tolerate such treatment of fellow citizens – male or female – in their name. Cleaning the place up and ensuring that the seriously ill had proper access to doctors would be a start.

The memory of those days will be with me for ever. More immediately they set my agenda for the next five years.

2

1934–1995

'I fail already; I'm over 60!'

HOW WAS IT THAT AN army general should have found himself inspecting Holloway women's prison, two and a half years after he had retired from active service? I wondered about that myself many times in my initial few months in office. I often thought back, trying to recall any experiences or individuals from my past that might help and guide me in making recommendations that could answer my own questions. What was there in my background and experience on which I could draw? Like most of the public, I knew little about prisons other than what I heard, read or saw in the media. However, I had seen some prisons in Northern Ireland and had encountered Argentinian prisoners of war in the Falkland Islands. Within the army itself, I had seen how soldiers were kept in detention and how they were treated in its prison, or the Military Corrective Training Centre as it was called, where the aim was to reclaim for military service the majority of those sent there. This made it very different from ordinary prisons.

Like most other people, I had views about the punishment of those

who committed crimes, and had long been against the death penalty. In Northern Ireland, for example, the person who ordered a murder would never be executed. These views and experiences were shared by many other people, so what had happened to me over the years since I was born, on 6 November 1934, at 13 Vicar's Close, Wells, Somerset, to suggest me for the post? Of more immediate importance, what could I draw on, not only to help me form views but also to make judgements on the conduct of imprisonment?

My father, then the Reverend John Ramsbotham, was in Wells as vice-principal of the Theological College and priest-vicar of the Cathedral, having been ordained on coming down from Cambridge. His father had also been a priest, dying in office as the Preacher of the Charterhouse in London, where he had also been an editor of the great Clarendon edition of *Tudor Church Music*.

My mother, born Eirian Morgan Owen, was a North Walian, Calvinist Methodist, whose adoption of Anglicanism was never accepted by her family, particularly when, in 1933, she married a priest. After school at St Paul's, where she overlapped with my father's two sisters, she also went up to Cambridge, where she read history at Girton. Almost three years older than my father, she got a better final exam result than he did but, like all women at that time, could not be awarded a degree. Highly intelligent and well read, she was descended from Owen Glendower from whom she felt that she had inherited a rebellious streak, and I have always wondered what she might have achieved had she not chosen to raise five children and be a support to my father.

In 1936 my father became Warden of the missionary training College of the Ascension in Selly Oak, Birmingham, where he remained until 1940, during which time my two brothers and the elder of my two sisters were born.

Between 1940 and 1950 my father was first rector of Ordsall, a village outside Retford in Nottinghamshire where my younger sister was born, and then vicar of St George's, Jesmond, a large parish in

Newcastle-upon-Tyne. In 1950 he was appointed suffragan Bishop of Jarrow and we moved to an incomparably placed house beside Durham Cathedral. Finally, in 1958 he was appointed Bishop of Wakefield, from where he retired in 1967 to Hexham in Northumberland, following a heart attack. My parents died within a year of each other, in 1988 and 1989. At my father's memorial service in Wakefield Cathedral, the then bishop described him as a 'pastor pastorum', who really cared for his clergy. No description could have been more accurate or pleased him more.

In 1943 I was sent to Hillbrow preparatory boarding school, which had been evacuated from Rugby to Featherstone Castle, near Haltwhistle, some 30 miles west of Newcastle. The headmaster, Mr Dixon, a deeply Christian man, was a pillar of rectitude, who loved Bach and climbing mountains. The castle was always bitterly cold and, when I went there, still lit by gas. In spring terms, when the ground always seemed to be covered with frost or snow or both, lessons were frequently stopped and the boys sent on a run to get warm.

It was here that I first came across prisoners. Immediately alongside the castle was a large prisoner of war camp. When World War II ended, some of the prisoners were allowed to work in the school. One of them, Hans Goetsche, a gentle and unmilitary man who had been organist at Bach's Marienkirche in Lübeck, taught us the piano. Others worked in the kitchen or the garden. The POWs also put on a performance of the mystery play *Everyman*, in German, at the front of the castle, for which they made costumes out of dyed sacking. Their obvious enthusiasm for the opportunity was my first exposure to the value of the contribution that the creative arts can make to the lives of prisoners.

In 1948 I followed my father to Haileybury College near Hertford. It had originally been built as the East India Company's training college, at the same time and by the same architect as the Royal Military Academy, Sandhurst. After the Indian Mutiny, when the company ceased to be responsible for running India, the buildings were bought by a group of local businessmen and turned into a school.

Throughout my time at Haileybury I was fortunate to be taught English by the Reverend Val Rogers, later headmaster of Portora Royal School in Northern Ireland, who was a major influence on my life. He made us think, his principal weapon – which he used, and taught us to use, mercilessly – being the word 'why'. His personal conversion from intellectual Communism through agnosticism to ordination, via a distinguished war record, coupled with his personal knowledge of the great writers of the pre- and immediately postwar period such as W. H. Auden, Christopher Isherwood, T. S. Eliot, Stephen Spender and C. S. Lewis, gave him a unique platform from which to take us on exciting literary journeys. Of course we covered the set books, but Val taught us not to be afraid to challenge accepted wisdom or practice if we felt it to be unsound or lacking in common sense. He was not popular with conventional reactionaries such as my housemaster, but his approach was inspirational and I owe a great deal to him.

At home in Durham we were continually visited by a wide variety of people. Two were unforgettable. Sam Watson, a staunch trades unionist and member of the Labour Party, had taught himself to read by the light of his miner's lamp while, as a boy, he worked down a coal mine. Always a realist, Sam was also a humanist – with a sense of humour. The same applied to Lord (Jack) Lawson, another miner and Labour politician, who later became Chancellor of Durham University. From people like these I learned what life in County Durham had been like between the wars, and the importance of education, training and employment for all. Both men made me realise the importance of communities, in which people know about and care for each other, whatever the circumstances.

Having passed the entrance exam to Corpus Christi College, Cambridge, again following my father, I decided to leave school as early as possible in order to get my two-year National Service over with, complete university, and get on with life before I was too old. I knew nothing about the army and, on my housemaster's advice, opted for the artillery. After being selected for officer training I was commissioned in March 1953 and posted to 2nd Regiment Royal Horse

Artillery at Hildesheim in Germany. Once there I realised that I was neither technically nor mathematically competent enough to be a gunner. I much preferred the infantry and was particularly taken with a regiment called the Rifle Brigade, with whom I was sent to work during an exercise, and a number of whose officers I met on various playing fields. They seemed to have a rare and exceptional ability to combine enjoyment of life with professional competence in a way that made a strong impression on me.

I went up to Cambridge in October 1954, where the two most important decisions that I made during my three years there had nothing to do with the university or the History Tripos. I met my future wife and decided on a career in the regular army.

Meeting, and subsequently marrying, Sue Dickinson has been the most wonderfully fortunate event in my life. Although our homes were only 25 miles apart when we lived in Durham, we actually met while skiing, with different parties, staying in the same hotel in Norway. She has influenced me more than words can say and I shall never be able to repay the many debts of gratitude that I owe her. When we married in 1958, we were officially classified as living in sin, because I was under the age of 25, which meant that we received no marriage allowance, nor qualified for an army house. Fortunately, however, when we moved to Germany soon afterwards, there were only five other married officers in the regiment and we were allowed to live in one of the eight houses made available to every unit when it moved. My selfish pursuit of my chosen career was never kind to Sue, not least because of the number of times that we had to move house. Despite this, she made homes in a wide variety of different houses, while bringing up our two sons, James, born in 1959, and Richard in 1962.

I decided on a career in the regular army, rather than the colonial service for which I had originally opted, not least because there did not seem likely to be many colonies left to service. For a time I considered various jobs in the City, but knew that I was not cut out for them. I

enjoyed the outdoor military life and the company of soldiers and so, with help and encouragement from one of Sue's grandmothers and uncles and other friends, I applied and was accepted for a commission in the Rifle Brigade.

Professionally, and in every other way, I could not have made a better choice. The ethos of the regiment was that the individual counts, and what Sir John Moore of Corunna, my only military ancestor, described as a 'mutual bond of trust and affection between all ranks'. We were 'excellently different' from the rest of the army. We wore green uniforms with black buttons; we marched faster than anyone else; we carried no colours because individual sharpshooters did not fight en masse and did not need to rally round a flag since everything was controlled by bugle calls. The Rifle Brigade had won more VCs than any other regiment in the army. At the beginning of World War II, almost to a man, the First Battalion had been part of a small force that was either killed, wounded or captured at Calais, helping to make the evacuation from Dunkirk possible. When I asked my first second-in-command, Tom Acton, who was one of those captured, how it was that the Rifle Brigade had done so well despite having not seen action since World War I, he replied that the regiment had always fought well and that they were among friends. Those remain regimental characteristics.

Very early on in my military career I was taught that identifying and developing talent was one of the most important responsibilities of an officer. The army is run by chains of command – everyone is responsible for a detailed task or role, for which they are accountable upwards to a known and nominated person responsible for supervising their performance. Non-commissioned officers (NCOs), who form the middle management of a regiment or unit, are its lifeblood. They are in closer minute-to-minute contact with riflemen than the officers, who form the senior management, and are responsible for overseeing the minutiae of practical skills. A regiment can be made or broken by its NCOs, and woe betide any that does not take their selection and training seriously.

The first date written into the regimental calendar was that of the annual course for training potential NCOs, weeks when the best in the regiment were made available to train those selected to be considered for promotion. Only the best would do for a rigorous and demanding process, because those who passed would have to lead riflemen in war.

In early 1960 I was posted to the regimental depot at Winchester to command the Junior Riflemen's Company, which consisted of some 90 boys aged between 15 and 17½. These youngsters had boundless energy, their fitness increased by daily PT and much sport. At regular intervals, or if the ill-disciplinary temperature seemed to be rising, I laid on demanding adventure-training exercises to burn off any surplus. I soon learned that full, purposeful and active days for this age group, who were very different from adult riflemen, had to be carefully planned and supervised.

From Winchester I was offered a post on the staff of the King's African Rifle Brigade in Kenya, in 1962, the year before 'uhuru' (independence). The brigade's headquarters was in Nanyuki, a small township on the Equator beside Mount Kenya, where the scenery alone made it a glorious place in which to soldier. Its commander was Brigadier Miles Fitzalan Howard (later the Duke of Norfolk) who could not have been a better choice for the time, or more fun to serve with. As far as he was concerned there was no difference between the British and African officers and soldiers and he teased and bantered with us both equally. As a result he created and maintained a very happy environment in which to serve, without a trace of racism. We were all friends, we all had a job to do to the best of our ability, and we depended on each other.

However, Sue, James, Richard and I were not, after all, in Kenya for 'uhuru'. I had to return to England to attend the Staff College, a most important year in a military career. Afterwards I returned to the regiment, and was due to report to Felixstowe in mid-January 1965. However, on New Year's Eve, while staying with Sue's parents, I saw a newspaper article saying that the Rifle Brigade was being sent to the

Far East for a year to reinforce those involved in defending Malaysia from Indonesian 'confrontation'. I rang up to ask if this included me, to be told I was to take over command of a company at once and would be leaving England by air seven days later. The battalion was to be unaccompanied, which meant leaving Sue and the boys in a house that we had rented but not yet moved into.

After an initial four months in Hong Kong and six weeks jungle training in Malaya, we were flown to Borneo for our six-and-a-half months on operations. Our entrenched base was on top of a small hill above a kampong (village) called Gunan Gajak which, because that is an English corruption of a Dyak name, is not on any map. As the crow flies, we were some two miles from the border with Indonesia that ran along a high, jungle clad ridge and took several hours to reach on foot. There being no roads or navigable rivers in the area, all our supplies had to be parachuted on to the kampong sports field or flown in by helicopter. There were only two ways of moving – on foot or by helicopter – to and from our main occupation: aggressive patrolling, lasting up to five days and aimed at denying the area to the Indonesians. The whole campaign was conducted in circumstances unrecognisable from those of today: not a single journalist visited us and nobody in England appeared to know anything about what we were doing or how.

One day I was told to expect a visit from the Director of Staff Duties from the Ministry of Defence, the officer responsible for planning the deployment of troops to tasks around the world. Major General Michael (later Field Marshal Lord) Carver had been a highly decorated brigadier in the war by the age of 29 and was said to have the finest brain in the army. Although I did not know it at the time, that meeting determined the course of my subsequent career. Having been introduced, he said he did not need to look around my base, about which he had been briefed, and asked if there was somewhere we could talk. Immediately we sat down he began asking detailed questions that revealed his understanding and knowledge of leading riflemen on such operations, including their training and motivation. It was stimulating to be in the company of someone who not only

knew the kind of questions that we were asking ourselves, but was willing to listen as well as offer his opinions. Such was my fascination during our discussion, which moved on to many wider topics, that I lost all count of time. Suddenly I felt the presence of my brigade commander, who told Major General Carver that he had had two hours of the 20 minutes on the programme and that, unless they left immediately, they would not get back to Kuching before dark. 'Thank you,' he replied, 'I have only two more questions' – which he had. He then got back into the helicopter and left.

In July 1970, five years and four jobs later, I was called back from Germany to be interviewed by General Sir Michael Carver as he now was, to be his military assistant when he was appointed head of the army, or Chief of the General Staff (CGS). He said that he wanted to remind himself that I was the person he had met in Borneo and asked if I wanted the job. What could I say? Quite apart from the promotion, here was the chance of working for an exceptional person, in a very privileged position. He pre-empted any complacency I might have felt by reminding me that he could always sack me.

And so, in June 1971, I began my first Whitehall job, at a time when Northern Ireland was moving to a crisis, Britain was involved in helping the Sultan of Oman in his war against Yemeni insurgents, and we were completing our withdrawal from the Middle and Far East. For the next two and a quarter years I saw at close hand someone who, in addition to being a master of his profession, was at ease with politicians, officials and academics, all of whom acknowledged his ability. Working for Sir Michael Carver was demanding and fascinating, made more so by knowing that I could never afford to let my concentration lapse.

When Sir Michael was promoted to Field Marshal and became Chief of the Defence Staff (CDS), I stayed on for a short time to see in his successor, General Sir Peter Hunt, before moving on to the high point of every soldier's career – command of your own regiment.

The regimental system is the bedrock of the British army. A soldier joins a regiment, wears its uniform, serves with it except when posted

to another organisation, and remains a member of it for life. I had been away three times on staff jobs and my final return was for a mandatory two and a half years. This has lessons for the Prison Service, which moves its commanding officers, or prison governors, around far too often, leaving them in post for much too short a time. The whole of an army officer's career is an apprenticeship for command. You know and have served with most of those whom you will lead. You have been trained in, and filled, a number of the subordinate posts and so should know your job. You hope that your time in command will include an operational challenge.

One of my challenges was a four-month unaccompanied operational tour in Belfast, where my headquarters was in the Springfield Road Police Station, just off the Falls Road. I was fortunate in my team and I could not have admired my young riflemen more for the way they conducted themselves on the streets, showing a maturity beyond their years. Winning the hearts and minds of the nationalist population was never going to be easy, but they were always prepared to try. My greatest satisfaction was that, at the end of a very active four months, I brought back every member of the battalion whom I had taken there. My faith that this was largely due to their professionalism was justified a year or two later, when someone found an IRA document confirming that close observation of the way that new arrivals first performed on the streets determined whether or not they would be taken on. Clearly, the battalion looked the part, a lesson that I later passed on to all those coming to Belfast under my command.

After a little over a year in Gibraltar – a happy break from operations – our next move was a return to Germany where, now promoted to the rank of colonel, I was posted to Headquarters 4 Armoured Division, commanded by another senior officer who was to become a great friend and influence. Major General (later Field Marshal Sir) Nigel Bagnall was a soldier's soldier, who had read and thought deeply about what was required of the army in operations against the Soviet army. He concentrated on how our men might fight

and on learning how they might be fought. Nigel's most important legacy to today's army, however, was his later introduction of a Higher Command and Staff Course. He was concerned that those destined for senior appointments received no training in the exercise of high command. All ranks up to and including commanding officer were trained and tested, but after that nothing. Too many people were promoted into positions for which they were neither qualified nor competent. They were never tested on exercises which they controlled and failings that could have been fatal in war were thus never discovered. This has lessons for any organisation, including the Prison Service. No one should be appointed to fill senior command positions without suitable and rigorous selection and training. Being put into a position that they are not competent to fill is as unfair to the person concerned as it is on those under their command.

At the end of 1978 I was promoted to brigadier, and returned to Belfast to command 39 Infantry Brigade for two years. This was operational command in a place that I knew, but it brought many different challenges.

In Belfast I had my first experience of going inside a prison. I was responsible for the protection of the outer perimeter of HMP Crumlin, which held all male prisoners awaiting trial in the province. The prison was connected to the Crown Court by a tunnel that ran under the Crumlin Road, which separated the two establishments. I knew its outside well because public protest, during and at the end of any emotive trial, invariably required soldiers to help the Royal Ulster Constabulary at the scene. However, my chief concern was that too many prison staff put their lives at risk by failing to vary the time and route of their journeys to and from the prison. Therefore, every four months or so, I spent an evening with the governor and his senior managers to remind them not to make themselves a target of the IRA. Sadly however, despite all the warnings, I twice found myself marching in the funeral procession of a senior prison officer who had been murdered on his way to work. Almost 20 years later I was to see their names on the memorial to

those members of the Northern Ireland Prison Service who had been killed in the troubles that stands just inside The Maze prison. There could be no starker reminder that, in such situations, prison staff are just as much in the law and order front line as any other member of the security forces.

After Belfast, and a year at the Royal College of Defence Studies, where 40 UK students, and 40 students from many other countries, come together for a stimulating year studying the world scene, I was appointed Director of Public Relations (Army) in January 1982. This task involved acting as middleman between the media and the army, promoting and defending it in the eyes of the public.

There will always be tension between the two sides, because journalists are bound to seek out the sensational that the army seeks to minimise. This tension is admirably summed up in the first paragraph of a small document entitled *Regulations for Correspondents Accompanying an Operational Force, 1958*: 'The essence of successful warfare is secrecy: the essence of successful journalism is publicity.'

Three months into my new appointment Argentina invaded the Falkland Islands. I shall never forget the first weekend of the war. My RAF colleague and I were told to go home because this was a purely naval affair. They were the last days I had off until early July! If there was tension between journalists and their 'minders' in the Falkland Islands there was also tension in the Ministry of Defence between the civil servants in charge of public relations and the three Services directors. We liked to brief correspondents personally, giving them the opportunity to ask questions in order to help them with their role of informing the public. Civil servants insisted on using prepared 'lines to take' and 'Q(uestion) & A(nswer) briefs'. The only problem with this was that no one believed the line, asked the Q or accepted the A. Above all, journalists wanted to talk to service people about service matters.

At the end of the war I flew out on the first aircraft to land at Stanley, with (Sir) Rex Hunt, the returning governor. Only British journalists had been allowed to accompany the task force that recaptured the Islands. My job was to plan a series of short visits by foreign

journalists to sites, including the battlefields, during the few weeks before the runway was closed for refurbishment.

During my week in the Falklands I visited the Argentinian prisoners of war, who were held in the old sheep-processing depot at San Carlos. They had separated themselves into groups according to rank – senior officers, junior officers, NCOs and conscripts. The senior officers had tried to maintain that the conscripts were still their subordinates, demanding, for example, that any one with bedding should surrender it to any senior officer who had none. No British soldier had had any experience of guarding prisoners before but, as far as they were concerned, all prisoners were treated equally and they quickly restored any purloined bedding to its rightful owner. It was sad to see the wretched conscripts – some of them still schoolchildren – following their British guards around, amazed that soldiers could treat them so humanely.

The normal chain of command operated within the camp. Soldiers were told to adopt the well-tried 'three Fs' observed on the streets of Northern Ireland – Firm, Fair and Friendly – in their relationships with prisoners. I was later to reflect that this approach seemed to come as naturally to the soldier guards as it did to those recruited by private sector companies to be custodial officers in contract prisons. It was by no means the norm in a number of public sector prisons.

Once the war was over, the House of Commons Defence Committee instigated an inquiry into why things had been so badly handled. The answer was, of course, quite simple: there were no proper contingency arrangements. There is a world of difference between public relations designed to protect ministers or project government policy, and the reporting of war itself. Of course officials are involved because they are responsible for projecting policy, but they ought never to forget that operational commanders have the right to insist on operational secrecy – particularly if they believe that the lives of any of those for whom they are responsible would be threatened by premature disclosure. Neither group can afford to forget that

public confidence cannot be taken for granted and has to be handled with care. If lost it can affect public support for a cause. Confidence is best achieved by being seen and heard. This applies to other operational services such as the Prison Service.

After two and a half years commanding 3rd Armoured Division at Soest in Germany, I returned to England to command the United Kingdom Field Army, which carried with it the additional task of being Inspector General of the Territorial Army. I was responsible for the training of all troops based in the United Kingdom for their many and various operational tasks at home and overseas, including the defence of the United Kingdom.

During this time I had my second experience of prisons. In 1989 industrial unrest caused the government to take over two army camps as temporary prisons. One of these, hutted Rolleston Camp in the middle of Salisbury Plain, was used largely by the Territorial Army. The other, Alma Dettingen, was a barrack complex in Surrey. At first we provided only external guards, but this expanded to include catering and works. All along we were determined that no soldiers, with the exception of military policemen and provost (prison) staff, should come face to face with prisoners – that was for professional prison staff. We were told that our commitment would end after three months.

One day I was told that I would receive a request for soldiers to censor prisoners' mail and that there were strong rumours that our involvement would continue beyond the three months. Fortunately Douglas (Lord) Hurd, the Home Secretary, was visiting Alma Dettingen that day, and I went to see him there. He assured me that there was no question of soldiers having to act as censors and promised that there would be no extension. He was as good as his word.

On a later visit a Royal Military Police sergeant major asked to see me to make a complaint. His story was that he had seen two prisoners exchanging cannabis, which he had reported to one of the Prison Service managers. He had been told to forget it because that was perfectly normal currency in prisons. Because soldiers faced instant

court martial and possible dismissal from the army if found in posses-
sion of drugs, he felt that it was quite wrong for a prisoner to be
allowed to get away with this without being charged. The acting
prison governor promised to investigate, but we never heard the result
before the temporary prison closed. This was my first exposure to an
attitude to drugs that I was to hear many times in the years ahead.

When I took up my last post as Adjutant General, No. 2 in the
army, at Christmas 1990, the active war in the Gulf had not yet
started. As the army's head of personnel, with a seat on the Army
Board, there was plenty to do in ensuring that all personnel matters,
particularly medical support, were in place. Immediately after the
land war ended, the CGS, General (now Field Marshal) Sir John
Chappell, and I flew out to Saudi Arabia and Kuwait to see and be
briefed by the soldiers on the ground and discuss arrangements for
their return. I shall never forget a sight from hell – horizon to horizon
burning oil wells – as we descended through clouds of smoke so thick
that you could hardly see the ends of the wing tips. It was nonetheless
a great thrill to see many people I knew, including one of my old
brigades, and to hear how well the young soldiers had performed in
completely new circumstances. One could not help being very proud
of our forces and the way they had been trained and led.

Now, Options for Change, the somewhat euphemistic title given to
the post-Cold War reductions in the Armed Forces, was looming
over us. This meant reducing the size of the army by a third over three
years. To do this we first tried to estimate its future shape in terms of
the number of units and other organisations that would be required.
Then we considered and projected the future of every individual officer and soldier, recognising that, inevitably, many would have to be
made redundant. Because there were no MoD or army funds for this,
we had to enter prolonged negotiations with the Treasury, who agreed
to make available 80 per cent of the cost. We spent hours trying to
explain to civil servants and financiers that cutting a living organisation
like an army is not like shutting a factory and dismissing all the
workers – recruiting and promotion must be continued to ensure

41

continuous viability. I was interested to see later that this was quite opposite to the way the Prison Service tackled its redundancy pro-gramme.

My main concern was that the Services' resettlement organisation was wholly unprepared for the strain it would have to take. I pointed out the potential embarrassment to Tom King, then Secretary of State for Defence, whom I had known since we were at Cambridge together, emphasising that something had to be done urgently to improve arrangements. Because the army was the most affected of the Services, I offered to lead this work on behalf of, but involving, all three Services. The result was what is now known as the Tri-Service Resettlement Organisation, which includes the use of job search com-panies to interview and help place servicemen in work.

The Department of Employment offered to set up a civilian Job Centre in Germany. When visiting this, I asked the staff, who had been sent out to run it, whether they noticed any difference between the soldiers and their families they were now seeing and the people they had seen in the centres in which they worked in England. All commented at once on the 'can do' approach of the soldiers. This was encouraging for their prospects, but sad that it would be lost to the army. One problem that soldiers faced when trying to find jobs had resonance with what I was to find later in prisons. No military courses carried certificates of skills worded in language that a civilian employer could understand. Luckily, Non-Vocational Qualifications (NVQs) were just being introduced, and we began working on relating all military qualifications to a NVQ equivalent, with the future in mind.

My ADC, Captain William Shipton, came up with a most im-aginative idea to match individual capabilities, revealed by an aptitude test, to job requirements, electronically. This would allow an employer to select potential employees on the basis of their skills without know-ing their background; selection would obviously depend on interview, but soldiers would have an equal opportunity to be selected for jobs based on their ability. The idea was taken up by the Department of Employment and introduced into a number of Job Centres, and

William later pursued the idea commercially. It has immense relevance for the employment of prisoners. They too could compete on level terms if employers listed job requirements in a way that could be matched to individual capabilities. The question of how and when they might have to reveal their previous conviction would have to be answered. But it could be done.

I still feel unhappy at how comparatively little we were able to achieve over housing. Although much was done to help those who were married, we were far less successful at finding long-term accommodation for single soldiers, many of whom had joined the army to escape their chaotic and dysfunctional backgrounds. Some hostel accommodation was available and service charities helped as much as they could. But our failure has resulted in too many ex-Servicemen ending up in prison, homeless and/or sleeping rough, something about which no one involved should feel proud. The problem is still there.

Another of my responsibilities was discipline, including the Royal Corps of Military Police and the Military Provost Staff Corps (MPSC) which ran the Military Corrective Training Centre (MCTC). This title was deliberately chosen to reflect the aim and purpose of the establishment, which contained two types of prisoner. By far the greater proportion were young soldiers who had made a bad start to their military careers and been punished for an offence against military law, often absence without leave. Their days were fully and purposefully occupied repeating their basic military training to give them a better chance of making a success of their chosen career on return to their units. Eighty-four per cent of them succeeded, thus vindicating the concept, and saving men for the army. The MPSC staff were the key to success. All were experienced soldiers who had to have reached the rank of sergeant in their own regiment before transferring into the Corps. They focussed on restoring and building up the self-confidence of their charges and enabling them to do what was asked of them.

The second part of the MCTC was for those being discharged from

the army because their services were no longer required. They were put through purposeful pre-release training designed to give them skills such as brickwork, woodwork, motor mechanics, painting and decorating and gardening, to help them gain employment in civilian life. This programme was modelled on what allegedly was available in prison. Unfortunately the only confirmation of its success was the occasional letter from a discharged prisoner to his instructor. This was my first introduction to the lack of data about re-offending.

Looking back over my 35 years of military service, I realised how fortunate I was to have had such a wonderful variety of experiences. I had commanded at every level from platoon at the bottom to army at the top. I had worked in Whitehall at the heart of government, with the Cabinet Office and many ministries in addition to the Ministry of Defence. I had had considerable practical staff experience, particularly on the personnel side, dealing with health and discipline as well as man management. As a member of the Army Board I had been responsible and accountable for a multi-billion pound budget and had planned and implemented a major redundancy programme. I had worked with the media. I had served in a number of countries outside the United Kingdom and retained friends and contacts in them. I had been lucky.

Shortly before I retired, (Sir) Malcolm Rifkind, then Secretary of State for Defence, asked me to return to the MoD as a consultant and write a paper on the management of the UK contribution to UN peacekeeping operations. I began this the day after I had completed my quaintly named 'terminal leave'. During its preparation I met Kofi Annan, then the UN's Under-Secretary General for Peacekeeping Operations, who asked me to join a small group who were preparing a similar paper on operational management for the Security Council.

I was also invited to join a firm called Defence Systems Limited (DSL), founded by two ex-members of the SAS, Alastair Morrison and Richard Bethell. My role, as Director of International Affairs, was to develop the work of the firm in support of both peacekeeping and

post-conflict reconstruction including de-mining, working with the UN and the World Bank. DSL fielded a very vibrant team.

I accepted, too, an appointment as chairman of the Hillingdon Hospital NHS Trust. Hillingdon is an interesting hospital with large maternity and mental health units. It is the nominated accident hospital for Heathrow and its catchment area includes large Asian communities in Southall and Hounslow. The professionalism and commitment of both the administrative and medical staffs at once impressed me. Philip Brown, the chief executive, was experienced, unflappable, and had the priceless ability to make people want to work for him. Of all the excellent medical directors there, I was particularly fortunate in the Director of Mental Health, Reg Freeman, who insisted that I trained as a lay assessor so that I could play an active part in the work of the unit. He was increasingly concerned about the impact of substance abuse on the young, citing evidence that it advanced latent disorders such as schizophrenia. This fear was heightened by a tragic suicide that took place soon after a young man was admitted to the unit.

However, my multi-faceted post-army life was about to change. One day in August 1995, just before Sue and I went off on holiday to Italy, we found a message on the answering machine asking me to call a number that I did not recognise. It was a head-hunter who, having admitted that we had never met, made the surprising remark that people had said I should allow my name to go forward for the post of Her Majesty's Chief Inspector of Prisons. When I asked 'which people' he said that he could not tell me. I asked what the qualifications were, to which he replied that I had to be under 60. 'I fail already,' I responded, but after further discussion I agreed to let my name go forward, and went to Italy.

On our return the head-hunter rang again, telling me that I was now on a shortlist of 15. 'From what?' I asked. 'Sixty' came the response. 'How did that happen?' I asked. 'I can't tell you,' he replied, and asked whether I was happy to take a psychometric test which, when completed, would be sent to an industrial psychologist for

45

analysis. Never having seen, let alone taken, one before, I was intrigued as to what I might learn about myself and agreed to the test. I was invited to meet the industrial psychologist, who told me that my profile exactly matched that of the job. When I explained that I was disqualified by age, she replied that her task was to analyse the potential of candidates without considering such limitations.

I was placed on a shortlist of six to be interviewed, before which the Permanent Secretary in the Home Office, Richard Wilson, whom I had never met, would like to see me. His approach reminded me of the best of the Ministry of Defence civil servants and I knew that we could work together.

I duly attended for interview, having learned something about imprisonment through reading as much as I could lay my hands on. I knew that all was not well with its conduct, in the eyes of the recently retired Chief Inspector, Judge Stephen Tumim. The inspection process did not worry me after a lifetime of inspecting everything from my riflemen's feet to operational units and headquarters. Quite apart from being over 60, I was perfectly relaxed about the outcome, having plenty of other things to do.

A few days later I learned that I was now on a shortlist of two, who were to see Michael Howard, the Home Secretary. I still could not imagine that I would be offered the post, as I was over age. Michael Howard asked me two questions. Firstly, he wanted to know how I would do the job. I told him that I regarded Inspectorates as members of the partnership of all those involved with what they were inspecting. In the case of prisons this meant prisoners – before, during and after sentence – ministers, officials, prison staff, and any agencies or voluntary organisations involved in penal affairs. An independent Chief Inspector had no executive responsibility, but I would hope to be included in discussions on both policy and practice, to which inspection experience could make an important contribution.

Secondly, Michael Howard asked how he could explain his appointment of another army general, when the report written by the previous one that he had employed, Sir John Learmont, had resulted

in the sacking of the Director General of the Prison Service. I told him that he was not taking on a general. I had retired from that position two and a half years before and, if he employed me, it was presumably because of what I could offer the job of inspecting and reporting on prisons. He thanked me for coming, we said good night, and I left his office.

The following morning I was telephoned by Richard Wilson's private secretary, who asked if the Permanent Secretary could come and see me at home that evening. When he arrived, and had accepted a drink, he said that I had got away too quickly last night. The Chief Inspector's job was mine but, after I had left, Michael Howard had asked him to call me back and ask whether I would take on the job of Director General of the Prison Service instead. Richard reminded me that he had mentioned this when we first met, and I had retorted that I would not touch the job with a barge pole. I had already been a line manager at many levels and was too old to start that again. Anyway, I felt that a Director General of the Prison Service, its professional head, should have risen to the top by proving him or herself to be the person best fitted for the job and recognised as such by all in the Service. Richard Wilson, however, was not deterred, asking me to think again and let him know my answer within a week. I discussed the point with my two referees, who quickly confirmed my original instincts, and I rang Richard's office to repeat my rejection of the offer before flying to Washington and New York.

When I arrived back some five days later I found a message from the Chief of the Defence Staff, Field Marshal Sir Peter (later Lord) Inge, an old friend and contemporary, saying that Michael Howard had asked him to try to get me to change my mind. Peter knew that I wouldn't, but had to ask. I stood firm, repeating my reasons, which I knew he would understand.

By now it was November, which did not leave much time for me to unscramble some of my other commitments before my start date of 1 December. Sadly, I concluded that I should resign from Hillingdon Hospital because, although I could probably still chair board meetings,

I wouldn't have time to be around the hospital as much as I currently was. However, I asked for two days a month with DSL to continue my work with the UN and World Bank on post-conflict reconstruction and de-mining, not least in order to maintain the contacts that I had made.

Her Majesty the Queen and the Prime Minister, John Major, having agreed my appointment, it was announced on Thursday 30 November, the day before I took up the post, on my return from addressing a peacekeeping conference in Cyprus. And so I arrived at the Home Office on 1 December 1995, met Colin Allen, and embarked on my next journey. It was to last for five years and eight months.

3

HM INSPECTORATE OF PRISONS

'A system without an independent element is not a system that accords with proper standards of justice.'

Lord Chief Justice Woolf

HER MAJESTY'S INSPECTORATE OF PRISONS, of which I had now become the fourth Chief Inspector since it was formed in 1981, provides Lord Woolf's independent element within the prison systems of England and Wales. It is also responsible for the inspection of prisons in Northern Ireland, the Overseas Dependent Territories of Anguilla, the Cayman Islands, Montserrat, Pitcairn (one cell), St Helena, the Turks and Caicos Islands and the British Virgin Islands.

The Chief Inspector's remit, contained in an amendment to the 1952 Prison Act, is as follows:

Her Majesty's Chief Inspector of Prisons is required to inspect, or to arrange for the inspection of, prisons in England and Wales and to report on them to the Secretary of State, in particular on the treatment of prisoners and on conditions within prisons.

It is also the duty of the Chief Inspector of Prisons to report to the Secretary of State on specific matters as

required, and to submit an annual report to be laid before Parliament.

I interpreted this to mean 'To monitor and influence the treatment and conditions of prisoners' – monitoring through visits and inspections, and influencing through recommendations contained in reports.

A new Chief Inspector, particularly one coming in from outside the Criminal Justice System as I did, has, first and foremost, to establish his or her credibility with all the stakeholders – ministers, Parliament, officials, the Prison Service, the public and prisoners. That is best done by publicly proving one's independence and objectivity. I was much amused by the amount of speculation about how a retired general would do the job. Those who thought that I would not follow the example of my predecessors in openly criticising poor treatment and conditions, clearly had neither read my remit nor understood soldiers. Soldiers are taught to obey orders. My orders were to report what I found. I could only assume that those who were disappointed that I did so neither understood my orders, nor wanted them obeyed.

Currently only England and Wales, Scotland and, for the last three years, Western Australia have an independent Prison Inspectorate. Discussions that I had with over 20 visiting ministers of justice from around the world who came to call on me suggested that this number could increase in the future. All were interested in 'quality assurance' and appeared to like our model. Other countries, such as Canada and the United States, have different arrangements. Canada audits its prisons for value for money, not for the quality of the treatment of prisoners. The United States has a voluntary system, operated by a private sector Corrections Association. This inspects any prison, on request, and for a fee. Out of 11,000 prisons barely 1000 are willing to pay.

Prison inspection in this country did not begin in 1981. The date most usually associated with its start is 1773 when John Howard – whose bust adorns one side of the main gate of HMP Wormwood

Scrubs, arguably the most instantly recognisable prison façade in the country – was appointed High Sheriff of Bedfordshire. He visited Bedford gaol, from which prisoners came to the court that he had to attend, and recorded his shock at what he found in a famous book, *The State of the Prisons in England and Wales*, published in 1777. His most quoted observation was that:

> The care of a prison is too important to be left to a gaoler;
> paid indeed for his attendance, but often tempted by his
> passions, or interests, to fail in his duty. To every prison
> there should be an inspector appointed . . . Sheriffs have
> this power already . . . But some excuse themselves from
> attention to this part of their duty, on account of the short
> duration, expense and trouble of their office, and these
> gentlemen have no doubt been fearful of the consequences
> of looking into prisons.

Bedford was one of more than a hundred 'Gaols, Bridewells, Houses of Correction, Penitentiaries and other Prisons, kept or used for the confinement of prisoners' at that time, paid for by local taxes. The system had been in existence since Anglo-Saxon times and most of such institutions were old, small and overcrowded. At the time of Howard's book, transportation to Australia had not yet begun. However, a number of longer-term prisoners, whose transportation to America had been temporarily suspended because of the War of Independence, were held in former warship hulks, moored in the Thames beside Millbank Prison on the site of what is now Tate Britain. These hulks were later used to house those awaiting transportation when it was resumed after the discovery of Australia. The letters POM – Prisoner of Millbank – stamped on their issued shirts, gave rise to the word used to describe those newly arrived from England.

The impetus for the better treatment of and conditions for prisoners that Howard began was resumed when the Napoleonic wars

ended. Among those who led the drive for reform were a number of East Anglian Quakers, famously including Elizabeth Fry, a bust of whom shares the gateway to Wormwood Scrubs with John Howard. She concentrated on the needs of women prisoners in particular, championing both prison visiting and mentoring released prisoners. With her brother, John Gurney, she hoped that, by their reforms, prisons 'may be rendered schools of industry and virtue, instead of the very nurseries of crime'. In 1835 their efforts were rewarded by the passing of an Act of Parliament for 'effecting greater uniformity in the government of the several prisons in England and Wales'. This was to be achieved by appointing:

> A sufficient number of fit and proper persons, not exceed-ing five, to visit and inspect every Gaol in any part of the Kingdom of Great Britain . . . inquire into all matters touching and concerning such Gaols . . . make a separate and distinct report in writing of the state of every Gaol and transmit the same in writing to one of His Majesty's Principal Secretaries of State.

By 1863 death or retirement had reduced the five inspectors to two. According to a House of Lords Select Committee the result was that:

> The amount of inspection given to the different prisons appeared to be less than originally intended to be, and that is in itself desirable . . . it appears by the evidence that in many cases prisons are visited by the inspector only once in the course of 18 months and that such visits average in duration about 2–4 hours.

Transportation to Australia ended in 1852, after which long-term prisoners were held in a number of what were called 'convict prisons', paid for by national taxes. In 1862 the generic term 'local prisons' was

introduced to cover the various types such as Gaols and Houses of Correction paid for by local taxes. These were both steps along the way to the 1877 nationalisation of both convict and local prisons under a Prison Commission, headed by a Prison Commissioner. One of the early actions of the first Commissioner, Major General Sir Edmund du Cane, was to abolish independent inspection by making the inspectors assistant commissioners. They still reported to the Secretary of State, but through the Commissioner. This self-regulation lasted for the next 104 years despite objections by the Gladstone Committee of 1895 that:

> The intention of the 1877 Act appears to have been that these officials, appointed by the Secretary of State, should be independent altogether of the Commissioners and act directly on behalf of the Secretary of State. This however seems to have fallen into desuetude, and the inspectors, by practice, have come to be looked upon as representing the Commissioners.

In 1962 the Prison Commission was itself abolished. The then Permanent Secretary to the Home Office, Sir Charles Cunningham, persuaded the then Home Secretary R. A. (later Lord) Butler that prisons, which took up the largest part of its budget, should be run like every other Home Office responsibility. He recommended that a Home Office Prison Department should replace the Commission, with a career civil servant as Director General. Although the logic of this appeared unassailable, the wisdom of trying to run prisons as a department of a Whitehall ministry was increasingly questioned over the years. In 1978, a report by the House of Commons Expenditure Committee reflected rising concern in the country about prison management, in particular self-regulation. Among other proposals, the report recommended the establishment of a fully independent Inspectorate, reporting directly to the Home Secretary and carrying out some of the duties given in other countries to an Ombudsman.

The report noted that, 'Such an office existed before the nationalisation of prisons in 1877, and, until then, played a very significant
part in shaping the policy and regulating the administration of our
prisons.'

In 1979 Prime Minister James (Lord) Callaghan appointed Mr
Justice May to head a Committee of Inquiry into the UK Prison
Service. In the course of this he received evidence from the Home
Office that three kinds of inspection were needed – efficiency audit,
propriety audit and inspection of the investigation of grievances.
However, not being keen on independent inspection of a Home
Office department, the Permanent Secretary, Sir Robert (Lord)
Armstrong said, 'The arguments appear to point in the direction of
improving the role of the present Prison Department Inspectorate
rather than establishing new independent bodies.'

But Mr Justice May was not persuaded. He accepted that 'in both
theory and practice, no inspection can be independent of Parliament,
and thus, in practice, of government'. He also accepted that 'both in
theory and in practice, no inspection carried out by a member of the
Home Office could be independent of that department or a Prison
Service that was part of it'. He therefore recommended that there
should be, 'A system of inspection of the Prison Service which . . .
should be distanced from it as far as possible.'

The Conservative government which took over from the Labour
administration that had set up the May inquiry, accepted the judge's
recommendation and appointed an independent Inspectorate, located
in the Home Office under a Crown appointee to be called Her
Majesty's Chief Inspector of Prisons. In his report, May strongly recommended that, in the interests of independence and objectivity,
the appointee should not come from within the Prison Service. This
has been accepted ever since. Sadly, the first Chief Inspector, Bill
Pierce, formerly Chief Probation Officer for Inner London, died
within a year of his appointment. A diplomat, Sir James Hennessy,
followed him for five years, and was succeeded by a judge, Stephen
(now Sir Stephen) Tumim, for eight. After just over five and a half

years, I, a soldier, handed over to Anne Owers, a Human Rights analyst.

Commenting on the first appointment, Mr Justice Eric Stockdale wrote:

> In view of the current overcrowding, the dilapidated state of the buildings, the use of industrial power by the Prison Officers Association and comparative impotence of management and all visitors, independent inspection is as essential as at any time since Howard wrote 'the care of a prison is too important to be left wholly to any gaoler'. It is devoutly to be hoped that the latest attempt to secure effective independent inspection of the prisons will not be frustrated as were the earlier attempts.

The Chief Inspector's remit covers efficiency and propriety, but not the investigation of grievances. It was not until 1994 that a Prisons Ombudsman was appointed to fulfil this requirement. Much of the time of the first appointee, Vice Admiral Sir Peter Woodhead, was taken up with trying to obtain a parliamentary remit similar to that of the Chief Inspector. Home Office officials resisted his attempts as stoutly as they had resisted the concept of independent inspection. The remit says nothing about the composition of the Inspectorate, frequency of inspection or content of reports. Mr Justice May recommended that the previous practice of formally inspecting every prison every five years should be continued. It is up to the Chief Inspector to decide which prisons should be inspected, when, and by what mix of inspectors. All that is laid down about the production of reports is that they must be addressed to the Home Secretary and, by law, published. The same applies to the annual report to Parliament.

When I looked at the arithmetic, however, I found that five-yearly inspection was impossible. I only had two inspection teams, each carrying out a programme of ten formal inspections every year and each lasting at least a week, whose dates were published in advance.

Preparing and conducting inspections, followed by writing reports, left barely enough time to carry out more than a few short and unannounced inspections, lasting two or three days. No inspections took place during August or over Christmas or Easter. Having only two teams meant that it needed seven years to inspect all 137 prisons in England and Wales, plus the four in Northern Ireland and the three Immigration Service Detention Centres, containing those asylum seekers and immigration detainees who were not held in prisons.

To combat this problem I spent a considerable amount of time during my first four years in office campaigning for a third team. In 1999, for example, 16 prisons had not been inspected for seven years and a further 12 for six. I had to remind ministers constantly that my minute budget was totally unequal to the task and was invariably overspent every year in completing even our inadequate programme. Eventually they gave way and increased funding, enabling me to form a third team, produce a five-year programme, and carry out more unannounced follow-up inspections. These concentrated on the implementation of previous recommendations to ensure that the momentum for change was maintained.

The three inspection teams are the 'guts' of the Inspectorate. Every team leader had to have governed a major prison before being appointed. In an ideal world such an appointment would be a recognised stepping stone for promotion within the Prison Service, not least because anyone working with the Inspectorate saw far more of the Prison Service in action than at any other time in their career. Not only did they learn a great deal about standards in the process, but were in a position to pass on the lessons when they returned to work in the Prison Service. I told team leaders what was wanted and left them to determine how that would be delivered. As with any other operation, success depended on their leadership and the resulting teamwork.

I was very fortunate in my team leaders, all of whom were distinctively individual. Tony Wood, who led at Holloway, was IT literate and fascinated by strategic issues, and I was not at all surprised when he was headhunted by Group 4 for his managerial skills. Rod Jacques, the

only team leader to remain with the Inspectorate throughout my time, was IT illiterate and a brilliant cartoonist, characteristics that caused amusement to all of us. Countless people in the Prison Service, from the Director General downwards, consulted Rod, however discomforted they may have been by his perceptive observations, judgements and recommendations. Geoff Hughes, a cheerful and ebullient Welshman who had previously governed a women's prison, Drake Hall, replaced Tony. John Podmore, a former governor of Swaleside on the Isle of Sheppey, came to lead the third team. Both Geoff and John had the necessary balance of professional skill, personality and sense of humour. All were friends and we functioned well as a team.

Each inspection team consisted of two permanent members supplemented by a third on temporary attachment. One was a Prison Service junior governor, hopefully with the potential to govern his or her prison. I was fortunate in those who served with me, all of whom became wedded to bringing about improvement. The second permanent member was someone with a non-custodial background drawn from Prison Service or Home Office civil servants, probation officers or a leader of a youth offending team. Their contribution was as broad as it was valuable.

The third and temporary member came from the Prison Service's Accelerated Promotion Scheme (APS), which brought in graduates and promoted existing prison officers to governing grades. The initial two APS years are spent in prisons, the first as a prison officer and the second as a principal officer, or middle manager. This is followed by promotion to Governor Grade 5, the junior grade, and what is called a 'Headquarters year' during which they work for a senior manager. I asked the Director General to send the brightest of them to the Inspectorate for their year. Seeing more of the Service than they might in a lifetime, and at a formative time in their career, could only enhance their education and training. Thus a succession of highly impressive young men and women were attached to inspection teams, contributing more and more as their year went on. I was very pleased

to hear that those on the APS regarded a year with the Inspectorate as the best of the 'Headquarters year' jobs. We had many requests to join us but, sadly, could not accept them all. Regrettably, the Prison Service has now stopped sending APS candidates to the Inspectorate.

Each member of a core team had specific inspection responsibilities that they also wrote up for the report. Sometimes teams called on a growing number of lay inspectors who included the wife of the Bishop of Huntingdon, a vicar from Leeds, and a former member of a Board of Visitors.

One or more research officers from the Research and Development Team, led by Monica Lloyd, our principal psychologist, supplemented teams. Intelligent, capable and motivated, all the graduate research officers were computer-literate young women with a very bright future ahead of them. Invariably, when we advertised the posts, we had hundreds of applicants. It was sad that, before joining us, so many of them had been unable to find work to exploit either their talents or their education.

Some six weeks before all programmed inspections, one or more research officers visited the prison and distributed questionnaires to a randomly selected ten per cent of all inmates, which they collected and analysed. If a chosen prisoner could not read, a researcher filled in the questionnaire with them. There were two purposes behind this. Firstly, all inspectors would know in advance the prisoner's view of the institution being inspected. This was invaluable collateral for subsequent meetings with randomly selected groups of prisoners. Secondly, questionnaires enabled us to begin building a unique database of the quality of the treatment of and conditions for prisoners throughout the prison system. Questionnaires, which differed for each type of prison, covered such issues as how prisoners were received, whether they were in work or education, whether they felt safe and whether they were being prepared for release. Analyses were published as quality assurance annexes to every report.

Research officers also conducted structured interviews with staff and prisoners during some of the unannounced inspections. In addition they carried out research for all thematic reviews. Monica led

much of this work herself. She also inspected offending behaviour programmes, which she had previously run in high security prisons. This included the treatment and conditions of those prisoners serving life sentences.

Each inspection team included a number of consultants, every one an expert in a particular aspect of imprisonment. The largest area was health care, led by a Chief Medical Inspector. I was fortunate in each of the two who worked with me. Malcolm Faulk, who took part in the Holloway inspection, retired soon afterwards. Very fortunately, we were then joined by Dr John Reed, author of the 1993 report for the government on the treatment of mentally disordered prisoners. John, a distinguished psychiatrist and experienced NHS executive, was the acknowledged expert on this much-neglected subject. His credibility within the NHS was to prove a priceless asset in our attempts to persuade all concerned that the NHS ought to take over responsibility for health care in prisons.

Dr Reed was helped by a number of other specialists, including a panel of nurse inspectors who looked at day-to-day nursing practice, inspectors from the Royal Society of Pharmacists who examined that important and expensive part of health care, and a number of dentists nominated by the Royal College of Dentistry. We appointed two drug treatment consultants to inspect the ever-increasing number of assessment and treatment programmes. As Prison Service health care was not then subject to normal NHS inspection, the work of this whole team was particularly important.

One day, Chris Woodhead, Her Majesty's Chief Inspector of Schools, admitted to me that he had 100 days of prison education inspection in his budget but did not know how to spend it. I told him that I could spend it if he made some of his inspectors available to my teams. We already had our own education inspector, John Stephenson, but if we used official ones, education providers in prisons would then be subject to the same standards of inspection as the education colleges from which they came. Chris and I could then submit the same annual report to our respective secretaries of state.

Chris Woodhead agreed and the scheme was implemented from April 1999. OFSTED (the Office of Standards in Education) and/or FEFC (Further Education Funding Council) inspectors joined every team, assessing not only the standard of provision, but how education related to the work of the prison as a whole. Later, when a TSC (Training Standards Council) was formed to inspect the provision of NVQs (National Vocational Qualification) and other certificate-awarding activities, I invited it to join us as well. NVQs, and certificates such as those awarded by the City and Guilds, are important in helping prisoners to get jobs on release. The new Adult Learning Inspectorate (ALI) and the readjusted OFSTED, formed from the amalgamation of the three organisations, now carry out inspections.

We used a working farmer, John Walker, to inspect prison farms, and a civil engineer to check buildings, fire precautions and compliance with health and safety regulations. Sandy Radcliffe, an absolute terrier for detail, had been literally everywhere, in every prison in the country, at least once; indeed, staffs went in awe of his encyclopaedic knowledge. On one occasion, by noticing that a boiler had been installed back to front, he saved HMP Canterbury from blowing up. On another, he saw that the wrong bolts had been used to fix landings to the wall of a new unit in Frankland, thereby saving them from collapsing, together with whoever might have been on them at the time.

Finally, on particular occasions, we used inspectors from other Inspectorates. Probation inspectors came to observe preparation for release and the treatment and conditions of lifers. Social Services inspectors examined the treatment and conditions of those under the age of 18, who were subject to the provisions of the Children Act 1989, and alerted us to the ways in which such provisions were being disregarded. As a result, we appointed a full-time consultant, John Rae Price, formerly chief executive of the National Children's Bureau, to take a particular interest in the inspection of this vulnerable age group. Social Services inspectors also inspected Mother and Baby Units in women's prisons, for which they had a statutory responsibility.

Every inspection began with a formal briefing to the team by the

governor and senior management team of the prison, during which the inspection programme and its concerns were discussed. A familiarisation tour of the prison, conducted by the person nominated by the governor as team liaison officer, generally followed the briefing. Members of the team then met with randomly selected prisoners in the wings on which they had been told to concentrate. This done, they followed their individual programmes, meeting together over lunch and every evening for debriefing by the team leader. The leader himself also inspected particular aspects of a prison, met the Board of Visitors, and had at least a daily meeting with the governor to discuss particular points as they arose.

On the last day of an inspection, the team formally debriefed the governor and senior management team of the prison, the chairman of the Board of Visitors and the prison's area or line manager. Each inspector in turn covered the issues for which they had been responsible, highlighting both those aspects that gave cause for concern and any examples of good practice. The team leader gave an overall summing up so that no one was left in any doubt as to what might appear in the subsequent written report.

I would have liked to take part in every inspection myself but, even when only two inspection teams were operating, this was impossible. I had to attend meetings and conferences, receive visitors, visit prisons other than for inspection, carry out between 70 and 80 speaking engagements a year and cope with a voluminous correspondence. I could not have done this without the help of my indefatigable PA, Barbara Buchanan. I also had to read and do the final edit of every inspection report as well as write the preface. Together with my indispensable driver and friend, Brian Bell, I covered over 200,000 miles during my time in office.

However, either Colin Allen or I tried to spend at least one whole day with each team during an inspection. I also used to lead in any particularly sensitive unannounced inspections, when the staff reaction to our sudden appearance was almost as revealing as the inspection itself. The dates of unannounced inspections were given to no one

outside the Inspectorate, not even to ministers. Briefed by the team leader, I then walked round the prison with the governor, giving him or her the opportunity of airing any problems with which the Inspectorate might be able to help. As we walked, I spoke with as many staff and prisoners as possible. At the end of the day, I discussed my conclusions with the team, stayed with them overnight, and took part in the debrief the following morning. Colin and I always tried to conform to the different styles of each team and its leader.

In line with all military inspections, the aim that I gave to the teams was to 'help establishments improve their operational efficiency'. Inspections were conducted as free consultancies rather than an inquisition. The teams, made up of experts, could be consulted by prison staff. Our approach didn't prevent us from being outspoken about things we found to be wrong, but anything publicised or recommended had to have a constructive purpose. This was emphasised by our inclusion of examples of good practice in every report.

The inspection process is the principal weapon in the Inspectorate's armoury, and absolute right of access to and within prisons is guaranteed by law. Also by law inspection reports have to be published, but I found that publication was taking far too long, sometimes well over a year. Timeliness is of the essence if recommendations are to help improvements. Delay, which was orchestrated by civil servants working for the Home Secretary as well as by the Prison Service itself, suggested that the content of inspectors' reports was – unsurprisingly, perhaps – not always welcome. The climax of long drawn-out discussion between the Home Office and the Prison Service, from which the Inspectorate was excluded, was little short of farcical. When finally cleared, reports were published with one press release from the Chief Inspector saying what had been found at the time of the inspection, and another from the Prison Service saying what action it had taken since the inspectors had left.

When Jack Straw took over as Home Secretary in May 1997, almost 30 inspection reports were still unpublished, one of which I withdrew

because it had been outstanding for over a year. Straw's arrival provided the opportunity for proposing change.

The reporting process began with the debrief, after which both the inspected prison and its line manager knew what the report would contain. Action on certain recommendations could begin at once, and some prisons even acted on them during the inspection itself.

Our aim was to get the report to the Home Secretary within five weeks. The Prison Service then had three weeks to comment on matters of fact. After any factual objections had been accepted or rejected, the Director General told ministers that he was happy for the report to be published. After publication, the prison would draw up an action plan for each of the recommendations, copied to ministers and to me. The Prison Service had the right to reject recommendations, provided that they explained why. However, to maintain the momentum of change, action plans would be updated at regular intervals and the prison receive an unannounced follow-up inspection. Jack Straw agreed to these procedures and issued the necessary instructions.

At the same time as introducing debriefs, I began writing personal prefaces to every report, drawing attention to anything particularly good or bad, anything that had echoes with other similar prisons or types of prisoner, or any matters that were beyond the capability of a prison to resolve. The inspection process, while focussed on monitoring and influencing the treatment of and conditions for prisoners, was also quality assurance for the Home Secretary. Therefore it was essential to know what quality of imprisonment he required.

Not long before I took over, Michael Howard had electrified the Tory faithful at their annual party conference by proclaiming that 'Prison Works'. What exactly did he mean? What was I meant to assure him was working? Eventually I learned what he wanted of prisons in a discussion centred on the words of one his predecessors, Leon (Lord) Brittan, who once said that prison *was* punishment, not *for* punishment. The punishment was the deprivation of liberty for a period of time determined by the courts, and it was not the business

of the Prison Service to add to that punishment through punitive regimes in penal institutions. This seemed so absolutely right that I repeated it in speeches and inspection reports, pointing out that some treatment of prisoners, and the conditions in which they were held, was clearly and unacceptably punitive.

Michael Howard, however, challenged me on this. I told him that I had presumed that it was his government's policy, since the statement had been made by a recent Conservative Home Secretary.

'I couldn't disagree more,' he said.

'What sort of prisons do you expect me to find when I inspect?' I asked.

'Decent but austere, with a positive regime for tackling re-offending, based on opportunities for work and education,' he replied.

'Where's the punishment in that?'

'I think that we will resume this conversation another time.'

We never did because he left office shortly afterwards, following the May 1997 General Election. It was difficult to disagree with his definition.

We had had an earlier conversation on another matter that, at the time of writing, still requires formal resolution. Prisons are points of delivery of treatment and conditions for prisoners which, as Chief Inspector of Prisons, were all that I was responsible for inspecting. No one inspected the means by which that treatment or those conditions were delivered, in other words the Prison Service itself. All other Criminal Justice System chief inspectors were responsible for inspecting their services. For example, the Chief Inspector of Constabulary inspected the headquarters of each force as well as the policing methods. Until the appointment of the Chief Inspector of the new National Probation Service, all inspectors came from the service they were responsible for – hardly a recipe for absolute objectivity. All were professional advisers to ministers, and also members of management teams in the appropriate ministry. The sole exception was prisons, on which the Director General of the Prison Service was, quite rightly, the adviser.

What I had seen at Holloway, and learned from the experiences of my predecessors, suggested that no Chief Inspector of Prisons could assure quality without also being able to inspect the relevant part of the Prison Service. When I discussed this with Michael Howard, he at once saw my reasoning, and agreed that I could ask questions of Prison Service Headquarters. Nevertheless, he had no intention of formally amending my parliamentary terms of reference and I had to look for another way of widening the context of individual inspections.

Quality assurance is the real value that independent inspection adds to the conduct of imprisonment. Each of the penal stakeholders requires different assurance. The public needs assurance that it is protected by ministers, officials, and the Prison Service who, they hope, are making every effort to prevent prisoners committing further crimes on release. Parliament needs to be assured that the electorate is getting value for the public money entrusted to those ministers, officials and the Prison Service. Ministers and officials need to know that the treatment of and conditions for prisoners, conducted in their name by the Prison Service, are of the required standard, while prisoners themselves need to know that there is regular, independent and impartial scrutiny of their situation. How could we express this in a way that all the stakeholders could understand?

Government is obsessed with league tables. Michael Howard had never mentioned them but Jack Straw did. I could see absolutely no point in wasting time trying to league-table prisons that differed in size, role, prisoner mix or geographical location, based on a five-yearly inspection cycle. I also questioned what ministers could possibly learn about the quality of current treatment and conditions from comparing out of date information.

We could tell ministers which prisons were failing by providing details of the quality of treatment and conditions that prevailed on inspection, and we could indicate where improvements were necessary. Quality failure was a matter of right or wrong, not league table placement. Therefore, to define quality more precisely, we began

work on what we ultimately called the 'Healthy Prison' concept. There are four aspects to a Healthy Prison:

- Everyone is, and feels, safe – staff, prisoners, and those who work in or visit the prison.
- Everyone is treated with respect as a fellow human being.
- Everyone is encouraged to improve themselves and given the opportunity to do so through access to purposeful activity.
- Everyone is enabled to maintain contact with their family and is prepared for release.

We felt that this concept was entirely in line not only with Michael Howard but also with famous words spoken by another previous Home Secretary. Had I been in the Strangers' Gallery of the House of Commons shortly before 10 p.m. on the evening of 20 July 1910, I would have heard the 36-year-old Winston Churchill wind up a debate on Prison Estimates as follows:

> We must not forget that when every material improve-ment has been effected in prisons, when the temperature has been rightly adjusted, when the proper food to main-tain health and strength has been given, when the doctors, chaplains and prison visitors have come and gone, the con-vict stands deprived of everything that a free man calls life. We must not forget that all these improvements, which are sometimes salves to our consciences, do not change that position.
>
> The mood and temper of the public in regard to the treatment of crime and criminals is one of the most unfail-ing tests of the civilisation of any country. A calm and dispassionate recognition of the rights of the accused against the State and even of convicted criminals against the State, a constant heart-searching by all charged with the duty of

punishment, a desire and eagerness to rehabilitate in the world of industry all those who have paid their dues in the hard coinage of punishment, tireless efforts towards the discovery of curative and regenerating processes, and an unfaltering faith that there is a treasure, if you can only find it, in the heart of every man – these are the symbols which, in the treatment of crime and criminals, mark and measure the stored-up strength of a nation, and are sign and proof of the living virtue in it.

Marvellous words that stayed on my desk from the moment that I first read them! What better guidance for a Chief Inspector required to assure the quality of the treatment and conditions of prisoners? What better description of a humane and purposeful Criminal Justice System? Churchill's sentiments are the clearest possible condemnation of punitive, as opposed to rehabilitative, imprisonment. They challenged the national conscience in 1910 by referring to the civilisation of the country. How strong was a nation that sanctioned what I saw in Holloway 85 years later? They provided the clearest possible answer to questions about what the Prison Service should be attempting to do with and for prisoners. After sentencing, while the convicted discharge their dues to society, prison should rehabilitate them with the aim of turning them into useful and law-abiding citizens. In order to determine what curative and regenerating processes to apply, it should discover the talents and abilities of even the most hardened criminals.

How much attention would the stakeholders pay to demands for the end of unacceptable treatment and conditions? If ministers chose to ignore anything condemnatory, and instigated no change as a result of Inspectorate disclosures, it suggested that they had another agenda. Some said that they simply wanted the Prison Service to keep prisons under control so that there was nothing for the media to highlight. Winning the next election was far more important than risking public outcry by trying to reform prisons.

So what should I do? Bearing in mind that my remit came from

Parliament, not from any political party, I resolved to continue the line taken by my predecessors and report what I found rather than what ministers and officials might want to hear. Because it affected them, too, I hoped that such disclosure might arouse the strength and virtue in the public at large, encouraging them to challenge their elected representatives to take their protection seriously by ensuring that imprisonment was properly administered and decently conducted.

4

THE CONDUCT OF IMPRISONMENT

'There is no such thing as a criminal class.'

CRIME IS ESTIMATED TO COST the country around £80 billion per year. More than one million crimes – 18 per cent of the total – are committed by released prisoners, at a cost of more than £11 billion. Every reconviction costs the Criminal Justice System more than £65,000. Court and legal fees are likely to amount to around £30,000; it costs, on average, £37,500 to keep an adult male in prison for one year, and this is less than the average of £47,500 required to keep a juvenile under the age of 18 in a Young Offender Institution, or the staggering £130,000 per child needed by a local government Secure Training Centre.

What, then, did Michael Howard mean by his assertion that 'Prison Works'? Of course prison works to the extent that those who are locked up cannot commit crimes or endanger the public. But an annual £11 billion caused by re-offending can hardly be said to be value for the £2.8 billion per year, and rising, that it costs to run the Prison Service. The Home Secretary also seemed to ignore the fact that all but a handful of prisoners – in 2002 it stood at 24 – were going

to come out. Surely the question that has to be asked about whether prison works is 'In what state of mind will prisoners be when they come out?' Keep them locked up all the time, as I had found in Holloway, recreating the conditions in which so many had lived their lives so far, and the chances were that many of them would come out embittered and re-offend.

All the evidence – admittedly largely from America – suggested that if prisoners were treated in the manner outlined by Churchill and *professed* by the Prison Service – challenging their offending and anti-social behaviour and rectifying deficiencies that had prevented them from living responsible lives – 30 per cent might well not re-offend. Add that to the numbers who might not 'because they only had one crime in them' and the re-offending rate should be relatively low. But it is not. Fifty-eight per cent of all adults, 78 per cent of all young offenders under the age of 21, and 88 per cent of all children aged between 15 and 18, re-offend within two years of release.

Those who take the opposite line to Michael Howard, believing that prison does *not* work because of the horrendous number who re-offend, are not telling the whole story either. Forty-two per cent of adults and 22 per cent of young offenders do not re-offend. If the prevention of re-offending is an aim of imprisonment, then whether or not it works should be judged by its success or failure rate. But how ex-prisoners are supervised after release is also a matter of prime importance. Inconveniently for those who wish to make a strong case one way or the other, there is little difference between the re-offending rates of those given prison and those given community sentences, as currently conducted, although the latter has, allegedly, fallen by some three per cent. This suggests that, in order to say confidently that prison does or does not work, account has to be taken of what happens to prisoners after release.

Perhaps Michael Howard was merely making a claim to satisfy the 'hangers and floggers' in the run up to an election. To such people no punishment can be too harsh for any incorrigible rogue who steals, mugs, rapes or murders. It is, they believe, pointless to waste money

on expensive rehabilitation programmes because criminals are bound to re-offend whatever you try. They deserve nothing more than to be locked up and the key thrown away. By making their views known so much more loudly than most, this reactionary element encourages those in authority to assume that they are more numerous than they probably are. Their prejudice is fuelled by the way in which some members and organs of the press present crime and criminals to the public.

I, however, believe there is no such thing as a criminal class. During my time as Chief Inspector, a former Cabinet minister, peers of the realm, officers from all three Armed Forces, ministers of religion, barristers, solicitors, doctors, nurses, policemen, prison officers, probation officers, social workers, school teachers, businessmen, and executives of responsible voluntary organisations all served prison sentences.

Colin Allen told me that prisoners were often popularly divided into three categories – the bad, the mad and the sad. Of these, the purely bad were by far the smallest proportion. This was quite contrary to the public perception of prisoners as a combination of serial killer, paedophile, arsonist, armed robber and con man. A maximum of five per cent of the prison population presents such danger to the public that they have to be held in very secure conditions. That is not to say that the remaining 95 per cent do not deserve imprisonment, but that their criminality and the risk they present are substantially less.

The mad are much larger in number, as was confirmed by the Office of National Statistics in October 1998. In a most important report called *Psychiatric Morbidity among Prisoners in England and Wales*, for which all prisoners in every prison were surveyed, the document revealed that 70 per cent of male and 50 per cent of all female prisoners were suffering from some form of identifiable personality disorder. This did not mean that they were sectionable under the Mental Health Act but that their behaviour was measurably not normal. In general they were likely to be young, unmarried, and charged with what are called acquisitive offences (burglary, robbery or theft). Many were drug dependent, most were poor, and a significant

number had experienced several stressful events in their lives including physical and sexual abuse. These prisoners were more likely to live off crime than earn an honest living.

The sad also far outnumber the bad. The Prison Service uses the demeaning phrase 'poor copers', to describe those who cannot look after themselves either in prison or in the community. These include a number of what are called 'short-term repeat offenders', who are the scourge of the police, magistrates' courts and prisons, who see them coming back over and over again for the same sort of crime. Their sentences are always a matter of weeks rather than years, so nothing sustained can be done with them. One morning, while visiting HMP Barlinnie in Glasgow, I saw an empty cell in the busy reception wing. I was told that it was being kept for a prisoner who had been released that morning but would undoubtedly be back by evening, having stolen a bottle of whisky. These wretched people are part of society's flotsam. There is no way that they can survive outside prison, where they are fed, housed and kept warm. But is expensive prison really the right place for them and what alternatives could and should society be finding and funding? This is one of the many questions that should be put to the Prime Minister, following his expressed intention to be 'tough on the causes of crime'.

The bad, the mad, the sad: all three categories were present in Holloway. None of their needs were being satisfactorily looked after. In theory, the needs of, and problems posed by, every type and category of prisoner should have been covered by the Prison Service's Statement of Purpose, prominently displayed at the entrance to every prison. This was written in 1983, by the then Director General of the Prison Service:

> Her Majesty's Prison Service serves the public by keeping in custody those committed by the courts.
>
> Our duty is to look after them with humanity and help them to lead law-abiding and useful lives in custody and after release.

Was what we had seen at Holloway an acceptable way of carrying out this duty? Whose duty was it to see that the Prison Service carried out its duties?

This same question arose following what have been described as the worst series of riots in the history of the British penal system. These began in Strangeways prison in Manchester in April 1990, were copied in six other prisons, and lasted for 25 days. At the time, along with the rest of the public, I remember being transfixed by television pictures of prisoners occupying the roof of the jail that they were steadily dismantling and hurling tiles at anyone who appeared to approach. The riots were inquired into by Lord Justice Woolf, assisted by my predecessor, Judge Stephen Tumim. In February 1991 they published their report, and I was advised to read it as soon as I could. One of the great penal documents of all time, it remains required reading for anyone interested in imprisonment.

Strangeways was one of a number of prisons built in the second half of the nineteenth century that were based on Jeremy Bentham's idea of a 'panopticon', a design that remains pertinent today. Wings, in which prisoners are held, radiate off a central hub from which staff can observe and control all movement. I was interested to find that new prisons in the Caribbean Overseas Territories, which I was later required to inspect, had been built to a similar design, the only difference being that there was a gap between the hub and the wings to allow fresh air to circulate.

Many of these Victorian prisons are still in use, but the treatment of and conditions for prisoners confined in them seem to have regressed from the intentions of those who built them. Two, and sometimes three, prisoners are now held in cells designed for one. Every cell in Pentonville, the first of the modern prisons, built in 1843, was equipped with a loom, since all prisoners were required to work. Now, too many have nothing to do. Every cell originally had a lavatory, emptied by pressure produced by a treadmill, operated by prisoners. When use of treadmills was stopped in 1895, so in-cell

sanitation ended, not to be restored until after the Woolf report. Much internal sanitation is now unscreened, making many cells little better than lavatories.

Lord Woolf found that overcrowding and idleness were two of the main causes of the riots, but his recipe for improvement began with something far deeper than that. He recommended a complete reassessment of the role of the Prison Service in order to give it a clear sense of direction. At the heart of the overcrowding problem was a lack of co-ordination between various arms of the Criminal Justice System, in particular between judges who were responsible for sending people to prison and the Prison Service which was responsible for holding them there. One overcrowded the other.

To resolve the idleness problem, as well as produce stability, the Prison Service had to balance three requirements:

> Security – the obligation to prevent prisoners from escaping.
> Control – the obligation to prevent them from causing disturbances.
> Justice – the obligation to treat them with humanity and fairness and prepare them for their return to the community in a way that makes it less likely that they will re-offend.

At Strangeways, failure to maintain control and achieve the necessary standards of justice had resulted in what could easily have been a collapse of security.

Lord Woolf pointed out that security, control and justice could not be held in balance unless the Prison Service changed its management style and structure. In particular, he focussed on the importance of proper relationships between management and staff and staff and prisoners, and identified '. . . a fundamental lack of respect and failure to give and require responsibilities at all levels in the prison system, which must be tackled if the Prison Service is to maintain a stable

system'. If managers showed that they respected their staff, then staff were more likely to treat prisoners in the same way and with humanity. The impetus for this has to come from the top, as Lord Woolf pointed out in criticising the civil servant, who was Director General at the time of the riot, for absenting himself from the scene and passing responsibility for its resolution to his Prison Service deputy. Visible leadership is required of a Director General, who is the operational head, in day-to-day charge of the service for which he is publicly accountable.

While the Prison Service's Statement of Purpose has the merit of being succinct and covering security, control and justice, it does not fully explain its role, which is to serve the public by furthering the aims of the Criminal Justice System. In other words, to protect the public by preventing further crime being committed by prisoners who have been in its charge and care. Lord Woolf's wide-ranging recommendations included increased delegation of responsibility to prison governors, enhanced roles for prison officers and a national system of accredited performance standards. He recommended that every prisoner should sign a contract, or compact as it is confusingly called in prison today, setting out what he could expect and what was expected of him. Better chances of retaining contact with families should be facilitated by keeping prisoners in community prisons as near to their homes as possible. No prison should be allowed to hold more than its certified number of inmates without Parliament being informed.

I also read Mr Justice May's 1979 report that had given rise to the formation of the Inspectorate. In it I found:

> It was argued (by witnesses) that the organisation and ethos
> of a Civil Service department was inappropriate for the
> management of an operational organisation dealing 24
> hours a day with the difficult human problems of both staff
> and inmates alike . . . Prison Officers in the field, it was
> said, find it frustrating and maddening to be told how to
> handle prisoners in a particular situation by someone who

has never had that experience himself. Whether rightly or wrongly . . . the Prison Officer, unlocking 40 criminals on a Wing in an establishment two or three hundred miles from London, saw the Headquarters of his Service as a faceless monolith, caring not for human beings but for efficient administration.

The more I looked at the Prison Service, the more I realised how much was still exactly as he had described. The numbers working in the 'faceless monolith' that was Prison Service Headquarters had grown from 168 in the days of the Prison Commission to more than 1800. From it spewed an endless stream of rules, regulations, operating standards, operating instructions, orders, targets and performance indicators. General Sir John Learmont memorably described what these amounted to in his 1995 report on the escape from Parkhurst.

Learmont asked a prison to record all correspondence received from Headquarters in a one-month period. The result averaged out at 230 letters, 65 faxes and 24 e-mails per day. Extrapolated to include every prison in England and Wales over the four months of his investigation, he estimated that this amounted to 47 tons of paper, equating to a pile nearly a mile high, or more than 800 feet higher than Ben Nevis! What madness! Who on earth could possibly have time to read all this paperwork? In 2000 the governor of Holloway told me that 80 per cent of his time was taken up with bureaucracy. No wonder managers in prisons had so little time for the supervision and oversight of the treatment of and conditions for prisoners. They were tied to their desks, submerged under a continuous, bureaucratic avalanche from which they could not free themselves and which prevented them from doing their required work with either staff or inmates. In such circumstances, how could they establish the relationships that Lord Woolf felt to be so essential for security, control and justice?

Mr Justice May's statement touched several chords. The people best suited to run large operational organisations are those with considerable practical management experience. Very few ministers or

officials have ever run any organisation themselves. Fewer still have had the experience of rising up through the various tiers of management, learning how to exercise operational responsibility at each level. True, as they climb the rungs of the Civil Service ladder, officials become responsible for the work of more people. But that is more to do with overseeing bureaucracy than the minutiae of command.

I discovered that all this had been recognised by Kenneth (Lord) Baker, Home Secretary at the time of the Woolf report. He too was concerned at the way in which the Prison Service was managed and decided to invite someone from the world of business and industry to examine and report on it. He chose Sir Raymond Lygo, a former Chief of the Naval Staff and chief executive of British Aerospace, then director of James Capel Corporate Finance.

In the covering letter to his report, Sir Raymond made two very interesting comments. 'The Prison Service,' he declared, 'is the most complex organisation I have encountered and its problems some of the most intractable.' He further observed that, 'It was very clear that, unless there was a preparedness on the part of the Home Office to take its hands off the management of the Prison Service in its day to day business, and allow itself to be constrained by matters of policy only, then it would not be possible to effect the changes which you deem desirable, and which have become very clear to me as being necessary, during the talks that I have had and the visits that I have made.'

What changes did Sir Raymond and Kenneth Baker feel were desirable? Essentially, that it was not appropriate for the Prison Service to be run by civil servants using civil service methods. It should be much more independent of the Home Office, run by a Board under a non-executive chairman who could speak out on its behalf and in support of its needs. The Director General should not be the most promotable civil servant available, but someone, chosen by open competition, who had 'the ability to manage and provide leadership and inspiration'. Both the 'confetti of instructions' and the over-large Headquarters from which they descended must be reduced. There must be clarification of who was in charge of whom.

Industrial relations could only be improved if managers were allowed to manage.

With the exception of the appointment of a non-executive chairman, all Sir Raymond's recommendations were accepted but nothing was done to implement them. In fact, neither the Home Office nor the Prison Service produced an action plan for either Woolf or Lygo, whose reports were followed by a White Paper – *Custody, Care and Justice* – published in September 1991, agreed to by all political parties in the House of Commons. Kenneth Baker's foreword began, 'This White Paper charts a course for the Prison Service in England and Wales for the rest of this century and beyond.' The Home Secretary continued, '[It] recognises, as the Woolf report recognised, that a better and more stable prison system requires a coherent and consistent strategy for the Prison Service. This White Paper provides such a strategy. It is the planned programme of change which the Woolf report advocated . . . It is a strategy which derives from identifying the obligations of the Prison Service if it is to serve as an effective part of the Criminal Justice System in the 21st century.'

The aim of *Custody* could not have been set out more clearly:

> The first priority of any Prison Service is to keep in custody those committed to prison by the courts. That requires effective physical security measures and an alert and well-trained staff confident in their own safety and in the procedures to be followed when a security incident occurs. It requires a positive approach to security and control in prisons. It must be based on the quality of relationships between prisoners and staff and on providing prisoners with an active and worthwhile day in a secure environment located as near as possible to their home communities.

On *Care* the White Paper said:

Staff have a responsibility not only for the custody but also for the care of prisoners. This must be reflected in staff training. It must be demonstrated through providing programmes and conditions for prisoners which treat them with humanity, dignity and respect.

Finally, on *Justice*:

Prisoners should be required to exercise responsibility for what they do. They should be consulted and given explanations for decisions that affect them. The procedures for handling discipline and complaints must be effective and fair. Prisoners must be given opportunities to help them live law-abiding lives on release.

These three issues were expanded into 12 priorities. Such priorities included the need to end overcrowding, to improve co-operation with other services, to delegate responsibility and accountability to all levels, to provide sentence plans for each prisoner and to recognise the particular requirements of unconvicted prisoners.

Custody, Care and Justice has never been implemented. As with the Woolf and Lygo reports, neither the Home Office nor the Prison Service produced implementation or action plans. Only two of the 12 priorities have been actioned, but for different reasons. Physical security was improved at a cost of hundreds of millions of pounds – some of it diverted from programmes for prisoners – following the escapes from Whitemoor and Parkhurst. The government had promised, after Woolf, to have integral sanitation in all cells by April 1996, and the Minister of Prisons, Ann Widdecombe, duly announced that this was so. However, having just visited Dartmoor, I had to say publicly that 'slopping out' had not yet ended there or in a number of other prisons.

To complete the rejection of all recommendations for change contained in these three reports, whether or not they had been accepted

by Home Secretaries or endorsed by Parliament, the incoming Labour government had one further reactionary measure in store.

In 1995 the Prison Service was made an independent agency which, in theory, distanced it from the Home Office. However, Jack Straw undermined this by appointing a career civil servant, Martin Narey, as Director General. Later, David Blunkett effectively destroyed it by then making him, at the same time, second Permanent Secretary in the Home Office. Most recently he completed the destruction by moving Narey to the Home Office as Commissioner of Correctional Services – the Prison and Probation Services and the Youth Justice Board – and Permanent Secretary responsible for human resources in the Home Office. This confirmed the total rejection of Lygo.

I had expected ministers to have given clear direction to both Prison Service and prisons on what they were to do with and for prisoners during their time in custody. I had expected to find financial provision based on this direction, in line with how the Ministry of Defence negotiated with the Treasury. I had expected to find that the Prison Service had its own mechanisms for ensuring operational efficiency.

None of these expectations were met. How, then, could the Prison Service function effectively? On the evidence that I had just seen at Holloway it couldn't – and it wasn't. Reading through how my predecessors had been ignored, discovering that little or nothing had been done to implement the recommendations of Woolf, Lygo, or the only White Paper on prisons, and learning from Colin Allen how inspection reports were handled, did not encourage me to think that I would fare any better. While individual recommendations concerning particular prisons might be listened to, the most difficult task would be to persuade ministers and their officials to change their whole approach to the management and conduct of imprisonment, which was so conspicuously failing.

To help me find my way through all this, I fell back on the very structured thought process that all army officers, from the very beginning of their careers, are taught to undertake when faced with an

operational problem. Making an appreciation, as the process is called, begins by analysing the aim of an operation, including any factors – such as constraints on time or resources, or whether what you are considering is part of something bigger – which might limit the aim. Then follows a detailed study of the ground over which you are to operate, noting which parts are impassable, or contain difficult obstacles. You then analyse the comparative strengths and weaknesses of your own troops and those of the enemy whom you are facing. Finally, you list the options that are open to you before coming to your conclusions and recommendations.

Within the Criminal Justice System, the role of prisons seemed very like that of hospitals in the NHS. Neither has any control over who is sent in; both have to try to make people better, conscious that the process cannot be completed within the institution, but in the community in the form of aftercare. The analogy can be continued. Some prisoners or patients will prove incurable, others will have to come back for further or different treatment. It is said that if you stay too long in hospital you risk picking up further infection from the fabric. If you stay too long in prison you risk being corrupted by other prisoners.

However, while the Prison Service had written itself a Statement of Purpose, ministers had given it no aim against which its performance could be judged and the planned programme of change contained in the White Paper had been ignored. I could find no current direction on what the Prison Service was to do or how that was to be resourced, other than Michael Howard's demand for 'security, security, security'.

I always cringe when I hear the word 'strategies' used in connection with government initiatives because, as *Custody, Care and Justice* specified, there can only be one overarching strategy for any major activity. A strategy is defined as the 'projection and direction of the larger movements and operations of a campaign' that can unite all those involved in their purpose. Subordinate and related actions are either tactics – 'the art of deploying (military) forces in order of battle, and of performing (warlike) evolutions or manoeuvres' – or stratagems – 'devices or schemes for obtaining an advantage'. Yet at Holloway I had been told that it had a

drug strategy, whatever that meant. Was that a strategy for Holloway alone or Holloway's part of an overall Prison Service drug strategy?

The Statement of Purpose could be turned into a strategy if the overall aim was to prevent re-offending, but no one had laid that down. Nor did it seem to have a place in the Prime Minister's declaration that he intended to be 'tough on crime and tough on the causes of crime'.

All my experience had shown me the vital importance of everyone involved in an operation knowing what part they had to play in it and how. On the evidence of the governor of Holloway, governors only knew that they had to prevent prisoners from escaping. This appeared to have more to do with the prevention of ministerial embarrassment than of re-offending.

When I looked more closely, I found that the lack of a clear strategy was reflected most obviously in the way prisons were managed. To implement a given aim or strategy, every operational organisation needs a chain of command, with accountability and responsibility vested in managers at every level or link in the chain. Managerial structures are usually designed around the tasks that have to be managed. Normal organisational practice is for named individuals to be made responsible and accountable for separate aspects of an operation. The Prison Service is an operational organisation containing a number of operational units, or prisons. Each ought to be run according to the type of prisoner it houses. If Woolf, Lygo and the White Paper were followed, separate managers would be accountable upwards for the standard of performance of all prisons of a particular type, and responsible downwards for overseeing and ensuring consistent treatment and conditions, wherever prisoners of their particular type were held.

At Holloway I had found that no one was responsible for women. Only high security prisons had their own director and he had only been appointed following General Sir John Learmont's recommendation in his report on the escape from Parkhurst. This seemed to bear out a widely held view that the Prison Service only made progress when forced to implement recommendations following disasters.

In her recent series of Reith lectures entitled *A Question of Trust*, Baroness Onora O'Neill, Principal of Newnham College, Cambridge, reflected on the fact that many now say that they can no longer trust our public services or the people who run them. They are viewed with suspicion, their word doubted and their motives questioned. Whether real or perceived, this crisis of trust is a dangerous development, particularly for government. In pointing out that complex systems of accountability and control damaged trust, which could only be restored by making people and institutions more accountable, Baroness O'Neill was repeating what Lord Woolf had pointed out in his Strangeways report.

The Prison Service's impersonal approach to management, where no one appeared to be held responsible or accountable for anything, is characterised by another development that is becoming all too prevalent in the public sector, namely the growing use of a myriad of targets and performance indicators. Targets and performance indicators are a useful management tool when sensibly designed and used. Identifiable success can be rewarded and failure subjected to sanctions. However, their value is degraded if they tell you nothing about the quality of the activity that is being targeted. The Prison Service insists on using a large number of targets and performance indicators that tell you nothing about quality, as three separate examples demonstrate.

First, the most effective way of challenging re-offending is to provide every prisoner with a programme of purposeful activity, compatible with a variety of factors such as type of crime, length of sentence, ability and gender. Extraordinarily, the Prison Service sets different purposeful activity targets for private and public sector prisons. A private sector prison, which does not provide the 30 hours of purposeful activity per week specified in its contract, risks being fined. Public sector prisons invariably have lower targets based on an average of 23 hours, but they are not disciplined even if, like Belmarsh, they only deliver 11.

What ministers and senior managers need to know is not how many hours of purposeful activity are provided but how many are

devoted to offending behaviour programmes, education, or the improvement of work skills. The Prison Service's insistence on measuring the success of its offending behaviour programme by the numbers of courses in a year is equally unhelpful. If your aim is to reduce the risk of re-offending you need to know how many offenders need such courses and how many have not yet had them. In other words, targets ought to help pinpoint the reasons for success or failure so that steps can be taken to rectify deficiencies.

Second, if it costs an average of £14,000 per year to keep a prisoner in a resettlement prison, and £51,000 per year in a high security prison, the average cost per year of all prisoners in all prisons tells you nothing about the adequacy of the treatment and conditions in any.

Third, to combat the prevalence of drug abuse, the Prison Service introduced mandatory drug testing of a randomly chosen 10 per cent of the prisoner population each month in every prison. Initially, 25 per cent tested positive, but by 2000 when the percentage of those tested had dropped to five per cent, the percentage of those testing positive had also dropped to 13 per cent. Prisons are judged on targets that require an annual reduction in the numbers testing positive. How honest are the reported results?

One day I saw nine certificates on the wall of a prisoner's cell.

'What are those for,' I asked.

'Testing negative on mandatory testing. They know I don't use, so they test me every month. I'll have ten if you come in two weeks' time.'

In HMP Rochester, which claimed to have almost no positive tests, we discovered that asylum seekers and immigration detainees were being included in the mandatory percentage. Not only was this illegal because they were not prisoners, but they were held separately from prisoners and had no access to their drugs.

However, prisons such as HMP Altcourse, where every prisoner was tested on admission, reported that at least 70 per cent of all prisoners admitted to having a drug problem on admission to prison. Twenty-five per cent admitted to using heroin or crack cocaine.

Mandatory testing initially sent a message around the prison system that drug testing was being taken seriously, but it is now largely discredited and certainly does not indicate the size of the problem with which the Prison Service has to deal. Intensive treatment is only available in 50 out of the 137 prisons.

Reinforcing my suspicion that it was an avid disciple of this brave, new, managerialist world, the Prison Service established a number of Operating Standards Audit Teams, responsible for auditing every prison every two years. Prisons are graded according to exact compliance with regulations, but gradings based on exact compliance with regulations do not tell ministers – or the public – how well prisoners are being prepared for their return to the community. Neither do they reflect the quality of their treatment and conditions.

Slavish attention to targets and compliance with regulations, as opposed to the treatment of and conditions for prisoners, made it inevitable that, in the absence of an aim, there would be a conflict between Prison Service gradings and Inspectorate assessments of Healthy Prisons. I determined to take my aim from the White Paper – the prevention of re-offending – which had all-party support in Parliament. Ministers would have to decide which version they preferred.

After the aim comes ground. Prisoners are the 'ground' of imprisonment. Prisons exist to contain prisoners and help them to live useful and law-abiding lives. What then are the characteristics of the prisoner 'ground' that the Prison Service has to cultivate?

Ninety-five per cent are male, 65 per cent of whom are between the ages of 21 and 39. Over 4000 are female, whose numbers are rising faster than any other part of the population. Almost 3000 prisoners are still officially children, subject to the 1989 Children Act. More than 1000 are over pensionable age. The proportion of prisoners from ethnic minority backgrounds is three times that of their proportion in the community as a whole.

When first received into prison, three-quarters of inmates are unemployed, a third are homeless, 65 per cent of all adult males have

a reading age of less than eight, and more than half the prison population has no educational qualification of any kind. Taken together with the numbers in the 'mad' and 'sad' categories, these are not exactly the figures of an advantaged stratum of society.

Who then were the enemy and who the own troops? Own troops were easy to define. It was already abundantly clear that I had a priceless asset in the Inspectorate, whose admirable members had shown that they were quite capable of doing what I thought inspectors *should* do. They had the knowledge, they had the enthusiasm, they knew precisely from their own experience – as well as their instincts – what was required, and they were a team. I looked forward to working with them not with gloom or despair but with keen anticipation.

However, they were not alone. Holloway had shown me that, in addition to the many good and dedicated members of the Prison Service at all levels, and the Boards of Visitors, there were countless other volunteers wanting to do the work with and for prisoners that the Prison Service was not doing. The shelves in my office were filled with booklets and documents from organisations such as the Prison Reform Trust and the Penal Consortium (of organisations interested in reform). I was greeted by a host of letters from interested experts and other well-wishers. We were part of a large team.

The enemy was equally easy to identify. It was not prisons, prisoners or the staff who worked in or with them. It was not Parliament. It was not the public or the media, although both would have to be convinced that the facts we reported ought to concern them as much as they did the Inspectorate.

The enemy was exactly the same group – although made up of different individuals – that had ignored, or resisted, all the efforts of so many distinguished and knowledgeable people over the years to improve the conduct of imprisonment. 'Same race, different rats' was how a similar group were once described by another general. The enemy of successful imprisonment was a triumvirate: ministers, Home Office officials, and the hierarchy of the Prison Service.

They were the enemy because their actions or inactions were the

barrier to progress. By subscribing to ineffective managerial practice they were perpetuating failings that many experienced observers had noted for years. The myriad of short-term initiatives that they produced might look good on paper, but because they were not related to any strategy they achieved little either long lasting or of substance. They could blame the Treasury for their lack of financial resources, but without a strategy, or any attempt to identify and eliminate the waste generated by current managerial practice, they did not even know how much money they needed.

On the evidence, there were only two courses open to me. Either I could acknowledge that a system, which had resisted and ignored advice for so long, would not change because it did not want to do so. Or, in the firm belief that improvement based on fudge inevitably *is* fudge and real improvement can only be based on fact, I could try to give my stakeholders a true understanding of the reasons why prisons were failing to protect them by preventing the appalling re-offending rate. Prisons were not responsible for failing to do what they had neither been directed nor resourced to do. Therefore, in honouring my parliamentary remit, I ought to draw attention to ministerial and official contributions to failure in every report, in the hope that they might at last recognise their responsibilities.

5

LOCAL PRISONS

'Brixton is not just a failing prison; it is a failed prison, failed by
Ministers and failed by the Prison Service.'

JUST AFTER 6 P.M. ONE WET and windy Thursday evening in May
1999, a large white lorry with a number of small, square windows
high up along its sides, turned into a short, steep road beside the
outer wall of HMP Exeter. It climbed towards the main gate, two dark
green, wooden doors set in an ornate stone arch above which were
the words 'Devon County Prison' and the date 1852.

It was quite obvious that the space available in front of the gates
was far too small to allow the driver to swing out sufficiently to be
able to turn into them. I stood and watched with interest while, for
what seemed like at least ten minutes, he gingerly edged the lorry
backwards and forwards, backwards and forwards, its rear end frequently sticking way out over a steep, grassy bank that fell away to a
busy main road. Eventually he positioned the vehicle so that he could
drive through the arch and make an immediate sharp left turn into
the prison itself. The splendid and imposing gateway turned out to be
a listed feature of a listed building and so could not be altered to allow
easy entrance to today's vehicles. It might have been suitable for

horse-drawn carriages to enter 150 years ago, but what was needed now was an alternative gatehouse, or a new prison.

Once inside, the driver had to manoeuvre the lorry again, in a small courtyard, until its rear was facing an open door into the prison itself, beside which stood a prison officer. The driver climbed out of the cab, carrying some documents which he took through the door into a gloomy room on one side of which was a long counter-like desk, behind which stood a number of other officers. Around the room were two or three grilled doors leading to small rooms with low benches ranged against their bare walls. The papers handed over, the driver, now accompanied by a prison officer, returned to the lorry, opened a side door and went inside. He soon re-emerged, carrying a plastic bag bearing the Prison Service logo and containing a number of items that I could not make out. Behind him, handcuffed to the officer, came a rather dishevelled young man, wearing a T-shirt and jeans, seemingly in his early twenties. Back inside the prison, the driver placed the plastic bag on the desk, where its seal was broken and its contents tipped out by another officer. The handcuffed man was asked to confirm their description as they were listed on a document that he was asked to sign. After further personal details had been recorded, the prisoner's handcuffs were removed and he was taken to one of the small, grilled rooms. This procedure was repeated for the other eight occupants of the lorry, six of whom joined the first man, while two were put into separate rooms.

For the next two hours each prisoner went through a variety of processes. Having been documented he was given a green prison dressing gown and towel and offered a shower. He was issued with a standard number of striped prison shirts, maroon T-shirts, trousers, socks and trainers, a set of which he changed into. At the same time his own clothes were taken away and their details recorded. He was called forward for interview by a nurse, who questioned him about his immediate physical and mental health. He was then issued with blankets, sheets and pillowcases and, in another room, offered a mug of tea and a plate of stew that had been heated up in a small microwave oven.

There was much waiting between these various activities, during which time the prisoners, together with some others who had arrived at the prison before them, sat listlessly in what were called waiting rooms. No one spoke much. No prison officers talked to them.

Eventually, shortly before 8.00 a.m., all but two of the men were collected by a prison officer and led away, carrying their belongings, to the wing where they would spend their first night in prison. Of the remaining two, one was clearly a serious drug addict – shivering, a vacant expression on his sallow face. The nurse felt that he should be under observation in the Health Care Centre, to which she and another prison officer took him.

The other man had been separated from the others from the moment that the driver of the lorry mentioned the word 'numbers' to the staff when bringing him into the prison. Apparently he was in debt to a drug dealer, already in the prison, from whom he wished to be kept separate for his own protection. Voluntary separation for those who ask for it is allowed for under Prison Rule 45, hence the slang use of the word 'numbers'. Such prisoners are classified as vulnerable and kept out of sight and sound of all others as far as possible. They include sex offenders, those who have been threatened or bullied, those who find it difficult to cope with life in prison and some who are in debt. In their own interests, vulnerable prisoners are unlikely to cause any trouble because to do so risks their being put in with those from whom they wish to remain separated. However, running a separate unit for them imposes additional strain both on staff and the organisation of a prison.

In some institutions determined efforts are made to try to persuade prisoners to remain in the main part of the prison because there is a stigma attached to those on Rule 45, which will move with them throughout the prison system. One prison, HMP Durham, bravely refuses to regard any prisoner as being more vulnerable than any other, holding all together, which requires a confident and competent staff. An exception was made for a particularly well-known police officer, who was sent to another prison. But the prison runs much

more smoothly as a result, justifying both the risk and the additional staff effort.

Back at Exeter, the other six new inmates were taken to the ground floor of the largest accommodation block of the prison. Initially they were all put in a room containing a television set and a number of wooden chairs. Here, the officer told them what time they would be woken in the morning and what time they would be unlocked from their cells so that they could collect their breakfast. He then gave each of them a plastic bag containing a safety razor, toothbrush, toothpaste, biro, writing paper and envelopes, a small amount of tobacco and some cigarette papers.

As their names were called out, the men were taken in pairs to their white-painted, high-ceilinged cells, in which mattresses and pillows were already on a metal, double-tier bunk bed. The only other furnishing was a small table, two wooden chairs and two small, wooden cupboards. High up on one wall was a small, barred window, and near the door a stainless steel washbasin and lavatory. They were shown how to activate a call bell to alert staff if they needed attention and were told, forcefully, that this was for emergency use only. Having been asked if they had any questions the cell door was slammed shut and they were locked in for the night.

This reception procedure goes on every day of the week in every prison in the land. It is one of the most important moments in a prisoner's time in custody. The attitude of reception staff, the manner they adopt towards prisoners, the care and thoroughness of the process itself and the general impression made by the surroundings in which it takes place, often determine the way in which prisoners will behave throughout their sentence.

The same procedure takes place, in reverse, almost every day of the week as well. From about seven o'clock in the morning prisoners who are going to court are brought to the reception area, their prison clothes taken from them and their own clothes and possessions handed back. Some of them may return in the evening, in which case the reception process is repeated, but some might be released straight

from court. After being given breakfast, they sit in the same waiting rooms as when they arrived, awaiting the same vans to take them to court. Cellular vans, as they are called, contain up to 12, small, individual cells '900-mm high, 810 mm between the forward facing plastic moulded seat and 650 mm between the door and the sidewall'. A concession is allowed for journeys of more than two and a half hours, when seats with moulded full-seat cushions are meant to be fitted. The contract states that there must be a 'taper from the front inner edge of the seat towards the door hinge panel, to allow foot entry and prevent parts of a body being trapped between the frame and a rapidly closing door'. The language reflects the impersonality of the whole operation. So seated, prisoners are then driven either directly to the court, or via other prisons to collect more prisoners.

After those who are due to appear in court have left, the next groups to go through the reverse reception procedure are those who are either being released or transferred to other prisons. Although reception areas are in use for much of the day, there are peak periods first thing in the morning and last thing at night. Unfortunately, this is not reflected in staff shifts, which don't allow for flexibility. This means that, all too often, late arrivals can sit around for over an hour waiting for reception staff to return from their evening meal. This, together with late arrivals from courts, because drivers also act as court officials and therefore can only return prisoners when the court has closed for the day, has particularly unfortunate ramifications. Too many prisoners only arrive on their wings just before day staff go off duty at 8 p.m., leaving totally inadequate time for their briefing.

Fortunately, this is beginning to change as an increasing number of prisons introduce 'first night' procedures. Specially selected and trained staff look after and brief newly received prisoners, who are held in separate accommodation. Hopefully, this will have an impact on the dreadfully high suicide rate among prisoners on their first night in custody.

To prove the point that improvements are possible, I was interested to discover how the problem was tackled at HMP Altcourse – far and

away the best-run local prison in the country. The experienced director, Walter McGowan, employed by Group 4 after governing a large, public sector local prison, clearly understood the vital importance of good reception procedures. He therefore introduced three simple but significant innovations. Firstly, he renamed the procedure 'admissions', which meant that it was not compared with reception procedures used elsewhere. Secondly, he took away the grilles and doors from all waiting rooms, which forced staff to visit newly arrived prisoners frequently to check on their safety, presence and wellbeing. Finally, he insisted on flexible shifts to ensure that there were always sufficient officers on duty to staff the various parts of the process.

I was intrigued to find further evidence of the difference between private and public prison reception practice at HMP Wolds, also run by Group 4. During our inspection the director took me to watch a rehearsal of a rock opera, performed by the prisoners. Among those taking part was a heavily tattooed and rather sinister looking man, who had written much of the script. He had been transferred to Wolds after being a ringleader of a serious riot at the nearby high security prison, Full Sutton. When I spoke to him about the rock opera, I also asked him about the prison.

'It's the best I've been in – and I've been in a lot,' he said.

'Why, particularly?' I asked.

'It's given me hope,' he replied.

He went on to tell me that this had started the moment he arrived. He had got out of the van and gone into reception, expecting to get the same old treatment he had become used to over the years, but '. . . it was quite different. It was spotlessly clean. An officer sat me down in a chair, called me Mister and asked if I would like a cup of tea. I thought I was being conned! But that went on the whole time when I was taken to my cell and it's gone on ever since. They all wear their names so we know who the staff are. It's harder to hit someone if they treat you like that!'

Reception ought to be followed by another very important process:

induction. All that can reasonably be achieved with confused and often frightened prisoners on their first night in prison is a briefing to help them cope with the first 24 hours. Thereafter, a much longer induction programme ought to be carried out, which, if done properly, cannot possibly be completed in less than two to three weeks. In addition to explaining the daily routine, prison staff ought to carry out detailed assessments of every prisoner, to determine what help they will need in order for them to live useful and law-abiding lives both in prison and once they have completed their sentence.

Ideally, induction and assessment ought to begin on the morning after reception. Unwisely, instead of following a common checklist, such as those used by pilots every time they take off or land, each prison has its own programme. Some say that the procedures can be completed in a day, some say two or three days, others take up to three weeks. Some facilities keep prisoners in separate induction accommodation; others remove prisoners from their wings for specific parts of the programme. Results are as inconsistent as delivery.

Risk and need have to be separately assessed. Obviously, risk comes first – the risk that prisoners present to staff and fellow prisoners and the risk to the public if they escape. Any risk that they might present to themselves is separately assessed by the medical staff. Very high risk prisoners will be sent at once to a special secure unit in a high security prison, such as was usual with IRA prisoners, or to a Category A prison known as a 'core local', of which there are a number around the country. Both are very expensive and only used in extreme circumstances. The risk assessment process will also confirm whether any should be held separately from other prisoners.

Assessment of need begins with trying to find out what has prevented a prisoner from living a law-abiding or useful life thus far, resulting in a prison sentence. Offending behaviour programmes, designed to challenge and tackle sex offending for example, are conducted in a number of prisons. Other programmes have been designed to tackle anger management. Careful assessment is an essential prerequisite to treatment, which ought to begin as soon as possible. Five

separate potential deficiencies are associated with failure to live a useful life; these may or may not also be factors in offending.

Assessment of educational ability ought not to concentrate solely on basic literacy and numeracy skills. Many who have no educational qualifications of any kind may well suffer from learning difficulties, such as dyslexia. These ought to be teased out by use of standard tests, conducted and analysed in the same way in every prison in order to ensure consistency and continuity in subsequent education provision. Sadly, this is not what happens at present, nor are results always passed on, leading to the unnecessary and wasteful practice of re-assessing prisoners every time they change prison. I would like to see every prison judged on the numbers of prisoners who cannot read when they come in and the number who still can't read when they leave.

Aptitude tests can discover job-skill potential. Ideally all prisoners, having taken an aptitude test, should have their potential exploited in courses related to job prospects in the community to which they will return. As with education, both analysis and recommendation ought to be recorded so that they can be followed up in any facility to which a prisoner is moved.

By social skills the Prison Service means the ability to live in the community. I saw a most imaginative course entitled 'Learning to Live Alone' in the Northern Ireland Young Offender Institution (YOI) Hydebank Wood, a unique establishment run jointly by the Northern Ireland Prison and Social Services. Designed by social workers, this consisted of courses in cooking, painting and decorating, plumbing and electrical repair, first aid home economics and coping with the bureaucracy of the welfare state. It seemed so obvious that I wondered why it was not made standard practice in every prison. Considering how many people live alone, or lack even the most rudimentary understanding of how to cope with the demands of everyday life, it could also be taught in schools.

Parenting skills ought to be included in prison education programmes. In addition to the number of adults, a truly appalling number of children and young offenders are, or are about to become,

parents. Many have spent years in care and have not the slightest idea of what a parent is, let alone how to be one. Imprisonment presents a real opportunity to teach them.

I have drawn attention already to the large number of prisoners with mental health problems of one kind or another. Plans for future care should be made on the basis of specialist assessment, including which prison is most suitable for someone with a particular disorder. Because almost all will be released, such plans *must* include the establishment of a lifestyle that they can sustain in the wider community. This emphasises the importance of regarding health in prisons as a public health issue. The same applies to the considerable number of people with serious physical health problems, including blood-transmitted viruses, such as HIV and Hepatitis C, associated with substance abuse, as well as TB – a growing problem, particularly among rough sleepers and immigrants from Eastern Europe. Prison presents an ideal opportunity to teach healthy living disciplines, including exercise habits.

Diet is a key ingredient of healthy living. Clinical studies in many countries have proved that correct nutrition is a cheap, humane and highly effective way of reducing anti-social behaviour. Recently this was proved yet again by Bernard Gesch, director of the charity *Natural Justice,* in a trial conducted with over 400 young offenders at HMYOI Aylesbury. Half were given a daily supplement to their diet containing essential vitamins, minerals and fatty acids, and the other half a placebo. Over the time of the trial, there was a 37 per cent reduction in serious offences such as violence in the group taking the supplement. Neither group knew what it was taking. The outcome was immediately recognised by prison officers, who are normally very sceptical of such trials.

The Home Office response was to insist that its nominated expert should examine the result. He reported that the data was 92 per cent statistically pure, an almost unheard of score. However, despite the obvious implications for anti-social behaviour within prison and for society in general, both Home Office and Prison Service remain obdurately opposed to publicly accepting the results or adopting the process more widely. It is difficult for them to argue on grounds of

cost. It would cost a mere £3.5 million per year from the prison budget of £2.8 billion to give such a supplement to every prisoner every day. A 37 per cent reduction in serious offences such as violence would not only pay for this many times over, but could have an incalculable impact on the economic and social cost of crime. If Tony Blair is so keen on tackling the causes of crime he would do well to examine the impact of inappropriate diet such as fast foods. Prisons could provide an appropriate testing ground. I realise that, on release, prisoners might well return to their fast food habits but, emphasising the relevance of correct nutrition to parents and schools, the experience may well alter the eating habits of some of them.

Finally, on reception every prisoner ought to be tested for drug abuse to discover who is or is not using them at the time. As at HMP Altcourse, those who test positive ought then to be kept separate from the non-users. Positive specimens should be further analysed to determine exactly what substance is being used. If the opportunity to tackle what is a national problem is to be seized, every local prison ought to be able to conduct thorough detoxification programmes for all those assessed as being in need of them. Proper detoxification is a far longer and more detailed process than the supervised withdrawal that currently passes for it in some prisons. Only by testing everyone will the Prison Service gain a true picture of the overall size of the drug problem that it then has to resolve.

If all these measures had been available to the eight men I saw received into ancient HMP Exeter that May evening, the prison would not have earned the damning report that it subsequently received. Much of what was required was outside its ability to resolve. It could not devote non-existent funds to improving its architecture. It had no control over the numbers of mentally disordered or otherwise vulnerable prisoners it had to try to house in totally inappropriate conditions, with wholly inadequate resources. It was not responsible for the boys from Stafford – over 200 miles away – whom I found sent from HMYOI Brinsford, at less than an hour's notice, to serve the last six weeks of their sentence at Exeter. It would not have chosen to close its already limited

number of workshops because there were no funds to pay instructors. It needed help to counter the activities of a particularly militant and obstructive Prison Officers Association Committee.

However, to my deep concern, Exeter was little different from any of the other 41 adult male local prisons that we inspected. Without exception they were overcrowded and under-resourced. Collectively, they were certified to hold 18,500 prisoners but held over 23,000. People think that local prisons house mainly unsentenced prisoners, but only 9000 are unsentenced. The majority are a mixture of lifers, long-, medium- and short-sentenced prisoners, convicted but unsentenced prisoners, sex offenders, the mentally disordered, serious drug addicts, asylum seekers and immigration detainees and, in some cases, young offenders. Catering for all their various needs is an impossibility. All that can be done is to compromise between sentenced and unsentenced, leaving both categories as losers.

Of the 41 local prisons, all but five are situated in the heart of inner cities, from which the majority of their prisoners come. Twenty-eight such institutions were, like Exeter, built in Victorian times or earlier. They have been adapted from time to time by the addition of other buildings, or the conversion of some areas into classrooms or workshops. But their age and unsuitable architecture, allied to lack of maintenance, mean that the buildings are major contributors to the Prison Service's £1 billion works bill that grows larger and more worrying each year, thanks to inadequate capital funding. This irresponsible Treasury housekeeping will eventually result in buildings falling down, or having to be taken out of use because they have been condemned as unsafe by health and safety inspectors, as happened at HMP Swansea. A responsible housekeeper would ring-fence funding of a coherent maintenance programme.

The problems that bedevil local prisons are at the heart of the problems of the Prison Service. The solution is clear and obvious but, like so many others, ignored. Local prisons lack both strategic and tactical direction. Having no clear aim, their governors do not know what

they should be doing with and for their prisoners. Direction must be provided. These problems have not just arisen. They stem from a fault line that stretches back to 1877. In that year local prisons, which contained in the main unsentenced or short-sentenced prisoners and debtors, were nationalised with convict prisons containing long-term prisoners. However, unsentenced and short-term prisoners require different treatment from long-term prisoners. For example, they need access to the due processes of law, such as making application for bail and having ready access to their lawyers.

Sentenced prisoners on the other hand require full, purposeful and active employment every day. Old, Victorian local prisons are quite suitable for unsentenced, or remand prisoners as they are usually called. Their cells are larger than those in their modern counterparts and are capable of holding more than one prisoner without being overcrowded, but they are totally unsuitable for sentenced prisoners. Their design did not include sufficient classrooms or workshops, whereas modern accommodation blocks also have lecture and other rooms suitable for training courses or group activities.

If they are to remain in use, which because of the inexorable rise in the size of the prison population seems likely for the foreseeable future, inner-city local prisons ought to be given specific roles appropriate to their location and their facilities. There is talk of selling some of them off and using the money raised from the prime sites on which many of them sit to build a number of large, multi-functional prisons on greenfield sites. I am chary of this because the majority of prisoners come from the inner city areas in which these prisons are located. They will always be favoured by prisoners whose homes are nearby and who will tolerate considerable discomfort to remain there. This validates Lord Woolf's 'community cluster' concept. Each region of the country should have a cluster of sufficient prison places to hold all the various types of prisoner. After sentence, prisoners would move to suitable training prisons near enough to their homes to enable them to keep in contact with their families, as well as allow community involvement in their rehabilitation and resettlement. I cannot

overemphasise the importance of maintaining family contact in the prevention of re-offending.

When inner city local prisons like Exeter were first built they had three roles. One was to receive prisoners immediately after arrest and hold them until trial and conviction. The second was to hold prisoners awarded short sentences. The third was to receive long-term prisoners from the local area for the last few months of their sentence, so that they could be appropriately resettled. These tasks are still valid. The treatment requirements of all prisoners held in local prisons suffer from compromise, the inevitable result of inadequate resources. A way out would be for anyone awarded a sentence of longer than six months to be sent immediately to a training prison of an appropriate category. Those awarded very long sentences could return to their local prison for a particular resettlement programme. Both modern and Victorian local prisons are ideally suited for the three tasks and would require little adaptation. If this happened, they could be redesignated 'community prisons'. They are located in communities. They hold and return prisoners from and to those communities. Communities could contribute to the work such prisons would be doing on their behalf.

There is nothing new about communities being involved with their local prison. Birmingham has adopted Winson Green, now known as the 'city prison'. It has paid for a project of teaching prisoners to teach other prisoners to read. Bristol supports an imaginative project initiated by Nick Wall, the governor of its prison, and funded by European and City money. This ensures that every remand and short-term prisoner has an opportunity to consult someone about housing, jobs, further education and drug or alcohol treatment. Everyone leaving prison has a named person to contact for further support. Nottingham Regional Health Authority pioneered the provision of occupational therapists to conduct day centres for mentally disordered prisoners. Norwich has initiated a most imaginative housing support scheme. Such examples of good practice, and many others, ought to be exploited and replicated by the Prison Service, but no one is in charge of local prisons or responsible for doing so.

One of the saddest aspects of local prisons is their inability to do more than scratch the surface of the huge variety of personal and other problems with which they are presented. One evening in Dorchester I learned that four prisoners had come in for the umpteenth time, having committed a crime that might give them early access to its detoxification programme. Talking to them, I found that two came from good families with whom they had lost touch, having been evicted from home because of their drug habit. Another had been living rough in Bournemouth, unable to get, or keep, a job. Detoxification was not available in the community, nor was immediate follow-on treatment. Their choice was obvious; their outlook bleak. Return to their former habits and ultimately the lonely death of an incurable addict, or hope for help in prison. Sadly, because of the shortage of treatment available in the community, whatever help they received in prison was unlikely to be continued for a number of months after their release.

I recall two conversations related to the fact that 65 per cent of all adult male prisoners have a reading age of less than eight. One was in Nottingham with a young man in his twenties who could not read or write and told me that he did not want to. When I asked him why he replied that he could not be bothered. I asked him how he knew which bus to catch or how to fill in forms in the employment office. He replied that he could always ask someone. All this was in the hearing of the other prisoner in his cell. Later that day I watched him collect his evening meal. When he saw me he came over and asked if he could have a word. I followed him out of the servery into the main corridor. He said that he had been thinking over our conversation and wondered if it really was possible for him to be taught how to read. He had not wanted to admit this in his cell, because his cellmate could not read either, nor did he want to. I passed his name, and his wish, on to the governor. I heard later that he was learning.

The other conversation was in Wandsworth, where I saw a number of prisoners carrying red books called *Toe by Toe*. These had been provided by the Shannon Trust, a charity called set up by a retired soldier

and businessman, Christopher Morgan, who, some years earlier, had answered a call by the Prison Reform Trust for people to write to lifers. Christopher published the letters that he exchanged with his lifer, Tom Shannon, in a very moving book called *The Invisible Crying Tree*. The profits from the book were put into a trust, whose objective is to teach literate prisoners how to teach illiterate prisoners to read. Thanks to a particularly determined prison officer, Neil Lodge, recently the recipient of a well-deserved Butler Trust Award, Wandsworth had accepted the scheme. Unfortunately for its further development Martin Narey would not give it his unqualified support on the grounds, he said, of cost in staff time, but, hopefully, that too is changing.

Prisoners who have been taught to use *Toe by Toe* teach other prisoners for half an hour each day, on their wings, which means that staff do not have to escort anyone anywhere. The result is two-fold. Obviously the mentee learns to read, but the mentor gains self-respect from doing something useful for someone else. A 46-year-old tearfully told me what it meant to him:

'For the first time I can communicate with my nine-year-old daughter, who was born after I came inside. She writes me stories and I am writing one for her. I now know what I have missed.'

'Do you think that not being able to read had anything to do with your being inside?'

'Yes, because I never had a decent job. I was sacked from some because I couldn't follow instructions.'

Most of the really disturbing reports that I published were about local prisons. The Prison Service ought to be thoroughly ashamed of some of the treatment and conditions that we saw and reported on in Birmingham, Brixton, Chelmsford, Exeter, Lincoln, Liverpool, Nottingham, Preston, Wandsworth and Wormwood Scrubs. And yet both ministers and the Director General seemed unwilling to accept that they alone could bring about change. Every time I published a damning report they claimed to be surprised and blamed the prison governor. Three examples show how wrong they were.

When we inspected Wormwood Scrubs in September 1996 we

were very concerned about the numbers of prisoners who had nothing to do all day. As at Holloway, the perpetual excuse was that the staff was overstretched. Only rarely were sufficient numbers on duty in the evening to allow prisoners to have showers or make telephone calls. The same applied to escorting prisoners to education or the gym. The only prisoners with permanent occupation were the wing cleaners, personally selected by staff.

More disturbing was the undercurrent of fear that was immediately apparent whenever we spoke to prisoners. Too many were guarded in what they said if staff were anywhere near. We were told that some staff were ill-treating prisoners, particularly in the segregation unit, but that management did nothing to investigate or stop this. The life of the prison was clearly undermined by the fact that no one appeared to feel safe. Prisoners told us that managers were never seen around the prison, meaning that they were not overseeing how staff treated inmates. This was Holloway all over again. Was it just gross inefficiency or were they deliberately turning a blind eye to something they knew was going on but did not have the guts to confront? Many prisoners told us that there was no point in making written complaints because they rarely got beyond the officer to whom they had to be handed. Prison officers were always believed rather than prisoners.

I described Wormwood Scrubs as a 'flagship dead in the water'. We reported the rumoured ill-treatment of prisoners as forcefully as we could, recommending that it be investigated at once. I also gave notice that I would carry out a follow-up inspection within two years of the report being published. The then recently appointed governor, Joe Mullins, suspected that all this had been happening for some time under his predecessor, and probably under several governors before that. This put him in something of a quandary because, not only was his predecessor still in the Prison Service, but had been promoted from his governership.

After the inspection Mullins tried to introduce a new staff shift system, or detail as it was called, requiring staff to be on duty when most needed to work with prisoners rather than when they wanted to

turn up. But both the inevitable and the unforgivable followed. Inevitably, the Prison Officers Association (POA) objected to his proposals because change was involved. Unforgivably, his immediate superiors, his area manager and regional director, supported the POA rather than face confrontation.

Soon the governor was to experience yet more unforgivable treatment from his superiors when he suspended an officer alleged to have assaulted a prisoner. This they over-ruled. Not surprisingly, this undermined his position within the prison in general and with the POA in particular. Dismayed at such lack of managerial support, when offered a senior post by one of the companies running private prisons, he accepted. In giving the statutory three-month notice of leaving, he warned the Director General not to delay in appointing a successor because the prison was in such a poor state that it should not be left without someone senior in charge. However, his warning went unheeded and the Scrubs was left without a governor for seven months.

Soon many disturbing stories about Wormwood Scrubs were circulating – homosexual relationships between individual members of staff undermining the management structure; increased numbers of unchecked assaults on prisoners by members of staff; appalling conditions in the Health Care Centre; the despair of decent staff members. When we went back in March 1999 I was extremely angry to find that nothing had been done to action our 1996 recommendations. The very strong rumours of prisoners' ill-treatment had not so much as been investigated.

The POA was conducting its own alternative form of management. Fifty-five different shift patterns were in operation, designed around the 'ease and comfort' of individual members of staff with no regard for the treatment of and conditions for prisoners. Almost no prisoners went to education or the gym because staff would not escort them. Conditions in the Health Care Centre were Dickensian; one seriously mentally disordered man's bed collapsed under him while John Reed was speaking to him. The Prison Service's own management consultancy had examined the Health Care Centre after our earlier report that staff

numbers were wholly inadequate for the large number of seriously mentally disturbed prisoners. Unbelievably, they recommended that the already inadequate staff should be cut by 30 per cent.

I had no alternative but to publish an even more damning report, asking ministers and the Director General why no action had been taken since 1996, and how the treatment of and conditions for prisoners had been allowed to deteriorate even further over the intervening two and a half years.

The result was instant and dramatic. The area manager was ordered to produce an action plan, underwritten by the Director General himself. The Prime Minister required Jack Straw to make a statement to the House of Commons explaining why nothing had been done to action previous recommendations. A solicitor came to see me with a number of sworn statements from prisoners who had been assaulted by staff, which I took at once to Jack Straw who passed them to the police. Their investigation resulted in a number of prison officers being brought to trial. However, their convictions at first instance were overturned on appeal.

None of this could have happened had there been a proactive, responsible and accountable management system, stretching from the Home Secretary down to every individual prison officer, that had taken the appropriate and required action years before.

The story of HMP Winson Green in Birmingham was, if anything, even worse. Birmingham has two local prisons, the old Winson Green, built in 1866 in the city itself, and Blakenhurst, built in 1980, situated some miles away and, until recently, run on contract by United Kingdom Detention Services. We inspected both prisons in 2000 and found the contrast between their treatment of and conditions for prisoners stark and remarkable.

Reception arrangements at Blakenhurst were carefully controlled and included separate accommodation for those spending their first night in prison. A comprehensive induction programme began at once with a briefing about the immediate future. Every prisoner was

issued with a telephone card and given the opportunity to phone home. There was work for many of the prisoners in a variety of workshops, for which both those remanded and those sentenced were eligible. I spoke to one cleaner, using an electric floor polisher in the dining room, and asked him whether this was his first time in prison.

'No,' he replied, 'but it's the first time I've been treated like a human.'

'In what way?' I asked.

'Well, if this was a POA jail there would have been two officers standing watching me. Here I'm told what to do and left to get on with it. They come and see that I have done it properly, and then take me to other jobs.'

'Have you done an industrial cleaning course?' (something that not only carries a qualification but also provides jobs for a number of prisoners on release).

'Yes, they put me on one before I was made a cleaner and I had to do a health and hygiene one. I've got certificates for both. This is the best jail I've been in.'

Again I asked in what way.

'Well, you can ask the officers anything and they don't muck you around.'

This could hardly have been in greater contrast to Winson Green. Admittedly it received more prisoners each day, but the reception area was dark, dirty, and lacked the businesslike and purposeful atmosphere of Blakenhurst. Induction arrangements were cursory to say the least, particularly in the evening when it was clear that staff could not wait to end their shift. What programme there was was subject to frequent cancellation, usually on the grounds that there were not enough officers to conduct it. Again, as at Holloway, the main reason put forward was the number of officers who were required to be away on other duties such as 'bed watching' prisoners in hospital.

However, that was not the worst. The dreadful, subterranean Health Care Centre was described by medical inspectors as the dirtiest they had ever seen, containing too many seriously mentally ill

prisoners who should have been in hospital, and there were no programmes for challenging sex offenders. Many of these were kept in
the prison for the whole of their sentence, in sharp contrast to
Blakenhurst, which moved them to a prison where they could
undergo treatment as soon as possible. I questioned why this was both
possible and normal practice in a private sector prison but not in a
public sector one. It was clear that one of the reasons was the attitude
of management and staff to their task.

As at Wormwood Scrubs there were strong rumours of staff ill-
treatment of prisoners. Middle management was ineffective, and too
many staff based the time that they came to and left work on
Birmingham's traffic problems rather than on the needs of prisoners. I
recommended that Winson Green needed the same kind of action plan
that had been drawn up for the improvement of Wormwood Scrubs,
and that the Home Secretary should intervene personally because only
he could ensure that it received the essential additional finance.

But why had Prison Service senior management not already done
this? Anyone with half an eye could see that the treatment and conditions in Winson Green were unacceptable. Even if they couldn't
see, they could have listened to the pleas of the governor, Chris
Scott, a thoroughly decent man, a priest and the chairman of the
Prison Governors Association. Anyone responsible and accountable
for the performance of all local prisons would have had to sort out
Winson Green years before. But no; it was in a different area to
Wormwood Scrubs, and therefore the responsibility of a different area
manager.

Even worse was to come. When we reinspected Winson Green two
years later, nothing had changed beyond what little the governor had
been able to achieve. I had visited him on a number of occasions in the
interim and listened to his despair at being unable to persuade Prison
Service Headquarters to listen, let alone respond, to what he was saying,
or to see that this was making him ill. No action plan was drawn up; no
extra money was made available. Instead, the Deputy Director General,
Phil Wheatley, sent in the same management services team that had rec-

ommended a reduction in health care at Wormwood Scrubs. At Winson Green they recommended a large budget cut!

Chris Scott had tried to brighten up the Health Care Centre with paint, but he could not brighten up the morale of its staff or the conditions for the number of seriously mentally ill patients who should not have been there. An overcrowded, understaffed local prison is no place for a doubly incontinent geriatric suffering from senile dementia. Such people need specialist nursing which prisons simply are not staffed to provide. On one wing, John Reed found a man who had not washed or changed his clothes for five weeks because staff thought that he was pretending to be mentally ill.

Having already appealed to Jack Straw to intervene on the evidence of what we had seen in 1998, I was now in something of a quandary. He had done nothing, so to whom did I now appeal? The Prime Minister? I wondered whether Jack Straw actually *wanted* Winson Green to be improved? What contrary advice had he received and from which officials?

Clearly the Director General, Martin Narey, had to respond, and a number of improvements have now been put in place. But the whole terrible and unnecessary story is yet another indictment of the lack of a coherent strategy and clear direction.

When we inspected Brixton in January 1996, we were briefed on a very carefully researched action plan, called Brixton 2000, that had been drawn up by Dr Andrew Coyle, now Director of the International Centre for Prison Studies at King's College London, when he was governor. The plan included the building of a new gate lodge, reception area, visitors' area, workshops and education centre, providing access to the gym and refurbishing the Health Care Centre. Andrew had taken everyone along with his plans, including the Prison Officers Association, but Michael Howard had killed it by cutting the Prison Service's capital provision, which Jack Straw had not restored.

Brixton was yet another Victorian inner-city local prison about which we were hearing disturbing stories. Because the number of fail-

ing prisons in London, including Feltham Young Offenders Institution, was putting such strain on the area manager, Martin Narey asked me to delay any further inspection of the prison until after our follow-up report on Wormwood Scrubs had been published. Unwisely, because of what I subsequently learned that this delay meant to the treatment of and conditions for prisoners, I agreed.

Early in 2000 the chairman of the Brixton Prison Officers Association Committee wrote a letter to the local paper complaining about the conditions at Brixton. In particular, he focussed on the numbers of mentally disordered prisoners with whom the medical staff could not cope. This was brought to the notice of the Prisons Minister, Paul Boateng, who immediately went to Brixton to see things for himself. Without consulting the Director General Boateng promised additional funding to put things right, saying that if conditions had not improved by the end of the year he would market test the prison.

The army has a well-worn 'lessons learned' system, by which experience is exploited to raise operational standards. Bearing in mind the action plans that had already been instigated in a number of other local prisons in London, I would have expected some of the lessons to have been passed on to Brixton. But this is not Prison Service custom. Had I hoped to find resulting improvements at Brixton when we finally inspected it in June 2000, I would have hoped in vain.

Everywhere we looked we found examples of what should never have been allowed to happen. On each of the top three floors of the Health Care Centre was a ward where 20 mentally disordered men, some of whom had attempted suicide, were confined. All day long they lay down or sat beside their beds with nothing to do, no television, and no one to talk to except each other or an occasional member of staff. The filthy windows – covered in pigeon droppings – and the dingy paintwork contributed to a deeply depressing atmosphere. Attached to one wall was a scratched perspex screen behind which members of staff sat, talking about patients in their hearing. Off each ward were the dirtiest, most dilapidated ablution areas that I have ever seen. Their windows were not merely covered but caked-in pigeon droppings,

which must have been there for years. The lavatories were literally encrusted with scale, and the rusty water pipes attached to the grimy showers and cracked washbasins were coming away from the walls. The floor tiles, too, were cracked and dirty. Had anyone dared to allow such conditions for patients in a National Health hospital they would, quite rightly, have been sacked, but Prison Service Headquarters and Brixton prison managers had tolerated the situation for years. Outside each ward were two small rooms that were occasionally used as classrooms for some of the patients. Other than medication, however, they received no day-care or any other kind of treatment programme. So, to avoid any later suggestion that we were exaggerating, I asked the Director General to come out and see it for himself while we were there, which he did.

When he examined the books, Geoff Hughes, who was leading the inspection, found that one of the nurses had falsified the records of one of the men on suicide watch. Observations are meant to be recorded every 15 minutes, or at whatever interval is ordered. At 2.15 one afternoon Geoff noticed that every observation that should have taken place between then and four o'clock, when the nurse went off duty, had been entered in advance and signed as having taken place. This could not have happened if the nurse knew that management would look at records.

This cavalier attitude to suicide was not confined to the Health Care Centre. On the main remand wing, containing the prisoners deemed most at risk, the cell call-bell audio alarm in the wing office had been sabotaged with sticking plaster. This, too, had obviously happened some days or weeks before the inspection. Martin Narey had written to all prisons about sabotaging alarms after we had reported similar instances in a number of other prisons. Clearly his edict had had little or no effect.

Utterly appalled by the conditions that I found in the Brixton Health Care Centre, I wrote at once to Jack Straw drawing his attention to the lack of equivalence with the NHS that the Prison Service claimed to provide. Immediately Mr Boateng, without consulting either the Director General or me, announced that Brixton was a failing prison and would be market tested.

However, in my report I had to say that while Brixton was failing to provide satisfactory treatment of and conditions for some of its prisoners, it was also a failed prison. Ministers and the Prison Service had failed to provide the necessary facilities that had been so carefully planned by Andrew Coyle. How could a prison succeed when it had had three governors and two interregnums in three years? How could it not fail to address re-offending when it had no education centre or workshops and its gym was outside the wall so that very few prisoners were permitted access to it? With none of the facilities needed to provide any – let alone 30 hours – purposeful activity per prisoner per week, what private sector company would take part in such an ill-considered market test? Mr Boateng's announcement was yet another example of the knee-jerk reactions that are the death of strategic planning.

Overcrowded, under-resourced, undirected local prisons are at the very centre of the Prison Service's problems. Unless and until ministers and the Prison Service resolve the problems caused by their having to hold such a wide variety of prisoners, whose treatment requirements they cannot meet, they will not begin to meet their responsibilities for reducing re-offending.

Local prisons are bound to be places with a high turnover, where it is impossible to carry out any sustained treatment programmes. Therefore it must make sense to remove all longer-term prisoners from such a frenetic environment. Those who remain need programmes suitable for short-term prisoners, whether sentenced or unsentenced. That is the only way in which two types of prisoner will receive their just penal deserts. That is the only way in which the public will be protected from their inevitable re-offending.

6

CLOSE SUPERVISION

'All persons under any form of detention or imprisonment shall be treated in a humane manner and with respect for the inherent dignity of the human person.'

UN Body of Principles

PRISONER R HAD BEEN KEPT in total seclusion on D Wing, the segregation unit of the Close Supervision Centre (CSC) at HMP Woodhill in Milton Keynes, for 206 days when we saw him in August 1999. He had been ordered to the CSC by the Director of High Security Prisons for threatening staff, and subsequently to its segregation unit for failing to conform to CSC routine.

Throughout those 206 days R had been denied access to work, education, hobbies, the gym or the chapel. The furnishings in his cell consisted of a concrete plinth on the floor, on which he put his mattress, a cardboard chair and table, a small fixed mirror and a prison issue noticeboard. He was not allowed a radio. He rarely saw another person. A senior officer and five prison officers, wearing helmets and visors and dressed in full control and restraint (riot) kit, unlocked him for his daily exercise in a small, caged yard in which he was left alone. Before his cell door was unlocked he was made to stand, arms outspread, against the back wall. Once the door had been opened, he was told to put his hands on his head. He was then given a pat-down

search, checked with a hand-held metal detector, and asked to open his mouth for inspection, before being allowed to walk out to his exercise. If the weather was bad a coat was put in the yard for him to use if he so chose. After what was invariably less than an hour he was taken back to his cell and locked in.

The same procedure took place when he took the three showers he was allowed each week. He could, in theory, have two closed visits every month – 30 minutes each in a small room, separated from his visitor by a reinforced glass window set in a solid wall. However, he refused any visits because he said that they were too short, allowed no physical contact with the visitor, and required his relatives to travel a long way from home. He was allowed to make two pre-booked, ten-minute, social telephone calls each week – one midweek and one at the weekend – but only in the mornings, the most expensive time.

R liked to keep his cell clean and was given a hand-brush and floorcloth to do so. But that was where normal hygiene stopped. Prisoners in segregation were not let out of their cells to clean the showers; this was meant to be done by civilian contract staff. However, there had been no contract for some months, resulting in the showers becoming so dirty that prisoners refused to use them. Staff therefore had no option but to clean them themselves. Like all other segregated prisoners, R selected his meals in advance from a weekly menu. These were plated up in the main kitchen and placed on sealed trays. At mealtimes staff pushed the trays through a flap in his cell door, through which he later returned them. We heard endless complaints from him and his companions about the standard of food, quite aside from its strange delivery. But this was part of the mechanism used to control prisoners such as R.

Prisoner B, in an adjoining cell, had an even more bizarre story to tell. One day, after he had finished his evening meal, he felt ill and had shouted in vain to attract staff attention. Staff preferred to watch D Wing cell doors on a CCTV monitor rather than patrol them, so B began kicking his door to make more noise. Still no attention.

Eventually he kicked it so hard that he broke a foot. At last staff responded, realising that he needed medical help.

No doctor was on duty in the prison and staff had to call for one from emergency duty on the nearby M1 motorway. When he arrived at the prison he was made to go through every detail of the very thorough security procedures before being taken to B's cell. There, instead of unlocking the door so that the doctor could examine his patient, staff told B to push his injured foot through the flap in the door. Having given what help he could, the doctor left, via the same time-consuming security procedures. Next day he complained vigorously about the time it took to reach B, let alone what happened when he eventually got there. As a result emergency medical procedures were changed.

Seclusion, as ordered for R and B, is used only as a last resort in the special mental hospitals such as Broadmoor, never as a standard method of managing risk. It can be authorised in response to a specific incident, but is terminated as soon as possible afterwards. Seclusion is defined as: 'The supervised confinement of a patient alone in a locked room, any time, day or night, for the protection of others from significant harm.'

It is used to supplement the belief that 'In the main, security and safety comes from a detailed knowledge of the patient, a level of staffing which provides for adequate observation and supervision, and the confidence of the staff in their own and their colleagues' professional skills to deal effectively with violent and dangerous situations.'

Finally, 'It is a fundamental principle of this policy that seclusion must end as soon as the risk to others has passed.'

In contrast to the intense scrutiny and supervision of patients in special hospitals by trained, professional people, prisoners in the basic and segregation units at Woodhill were held in enforced total isolation, in punishment conditions, with only one hour's daily respite – for solitary exercise – per day. The main differences between the two units were that those 'on basic' were allowed books, a radio, a daily shower and open visits, and staff did not wear riot gear when unlocking

prisoners. However, both categories stayed there until released by the sole authority of the Director of High Security Prisons. The nine prisoners in the two units at the time of our inspection had been held in these conditions for periods of between 27 days and 18 months, with an average stay of eight months.

In view of all the experience and knowledge available in special hospitals, and all that the Prison Service claimed about the decency and humanity of its treatment of prisoners, it is scarcely credible that it could have introduced such a system as late as 1998. The Director of High Security Prisons, Phil Wheatley, who was responsible for implementing its introduction, has recently been appointed Director General of the Prison Service.

The most difficult problem faced by all prison systems in the world is that posed by a small number of really difficult, dangerous and disruptive prisoners, such as R and B, who attack staff, take hostages, assault and murder other prisoners and/or refuse to conform to normal prison rules. It is a problem that cannot be ignored and which, despite many attempts, no one has yet satisfactorily solved. Any solution is complicated by the fact that many of the prisoners concerned have a history of severe mental disorder, making normal control methods often inappropriate. Their treatment is bound to be staff intensive, and therefore very expensive. As well as producing its severest test, how any prison system holds its most disruptive prisoners is also the clearest indication of its decency.

These disruptive prisoners are not necessarily those who have committed the most serious crimes, carrying the longest sentences. They form a very small sub-set of any prison population, numbering no more than 0.1 per cent of the total in England and Wales, or 70 individuals at maximum. Other European countries make special arrangements for about 1 per cent of their prisoners; the United States does so for 1.8 per cent. But, as with so many of its problems, the Prison Service cannot solve this one in isolation.

The management of prisoners who presented very serious control problems was sharply criticised in the Woodcock and Learmont

reports on the escapes from Whitemoor and Parkhurst high security prisons. At that time it was based on the recommendations of a Control Review Committee (CRC) which reported in 1985. By 1995 20 prisoners were held in small, self-contained units which operated relatively unstructured regimes. However, a number of equally disruptive prisoners who were unable to cope with these regimes and refused to conform were held in long-term segregation, under what was called a Continuous Assessment Scheme (CAS). This amounted to regular transfer every 28 days between the segregation units of different dispersal and other high security prisons, a process known familiarly as the 'merry-go-round'. Only their fitness to return to normal prison conditions was assessed.

The intention behind the CAS was to ensure that no one prison was burdened with a particular disruptive prisoner for too long. After that, any positive intention ceased. It was a short-term expedient, focussed on the wellbeing of a prison rather than a prisoner. Little was done beyond ensuring the containment of those in segregation. They were never in any one prison for long enough to participate in any rehabilitation programmes. Most dangerously, in relation to the Prison Service's obligation to protect the public from re-offenders, many prisoners who, one minute were regarded as being so dangerous and disruptive that they had to be held in specially secure conditions, were the next minute released straight from a segregation unit into the community. Hardly surprisingly, many were re-arrested almost immediately. No matter where or how they are held, all prisoners ought to have their fitness for release assessed and receive some form of preparation.

Following the criticism, the Prison Service commissioned a serving prison governor, Mike Spurr, to study current arrangements and recommend improvements. He proposed a system based on progression through a number of different stages, movement being earned by co-operative behaviour. The final 'carrot' was return to normal prison conditions. Those who refused to co-operate would remain at an appropriate stage until they did so. His recommendations were

accepted and, in February 1998, the first Close Supervision Centres (CSCs) were opened.

The Statement of Purpose of the new system was:

> Close Supervision Centres will operate as part of a national management strategy which aims to secure the return of problematic or disruptive prisoners to a settled and acceptable pattern of institutional behaviour.

To achieve this, the functions of the CSCs were to be:

- To remove the most seriously disruptive prisoners from mainstream high security or training prisons.
- To contain highly dangerous or disruptive individuals in small, highly supervised units, with safety for staff and prisoners.
- To provide the opportunity for individuals to address their anti-social disruptive behaviour in a controlled environment.
- To stabilise behaviour and prepare for a return to the mainstream [prison system] with minimum disruption, whenever possible.
- To contain, for as long as necessary, any prisoner presenting so great a threat to the safety of staff and prisoners, that long-term containment is the only option available.

The most modern prison in the country – HMP Woodhill in Milton Keynes – was selected to house the majority of prisoners under close supervision, in one of the imaginatively designed house blocks put up when the prison was opened in 1992. Triangular in shape, they can hold up to 62 prisoners in cells on three landings on the two shorter sides. These face a long, glazed wall and overlook a large, well-lit area in which many activities can take place. At the apex of the triangle is a central administrative area.

The house block allocated to the Close Supervision Centre was divided into five self-contained units, one solely for women prisoners, the first of whom was received in July 1998. The other four were given over to the various stages known as levels. Prisoners who showed signs of progress could move up from reception level two to standard intervention level three. Those who offended, or refused to conform, could be demoted to basic restricted level one. Later, the segregation unit, described as a very restricted regime, was added for those deemed to be below level one.

Initially, level four was housed in two separate prisons. HMP Hull operated an activity-based unit, to which prisoners could progress from Woodhill. Its regime was designed to prepare prisoners for their return to the mainstream. HMP Durham housed a therapeutic regime unit, known as level four (mentally disordered), for those whose behaviour was so disturbed that they were not considered suitable for the staged system. However, after little more than a year, the Hull unit was transferred to Durham.

I first saw the new system in operation when we inspected HMP Woodhill in July 1998. We were disturbed immediately by several aspects of the strange situation that we found. Firstly, neither the prison governor nor its Board of Visitors had any jurisdiction over the Close Supervision Centre, which was the responsibility of the Director of High Security Prisons at Prison Service Headquarters. It all seemed suspiciously unconstitutional.

Secondly, the treatment of and conditions for the prisoners in the CSC appeared to be at best punitive and at worst way outside the rules. Thirdly, it was clear that, compared with the NHS special hospitals in which similarly disturbed people were housed, there were insufficient numbers of psychiatric or psychologically trained staff to supervise appropriate clinical or other regimes.

Finally, we disliked the staffing arrangements. Not every prison officer is capable of or suitable for working with such disruptive prisoners, for which they ought to be specially selected and trained. All who work with similar people in special hospitals undergo careful

initial, and frequent continuation, training. All that the staff of the Woodhill CSC knew were the traditional custodial methods for dealing with violent prisoners, such as the control and restraint techniques that were taught to all prison officers. Although they took part in case conferences about every individual, they had little understanding of the particular problems posed by those whose behaviour might be conditioned by mental disorder. A number of officers expressed concern about this; some questioned the legality of what they were asked to do; others commented on the inadequacy of arrangements for their support in such stressful employment.

However, the new system had only been in existence for five months and had not had time to 'bed in'. Inspecting it so early could lead to claims that we were witnessing teething problems. I therefore decided to do no more than mention it in the Woodhill report, saying that I would inspect the system as a whole a year later, by which time it should have settled down. Nonetheless, because of the emotive nature and human rights implications of ill-treatment of prisoners, I reported my concerns to Richard Tilt, the Director General. I also told him that, because we would be inspecting a system and not a prison, I would involve the relevant staff from Prison Service Headquarters in the drafting of our report. If anyone wished to disagree with any of our findings I would rather they did so with me before the report was published, because I would be making recommendations to ministers for action that I hoped would quickly follow. However disagreeable, we would report accepted facts.

Shortly before we began our inspection in August 1999, the government published a White Paper called *Managing Dangerous People with Severe Personality Disorder* (DSPD), of whom there were estimated to be 2500 in the country. Of these, 400 were in the three special hospitals, Broadmoor, Rampton and Ashworth, 700 were somewhere in the community and 1400 in prison. However, no one appeared to know who the 1400 were or in which prisons they were held, because none had been formally assessed as suffering from DSPD. We felt sure that

they included the vast majority of the 41 then in the Close Supervision Centres. But who and where were the other 1359?

Few, if any, mentally disordered prisoners anywhere in the prison system were cared for to normal NHS standards, let alone the standards in special hospitals. Michael Howard had ordered the closure of the only unit that attempted to care for psychopaths – G Wing at Parkhurst – when that prison had its high security status removed. The prisoners confined there at that time were sent to different dispersal prisons, which lacked specialist staff able to continue the regime to which they had been accustomed. In the report of our July 1998 inspection of Woodhill, we had criticised the standard of health care generally. We knew that Durham had been one of the first prisons to establish a partnership with a local NHS Mental Health Trust, some years before. We knew of no special arrangements to support CSCs.

In preparation for our inspection, we spent some time learning how those with severe personality disorders were cared for and held in special hospitals. I visited both Broadmoor and Rampton. I also co-opted Dr Julie Hollyman, the chief executive of the Broadmoor Hospital Authority, as a professional adviser. We learned that, in general, there are two broad categories of violent offender. The first are the over-controlled, who are able to regulate their behaviour, who tend to be solitary, isolated and withdrawn. Their offending is likely to take the form of less frequent but serious violence, resulting from inter-personal problems. The other category, the under-controlled, are more extrovert, impulsive, and generally under-socialised. They tend to have a more extensive criminal history, are psychopathic and have more convictions for violence and serious acquisitive crime. Within these two there are various sub-groups, but it was apparently rare to find any under-controlled in special hospitals. This was usually because of their confrontational behaviour, or their refusal to recognise their condition.

Such a person was C, a notorious fitness fanatic, who had a dreadful record of hostage-taking, violence, and attacking other prisoners. Every day he put himself through an endless routine of press-ups and running – either on the spot, up and down his cell or round the

exercise yard whenever he was allowed out. He could hold a reasonable conversation with some people, particularly when he came to know and trust them. His self-promoted reputation was such that he was an inevitable initial entrant into the close supervision system, through which he had progressed to the final stage, level four, at Hull by July 1998.

However, one morning his regular education instructor was ill. Very unwisely, the prison staff did not think of mentioning this to C, or asking him whether he would like a substitute or prefer to wait until the person whom he knew returned. Instead, they sent another instructor, whom he had never seen before, into his cell. At once C became disturbed and took the man hostage for what must have been a terrifying 24 hours. Eventually the situation was talked down, the education instructor released, and C moved to the segregation unit at Woodhill. Despite his extreme record of violence, he explained all this to us reasonably and logically. It was a classic example of how carefully such people have to be managed, and emphasised how important it is that staff understand the nature of those whom they are required to look after.

The best example of an over-controlled person that I came across was X, one of the few prisoners who has been told that their life sentence means for the remainder of their natural life. His crimes were particularly horrendous – his name is mentioned every time the most notorious murderers are listed. He was not in a Close Supervision Centre, but I met him later in HMP Whitemoor.

One of the most positive and rewarding prisoner activities, now adopted in a number of prisons, is transcribing reading material into Braille. Much of this is due to the work of a charity called the Inside Out Trust and its inspiring Director, Margaret Carey. Some prisons concentrate on the needs of blind children in particular, producing both stories and textbooks. However, one type of textbook had always been denied to blind children – those containing scientific diagrams. X had changed that. After four years of detailed and continuous work, he had painstakingly described all the diagrams in such a book, in language that

a child could understand, which he had then transcribed. For the first time ever, therefore, blind students had access to such scientific material. Any normal person would be justifiably pleased with the result, but what was so frightening about X was that, when I commented on his achievement, he showed absolutely no emotion. It was as if doing something positive for a fellow human being did not enter into his life's equation. Clearly, such a person will always present a danger to the public, and any remote possibility of his release will have to be very carefully considered. That he was doing something useful with his life was due to the perception of someone who understood that such detailed and lonely work was appropriate for such a person. It had not been of X's choosing.

There were other under- and over-controlled prisoners in the Close Supervision Centres, but the most difficult to treat were the psychopaths. They were unsuitable for hospital treatment and had severe problems in adjusting to the norms of society, whether in prison or not. Experience in the now closed G Wing at Parkhurst suggested that a sustainable life-style could be determined, but that treatment was no longer available. An expert, whose work we consulted, pointed out that any treatment had to be based on a clear understanding of each particular individual and involved a combination of medication and re-learning opportunities. Some form of medication is essential if emotionally charged attitudes and beliefs are to be reduced to a level where psychological help can be given. This confirmed the need for both clinically trained staff, who could administer medication, and those who could deliver active programmes.

Monica Lloyd and Dr John Reed also reviewed the literature on the effects of isolation on disordered personalities. This confirmed that, while some prisoners might actively seek to avoid any contact with other people, seclusion was nonetheless generally detrimental to mental health and wellbeing. Indeed, it was likely to make violent people more violent, and releasing them from isolation would be rather like letting a puppy off a lead. They were likely to react by threatening staff, destroying property, setting fire to cell or self, or

indulging in what are called 'dirty protests' in which they cover themselves and their cells with their own excrement. Such behaviour
invariably encouraged staff to keep them in isolation. And so the
vicious circle continued.

At the time of our inspection there were 41 prisoners in the system:
23 in Woodhill, 12 in Durham, and, disturbingly, six who had been
temporarily transferred to specially designated 'high control cells' in
other dispersal prisons shortly before the inspection. The Director of
High Security Prisons assumed his authority allowed him to hold
selected prisoners in Close Supervision Centres, but we could find no
legal basis for him being able to do so elsewhere for up to 56 days. It
seemed that the old 'merry-go-round' was not yet dead. Letters from
two of these prisoners suggested that the timing of their sudden move
had not been entirely accidental. They had given advance warning
that they intended to tell us exactly how prisoners were treated within
the system.

All our previous concerns about Woodhill were confirmed. Every
prisoner had been sent to the Close Supervision Centre following a
breach of prison rules. Those in segregation were there for:

Hostage-taking.
Demonstrating violent behaviour, even when under
restraint.
Disrupting the regime and threatening staff.
Refusing to enter the induction wing on arrival and
assaulting staff.

The prevalence of untreated serious mental disorder, however, was
obvious. Medical records revealed that:

Only two prisoners had no recorded mental disorder.
Eight prisoners had already spent time in a special hospital.
Two prisoners were waiting special hospital admission.
There were inadequate notes on eight prisoners.

What was also interesting – and raised a concern that I believe to be worthy of further study – was that 50 per cent of these prisoners had suffered some form of head injury sometime in their past. Earlier in the year I had visited St Andrew's Hospital, Northampton, the largest privately run mental health establishment in the country. I was particularly interested in the work of its pioneering head injuries unit, where I learned that it was possible to predict some of the behavioural changes that might result from damage to particular parts of the brain. Armed with such knowledge, it was possible to design suitable treatment programmes, maximising what patients were capable of doing. A considerable amount of physical exercise was included because programmes that lacked stimulation were likely to make a patient worse rather than better. Often that meant they would become more rather than less violent. No activity was allowed to last for too long because of their diminished ability to concentrate.

As we had suspected, because the management at Woodhill only recorded details gathered since an individual was received into prison, many medical records were incomplete. If head injuries are a factor in violent behaviour, it would seem sensible that they should be noted in all initial medical examinations. If the St Andrew's example were copied, suitable treatment arrangements for those suffering from particular types of injury could then be made in certain prisons. This would both prevent some violent behaviour and enable better preparation of individuals for their return to the community.

Interestingly, designing a sustainable lifestyle was the intention behind a creditable attempt to treat a group of prisoners with particular mental health problems in HMP Dartmoor. A number had been sent to what was described as 'the dustbin of the prison system', because they appeared unable or unwilling to conform to normal routines and conditions in other prisons. Having examined them, the attached psychiatrist decided to test their IQ rating and found that this ranged between 48 and 68. An IQ of 80 is needed to be able to understand what you are being told. It was therefore hardly surprising that those who could not understand did not conform.

The psychiatrist decided to recreate the old asylum system that had been abolished in favour of so called Care in the Community. All disturbed prisoners were brought into the Health Care Centre to have their capabilities assessed and a daily routine planned. After this had been trialled and confirmed, they were returned to a normal wing where they were under the supervision of a psychiatric nurse. Whenever anyone showed signs of being unable to cope, he was returned to the Health Care Centre for refresher treatment. The system worked well, prisoners responding to the way in which they were treated and learning a routine that they could sustain on release. However, like too many other good initiatives, the experiment ceased when the Prison Service tried to move the psychiatrist to another job. She preferred to remain near her home and resigned. Despite our recommendations in an inspection report, the system's potential was never recognised or adopted. It could have prevented unsuitable treatment of prisoners with similar problems.

The situation in the Close Supervision Centre at Durham was in stark contrast to that at Woodhill. Both the governor and the Board of Visitors played a proactive role in the life of the Centre. Because Durham housed the only women's high security unit, staff already had some experience of managing high-risk and disruptive prisoners.

At first sight it appeared that the Home Secretary personally made each and every decision about a prisoner in the CSC system, in accordance with Prison Rule 46. It was allegedly on his authority that a selected prisoner was not allowed to associate with other prisoners. The Rules also stated that the Home Secretary would take account of medical considerations when reaching any decision about the allocation of prisoners to, and within, the close supervision system. In reality, however, having assumed the Home Secretary's responsibilities under Rule 46, the Director of High Security Prisons was sole judge and jury of everyone and everything in the system. I very much doubted whether any Home Secretary answerable to Parliament would knowingly have allowed R – or any other such prisoner – to

remain in the punitive conditions in which we found him for 206 days. Such treatment, if known, would have received immediate censure from the European Convention on the Prevention of Torture and Inhuman Treatment, which had already criticised the prison system in the United Kingdom for some of its practices. Had anyone, we wondered, explained to Jack Straw what was being done in his name? Other than the Inspectorate, the only other independent 'watchdog' that could have told him – the Board of Visitors at Woodhill – had had its responsibilities for the Close Supervision Centre suspended. So we looked into what alternative checks and balances had been built in to the system to prevent such treatment.

We found that a CSC monitoring group, required to meet quarterly under the chairmanship of the Director of High Security Prisons, had been set up in April 1998. It was made up of representatives from the Prison Service, the Boards of Visitors and the Probation Service, together with academic, psychiatric and psychological experts. Its role included reviewing and advising on regime development, co-ordination and operation of programmes, and assessing public reaction to the system. But the group was never given a specific watchdog function, nor was it independent of the Prison Service. I invited its members to comment on our findings.

From them we learned that only one member of the group regularly visited the units. The others, who were genuinely horrified at what they now learned had been happening in their name, relied on reports given to them by unit governors. They had not been told about what happened to individual prisoners on a day to day basis. They were given no information about the psychiatric profile and treatment needs of the population they were supposed to monitor, to enable them to assess the appropriateness of what was provided. Some admitted that they felt awkward about challenging management decisions that had been authorised by their chairman. Few were aware that he alone determined that certain prisoners were kept in open-ended punishment conditions. Thus the monitoring group had neither been doing, nor was enabled to do, its job. While we could wonder why

such experts had not asked for more details or gone to observe conditions for themselves, we could not accuse them of deliberately withholding information from ministers or the public.

What all this confirmed was that the system, as it was being currently operated, was in urgent need of re-focussing. The assumption that dangerous and severe personality disordered prisoners had both the inclination and the ability to co-operate rationally with prison authorities had never been properly tested. Furthermore, if the mental health of all prisoners was properly assessed on reception, the missing 1359 alleged to be suffering from DSPD could be identified the moment they were received into prison.

In commenting on what we had found, I drew attention to the first of the United Nations Body of Principles, which states that, 'All persons under any form of detention or imprisonment shall be treated in a humane manner and with respect for the inherent dignity of the human person.' The European Convention on Human Rights was about to be enshrined in British law. It seemed wholly inappropriate for the Home Secretary to delegate to an official all responsibility for decisions regarding those in the close supervision system. I cited a precedent in the Ministry of Defence where ministers are required to authorise the holding of soldiers in close arrest for longer than a specified number of days. The same should apply in the CSCs. The way custody is applied must be within the law. Ministers are answerable both for the policy and the operation of the close supervision system.

Following our report, the Prison Service took a number of steps to alter the way in which CSCs were managed and those suffering from dangerous and severe personality disorder assessed. The monitoring group now functions as such, and ought to be able to ensure that there are no further abuses.

In November 2000 we inspected HMP Whitemoor, which had been selected as a pilot site for the identification of dangerous and severely personality disordered prisoners. We arrived in week six of a three-month assessment of the likelihood of some volunteer prisoners responding to group interventions. The assessment procedure was

broken up into three periods of four weeks, each of which had a different objective. Prison staff were working alongside staff from Rampton Special Hospital.

It was obviously too early to get any considered reaction, but I spoke to several of the volunteers. What was most interesting was their completely different attitude to prison staff. Many said that this was the first time that staff had tried to interact with them, or appeared to take any interest in them as people. One was most anxious to show me some drawings that he had never thought of doing before. Another showed me some short stories that he had written. Both talked very favourably about the help and encouragement they were getting from instructors, staff and fellow prisoners alike. Prison staff, who had worked with them elsewhere in the prison, confirmed that they were noticing change. Some previously intractable prisoners were becoming more reasonable and were causing no trouble.

The psychologists, psychiatrists and clinical staff from Rampton were impressed at the eagerness of the prison officers to learn about how to manage – rather than merely lock up – severely personality disordered prisoners. However, they were very concerned about how prisoners would react when they realised that they would have to return to the main prison after their assessment was complete. Prisoners clearly hoped that follow-on programmes would maintain the momentum of change that had begun. However, no such programmes had, at the time, been either funded or planned. It was hoped that funding would be available in April 2001 and that they could start in October of that year, eight months after the assessment pilot had ended. In the event, the fears of the Rampton staff were entirely justified. Several prisoners protested volubly and violently when they realised that no follow-on was available. Some self-harmed.

This outcome was both unfortunate and avoidable, and demonstrated once again the dangers of not thinking through the full implications of a good initiative. Close Supervision Centres are centrally managed from Prison Service Headquarters, with little responsibility delegated to the governors of the prisons in which they

are housed. Those suffering from dangerous and severe personality disorder, however, are left at the mercy of the prison in which they are currently housed, few, if any of which, have any staff trained to look after them.

There are two abiding lessons to take from all these thoughts and experiences. First, considerably more attention has to be given to managing the risk posed by the most difficult, dangerous and disruptive prisoners than to any other type. Necessary special arrangements must include close and continuous supervision. But special arrangements are also needed for the management of all those whose mental disorder is so severe that they present significant risk, whether or not they have offended against prison rules. Management of both groups ought to be a hybrid of control and appropriate mental health treatment, based on thorough specialist assessment. All staff working with such prisoners ought to be carefully selected and fully trained.

The best way of ensuring this is to link all prisons holding both categories of prisoner to NHS special hospitals for advice, support and training. This was not possible in the past because the Prison Service was not part of the NHS. As from 1 April 2003, however, the NHS became responsible for funding primary, secondary and mental health in prisons. This also allows specialist medical advisers to be consulted whenever it is felt that any form of seclusion is necessary.

Additionally, the treatment of those needing close supervision, and the conditions in which they are held, must be scrupulously managed in accordance with the law. As with so many aspects of imprisonment, public confidence that all is well must be boosted by ministerial accountability and regular, independent and objective inspection.

7

SEX OFFENDERS

'Beast, nonce, animal.'

Prisoners to sex offender, HMP Liverpool

ONE MORNING, WHILE WE WERE inspecting HMP Cardiff, an 18-year-old sex offender came out of his cell on the landing reserved for such prisoners in the Vulnerable Prisoner Unit (VPU). As he did so he saw, coming out of a cell at the other end of the landing, the man who had sexually abused him when he was five. Because of overcrowding there was not enough accommodation to hold young and adult sex offenders in separate parts of the prison. Fortunately, the teenager had the presence of mind to report this to prison staff, who had no previous idea of his relationship with the older man.

Someone, however, must have known, because the older man had been sentenced for the offence. Police, probation or social services must have had both names in their records and could have alerted the Prison Service, but exchange of such information is, unfortunately, not common practice across the Criminal Justice System. The same lack of shared information features in all too many of the sensational incidents that so inflame public opinion. If the public is to be properly

protected, and the risk that sex offenders present kept under control, this is something that must be improved.

This incident introduces the fact that more than 5000 people – the vast majority of them male – are in prison today accused of, charged with or sentenced for sex offences. This is considerably more than the number of life-sentenced prisoners who, unlike sex offenders, are managed by a separate unit in Prison Service Headquarters. They are to be found in every local, and many other, prisons around the country, many of which have no staff specifically trained to run special sex-offender treatment programmes.

Sex offenders attract more emotive attention, in or out of prison, than any other type of prisoner, with paedophiles provoking the most antagonism. All those in prison know that they will be unpopular and at risk of attack by their fellow prisoners. Many apply to be held separately for their own protection from the moment they are first received – indeed, solicitors, policemen and cellular van drivers often advise them to do so as a matter of course. Separation is allowed for under Prison Rule 45 and no application may be denied. Every prison reception area has separate cells and waiting rooms in which those who ask for protection can be processed apart from other prisoners. All those held under Rule 45 are housed in Vulnerable Prisoner Units (VPUs) that are a feature of almost every prison. However, the prison grapevine will ensure that their presence is known whenever and wherever they move.

As far as possible vulnerable prisoners are kept out of sight, and hopefully sound, of other prisoners. Constant verbal abuse, shouted from cell windows, can have a devastating as well as an intimidatory effect and has contributed to self-harm and suicide. Staff at Exeter, for example, acknowledged how much easier it was to hold vulnerable prisoners in the refurbished resettlement hostel out of sight of the main prison, than on the top landing of one of the accommodation blocks. Previously all 'normal' inmates had to be locked in their cells whenever vulnerable prisoners were moved, causing extra work for staff as well as disrupting the day's routine.

Vulnerable prisoners tend to be compliant and don't cause trouble. However, while they might be easier to manage, they are always escorted to and from activities. Work usually takes place in separate workshops, and education may well have to be conducted in the VPU because no separate classroom can be provided in education centres. Separate visiting arrangements must be made, and health care has to be carefully managed in separately arranged accommodation for those who need in-patient treatment. Staff who work in VPUs must be alert to changes of mood and swings in morale, particularly in those nearing release.

When I asked governors which type of prisoner's release caused them the greatest concern, they almost invariably said sex offenders. Despite all the treatment programmes, they felt that they could never be quite certain that they would not re-offend. After all, they would be returning to the circumstances in which they had offended before and where the same temptations remained. This was why many governors favoured the introduction of halfway houses, from which sex offenders could be gradually reintroduced into society before gaining full release. However, any such proposal was bound to attract an outcry from those living nearby.

A governor of HMP Channings Wood in Devon once told me that he had been about to release a sex offender who had behaved so well, and appeared to present such low risk, that he had been made a 'redband' or trusted prisoner. However, the day before his release, his cell was searched and a large quantity of pornographic material discovered. On further investigation it was found that he was a member of a paedophile ring, inside and outside prison, who regularly exchanged such material. Naturally his release was cancelled.

A common factor among sex offenders is that almost all of them have themselves been abused in childhood, an experience that has damaged them psychologically in ways that it is difficult for someone from a normal, protective, family upbringing to appreciate. What should give society even greater cause for reflection is that most of this kind

of abuse takes place within an offender's own family, unreported and undetected. As one sex offender put it: 'Paedophilia is not a stranger danger. Most child-molesting activities go on for a long time, undetected, because the majority of children involved know their perpetrator. Very often the youngsters don't say anything, because they don't want to betray confidences, or they're afraid that they will lose the perpetrator's trust.'

I have mentioned earlier that prisoners are often categorised as 'mad, bad or sad'. Many sex offenders could wear all three caps. One such was a 76-year-old man, arrested and brought into the VPU at HMP Norwich while we were inspecting. His wife had reported him, on their golden wedding anniversary, for sexually assaulting his two granddaughters over 20 years earlier. Clearly, what he had done had been criminal, but he was old and confused and it was difficult to visualise a treatment programme that might be appropriate for him.

Such betrayal of family values, and abuse of safety among one's own kith and kin while growing up, often has a profound influence on the outlook of those who undergo such assault. It encourages some offenders to see themselves as victims, a concept that is difficult for their own victims to understand. Those responsible for looking after such prisoners must – however much they may abhor the crime that led to their imprisonment – try to avoid making things worse by treating them as pariahs and outcasts.

The feeling of victimisation is often a factor in sex-offender behaviour. They inflict on others what has been inflicted on them. This is yet another reason why governors and others feel that every release is a potential risk. I agree with those who argue that serious sex offenders should be awarded indeterminate sentences so that this risk can be kept under constant and regular review. Uncertainty usually encourages caution, which is to be encouraged where the protection of the public is concerned. Release should be conditional on risk evaluation and the successful completion of a statutory treatment programme.

Certain prisons specialise in treating sex offenders, some – such as

Usk – exclusively, others – such as Albany and Acklington – devoting a wing, or a number of wings, to the purpose. These facilities tend to be far away from offenders' home ground, accentuating the need for management and oversight of where they are held during their sentence and from where they will be released. Currently, the Prison Service has no way of ensuring that all sex offenders are assessed or put through a treatment programme before being released.

Confusingly, the Prison Service uses the word programme to describe what it calls its 'core' Sex Offender Treatment (Programme) (SOTP) course. This takes about nine months to complete, during which trained tutors take a group of offenders through a number of modules, focussing on sex offending in general and each individual's offence in particular. Particular emphasis is paid to the impact of the offence on the victim. However, there is a catch. In order to qualify for treatment offenders have first to admit their offence. Following this, to prepare them for the way in which the course will be conducted and to strengthen their acceptance of guilt, they are usually put through a 'cognitive skills' course, in which they are taught to work in groups and reason the difference between right and wrong.

There are also specialist sex offender programmes in two therapeutic prisons, Grendon Underwood and Dovegate. Group therapy was pioneered at Grendon Underwood, where remarkable work with some of the worst sex offenders has taken place since the prison opened in 1962. Group work is widely held to be the best method of treating sex offenders. Prisoners stay at Grendon for at least 18 months. Those who are then returned to the prison system are twice as likely to re-offend after release as those released either directly from Grendon, or through its co-located open prison, HMP Spring Hill. This is presumed to be because other prisons do not understand the way therapeutic communities work and are unable to follow on the treatment that a prisoner has undergone. The benefits are therefore dissipated. The value of such therapy has been recognised by the Prison Service, which has now opened another similar institution,

Dovegate, to provide a 'Grendon in the North'. Because such therapy is expensive it is best applied to the most serious offenders who need it most.

Therapy takes place in groups, to which one or two uniformed officers are allotted. They are encouraged to take an active part in the work, as facilitators rather than leaders, which has the effect of developing mutual trust, building confidence and inducing a feeling of safety in the group. It is a demanding but immensely satisfying role, as many of them told me when explaining that I was only allowed to meet groups by invitation, not by right.

There is more to treating sex offenders than cognitive skills training and the core 'programme'. Both are elements of a treatment programme that ought to include initial assessment, regular reassessment throughout a sentence and after release, relapse prevention and booster courses, pre-release checks, and follow-up after release. These do not have to take place in the same prison. Some can be repeated or even conducted in the community. The programme as a whole – not solely, as now, the cognitive skills and 'core' courses – ought to be accredited to ensure that whatever is done anywhere is consistent and effective.

I suspect that very few people appreciate the heavy demands made on the tutors who conduct offending behaviour treatment courses. Usually, they work as a team consisting of a trained psychologist, a prison officer and a probation officer. The complex nature of the problems they face with offenders is encapsulated in the story told by a prisoner in HMP Grendon Underwood:

'It was appalling of me to abuse my daughters' bodies, as well as their trust in me as their father. But I don't believe I am sick. I think I'm emotionally immature, vulnerable. I know it's got something to do with my failure to cope with success . . . I was successful at the time, a local hero, and it just went straight to my head. I had affairs with other women. And my parents split up after more than 30 years together. But I just tucked away my feelings and refused to think about it. It was the power that went to my head. I wanted power over

my children, but it came out as sexual, when what I wanted was their love and admiration.'

I asked to meet with some prison-officer tutors when I first visited HMP Wandsworth. They surprised me by asking if we could talk in an unoccupied cell. Once inside, they told me that this was because they were anxious not to be seen talking to me by some of the older prison officers who were not involved in sex-offender treatment. These officers constantly ridiculed tutors and their work, calling them 'groupies' because of the groups in which treatment was conducted. They clearly had no idea of the skill, or the stress and strain involved.

I saw what the tutors meant by stress and strain when, in another prison, I met some tutors who had just finished a session in which offenders have to role-play their offence. They were flushed, sweating profusely, and their hands were shaking. They told me that this role-play was the key part of the whole programme, but it was raw and emotionally draining. It was not something that they would like to talk about at home. It even made them ask questions of themselves when bathing their own children.

Soldiers are often put into stressful situations, but I can think of none that makes greater emotional demands, course after course, than this. My admiration for the tutors increased the more I saw and heard of their work. So did my concern that the Prison Service was not supporting them sufficiently. Psychiatric and mental health nurses are trained to identify signs of stress both in themselves and in others, and counsel each other through frequent meetings and discussions. This does not always happen in prisons. Psychologists and psychiatrists can take care of the more clinical aspects of support, but to protect the public it is important that there are enough tutors to conduct the number of courses required and ensure that all offenders are treated. Allowance must be made for tutors to take breaks between courses so as to prevent burn-out.

One day at HMP Albany on the Isle of Wight, I was invited to sit in with a group on a sex-offender treatment course, where an emotional

event had taken place the previous day. As I had come to expect, a number of middle-aged men were gathered in a room, bare except for a blackboard and the hollow square of chairs on which they were sitting, their tutors among them. An empty chair had been left for me beside one of the prisoners. After we had introduced ourselves, I was told that P, who was sitting next to me, had finally admitted to the offence that he had committed 22 years before. The rolls of kitchen paper on the tables between the chairs, suggested that this had been emotional not only for P, but for all concerned.

'What was the trigger for that?' I asked.

'Well, we have been told that we must tell the whole truth if we are to be helped and then released. I never trusted anyone not to tell stories that they heard in prison, and so I kept my mouth shut. I've waited for a long time. But no stories go outside this room. All the others have told theirs. I trust the tutors,' he replied.

'Does today seem any different to yesterday?' I questioned.

'I'll tell you straight. It feels as if I have taken a sack full of stones off my back' came the response.

This introduces the subject of denial, which has a significant impact on the custody, treatment and release of sex offenders. A number of prisoners resolutely protest their innocence throughout their sentence. Sex offenders cannot go before a Parole Board unless they have successfully completed a sex-offender treatment programme, and to qualify for a programme, they are required to admit their offence. Fortunately, a Criminal Case Review Commission is now able to examine all such protestations, and is very active in its work. But that all takes time. Many 'deniers' remain in prison long after what might have been their release date. The same catch-22 situation applies to a number of other long-term and life-sentenced prisoners who are told that they will not qualify for parole unless they admit their offence.

When we inspected HMP Usk in Wales, a small, well-run prison solely for sex offenders, we discovered that a number of men were not

on courses because they were 'in denial'. They ought to have been sent back to the prisons from which they had come, so making space for those willing to undergo treatment, but those prisons did not want them back because they did not want to hold more prisoners in their Vulnerable Prisoner Units. This is precisely why there ought to be a sex offender unit in Prison Service Headquarters, arranging for a number of prisons to hold 'deniers', thus preventing them from clogging up space in specialist institutions such as Usk.

'Deniers' presented a risk within such a prison. While treatment programmes make demands of staff, they are rightly designed to make demands of offenders. One reason for conducting treatment in groups is that members are able to help and encourage each other to stick at the programme. Individual commitment to treatment may, at times, be fragile, and the best way of maintaining it is to make certain that the participants are protected from anyone, such as those in denial, who might undermine it.

At the time we inspected, Usk was entering a partnership with the nearby HMP Parc near Bridgend, run by Group 4. Here, the director had adopted a course designed by the West Middlesex Probation Service for challenging deniers. This included examination of the difficult question of their own feelings of victimisation. When I visited the course I found that three of the ten offenders on it had admitted their offences within the first week, which suggested that the course was worth repeating in other prisons. Both the introduction of the 'deniers' course and the partnership between the two prisons resulted from the personal initiative of their governors. Their efforts have now been officially recognised and the course accredited by the Prison Service. Its absence for too long emphasises the need for someone to be made responsible and accountable for managing sex offenders.

Later, we learned of another serious attempt to understand and challenge 'deniers' at HMP Acklington in Northumberland. Very understandably, the governor and those responsible for looking after sex offenders were concerned that 65 per cent of those who had been sent there for treatment were in some form of denial. He and the staff

who ran the treatment programme were alarmed at what this meant in terms of risk to the public when they were released, since there were no accredited treatment programmes for those who refused to acknowledge their offence.

The probation staff and psychologists at Acklington felt that it was essential, and in the public interest, that their colleagues in the community should be involved in the process of preparing sex offenders for release. To make this possible prisoners should, as far as possible, be held in prisons in their home areas. It therefore made little sense for sex offenders from all over the country, including Parc in South Wales, to be sent to Acklington, the most northerly prison in England, simply because there were bed spaces available. This, too, reinforced the need for centralised management.

The Prison Service has a curious way of measuring the success of its Sex Offender Treatment Programme (SOTP). In keeping with its obsession with targets and performance indicators, it only records the number of courses completed in a year. In 2000–2001 it completed 786, reaching only 14 per cent of sex offenders. For the third successive year this was below its self-imposed target. The statistic is meaningless. Ministers – and the public – need to know how many sex offenders need such courses, how many have not yet undergone them, and what resources are needed to make certain that they do so before their release. The cost of all aspects of the programme, both in custody and in the community, ought to be worked out and published.

Recent events, such as the hysteria whipped up by the *News of the World* in Portsmouth, indicate that the public needs reassurance that every effort is being made to prevent any re-offending by this particularly emotive group of prisoners. Interestingly, support for the paper's campaign came from a sex offender in Grendon, who said, 'I believe the newspaper is right. When a convicted paedophile is released and he goes back into the community, that community has a right to know about his offences and his background. I believe that the public has a right to know about convicted child molesters as well as those who have not been criminally convicted, but pose a serious and

known risk. Any neighbourhood with children has a right to know who lives next door.'

The electorate also has a right to expect that ministers and the Prison Service will take seriously their responsibilities for protecting them by doing all it can to prevent sex offenders from re-offending.

8

RESETTLEMENT PRISONS

'58 per cent of all adults, 78 per cent of all young offenders aged 18–21 and 88 per cent of all young offenders aged 15–17 re-offend within two years of release.'

DURING ONE OF MY EARLY visits to HMP Parkhurst I was introduced to J, one of the prisoners on the Continuous Assessment Scheme described in Chapter Six. He was moved between the segregation units of various prisons every 28 days, usually because he had assaulted a prison officer or a fellow inmate. As a result he was well known, and talked about as violent, difficult and dangerous throughout the Prison Service.

That Parkhurst was the 36th prison that J had been in during his current ten-year sentence came out during our initial, rather stilted, conversation in his cell. However, he clearly had something more that he wanted to say to me, because he asked if we could continue outside the hearing of prison officers. We moved to a nearby classroom, with a glass panel in the door, where we could sit down at a table.

Prisoner J was a tall, thin man, with the typical pallor of one who spends much of his time inside a cell. He was obviously not unintelligent, and was trying to keep himself under control because he was

disturbed, if not angry, about something. The first thing he told me was that he was a 'loner', which was why he preferred to be in the segregation unit. He had tried to explain this to prison officers, but they seemed unwilling or unable to understand what this meant. So, in order to ensure that he remained in segregation, he felt compelled to commit an offence, such as assaulting an officer, every 28 days. He realised that this was not normal behaviour, but feared that it would be the pattern of his life throughout the final two years of his sentence.

Our discussion prompted him to ask if he could fetch some papers from his cell that he had written on the subject of wanting to be alone. When he returned and I had a chance to look at them, I noted that he mentioned something of his background, which, as I suspected, included interrupted schooling, domestic violence and family rejection. When out of prison he had had a number of jobs, but invariably left them when required to mix with other people.

He had been in and out of prison a number times, his last period of freedom having lasted little more than a day, when he had gone into a pub for a drink. There, he had left his coat, with his wallet inside, over a chair while he went to the lavatory. He came back to find that a number of other people had come into the pub and, incredible as it may seem to most of us, he simply could not bring himself to retrieve his coat from among them. He left the pub, and his wallet, behind, committed a burglary, was arrested, and found himself back inside.

J's papers amounted to a very well reasoned plea to be left alone and not have to conform to all the minutiae of daily prison routines. This plea had been refused. As I read his very lucid self-examination, I found myself wondering whether this whole expensive, unnatural and negative process could not have been avoided. It was quite clear that J needed psychiatric help but none had been made available. Could his condition have been treated if his symptoms had not been ignored? What would his future be?

Throughout our interview I was interested to note that, no doubt because of J's reputation, prison officers had peered through the glass panel in the door at frequent intervals to check on my safety.

I put all this to the governor when J had returned to his cell. He said that he would look into it, but didn't promise that anything could or would be done.

Two years later I saw J again. He was now in his 57th prison, and six weeks away from his release. This time he showed me a letter from Prison Service Headquarters saying that he was to be kept segregated for the remainder of his sentence. Specifically, he was to be given no preparation for release. What a demonstration of the Prison Service's negative attitude to rehabilitation! How could anyone in authority issue an instruction that was so far removed both from the announced aim of the Prison Service and from basic common sense?

Two prisons later, J was released straight into the outside world from the segregation unit of a high security prison. He was rearrested at five p.m. the same day.

This story can, unfortunately, be matched by too many others. It illustrates all too clearly how lack of preparation for release contributes to the appalling rate of adult male re-offending, something that applies equally if not more so to women and young offenders, whose treatment I mention in further chapters. How could the situation be improved?

All except 24 of the 73,000 prisoners at the time of writing will be released. These few are those who have been told that, for them, life means the whole of their natural life. The Prison Service's own Statement of Purpose states that it is their duty to help the other 99.9 per cent to live useful and law-abiding lives after release. But, if 58 per cent of all adults, 78 per cent of all young offenders aged 18–21 and 88 per cent of all young offenders aged 15–17 re-offend within two years, what does that say about the quality of that help?

I remember my parents talking about the difficulties experienced by some of those returning from active service in World War II in re-adjusting to family and civilian life. When I returned to my own family after a year away in the Far East, I realised that I had missed a part of my young sons' lives that I could never recover. How much more difficult for those who have been in prison for many years, whose return

disrupts whatever pattern of life a family has established during their absence, and who find that they have to adjust not only to life outside an ordered institution, but to changed conditions in society. The longer a prison sentence the more difficult the re-adjustment.

If the Prison Service's own Statement of Purpose is to mean what it says, resettlement should be at the heart of all that it does with and for offenders. Every assessment, every programme, every decision about where prisoners serve their sentence, should be aimed at helping them to return to society and not re-offend. Preparation will take time, as will throwing off the effects of institutionalisation and learning to look after themselves and make their own decisions. It must, of course, include making them face up to their criminal or anti-social behaviour – essential if the aim of the Criminal Justice System and the Prison Service to protect the public by preventing the next crime is to be achieved. But more is needed.

The word 'resettlement' is not a wholly accurate description in every case because many prisoners have never had a 'settled' existence even before imprisonment. If 'settlement' is to have any hope of success, the ways of living law-abiding and useful lives must be inculcated into prisoners from the moment they are received into prison. This requires the Prison Service not only to determine how each prisoner can be motivated and equipped to enable them to do this, but also to design every activity around the resettlement, or settlement, process. Examples set will be examples followed, good or bad.

However, the Prison Service's attitude to resettlement is by no means as clear and unambiguous as that. Only recently did they appoint a Director of Resettlement. However, this was not a new post, but merely a change in the title of the Director of Regimes, a well-meaning career civil servant who had not worked with prisoners. Although responsible for policy, the Director of Resettlement has no operational or financial responsibility for how prisoners are prepared in, or resettled from, individual prisons.

Lack of direction was highlighted in two recent and important

reports. The National Audit Office, in *Reducing Prisoner Reoffending* published in January 2002, commented:

> The Prison Service has rapidly expanded its provision of offending behaviour, drug misuse and education programmes so that more prisoners could benefit. The expansion, however, has been carried out without any clear overall plan for how the programmes should complement other prison activities aimed at preparing prisoners for release . . . A prisoner's access to programmes still owes much to where he or she is sent. We found that the scale and range of programmes offered within prisons of similar type and size varied significantly . . . When we completed the fieldwork for this examination [in June 2001], the Prison Service had no national record of the resettlement activities currently available within prisons at local level, or data on the extent to which individual prison performance on resettlement varies.

Even more importantly, the Cabinet Social Exclusion Unit report *Reducing Re-offending by Ex-prisoners,* published in July 2002, contained the following:

> Although the Prison Service and the Probation Service have improved their focus on reducing re-offending, the current balance of resources still does not enable them to deliver beneficial programmes such as education, drug and mental health treatment, offending behaviour and reparation programmes and many others, to anything like the number who need them.
>
> No one is ultimately responsible for the rehabilitation process at any level – from national policy, to the level of the individual prisoner. Responsibility and accountability for outcomes can be very unclear.

In prisons, processes on reception and release could be much better designed to promote rehabilitation and to identify and tackle factors influencing re-offending. Prisoners are losing housing and employment, and accruing debt for want of basic procedures, dedicated resources and expertise.

Not enough has been done to engage prisoners, their families, victims, communities and voluntary and business sectors in rehabilitation.

Tony Blair wrote in his foreword, 'We need to redouble our efforts to rehabilitate prisoners back into society effectively.'

None of these statements is new. Every one of them is contained in my annual reports and those of my predecessors. Perhaps, at last, those who up until now have refused to listen will pay attention to their Prime Minister.

I described the overall prison system in Chapter Four. Seventy-one, or more than half the total number of prisons in England and Wales, are training prisons, in which the majority of prisoners ought to spend the bulk of their sentence. The facilities are categorised A, B, C or D according to the risk presented by the prisoners they contain. Twelve of them are Category D, or lowest risk, also called 'open prisons' – something of a contradiction in terms. Their role is resettlement, but that is not their title. Instead, illustrating the topsy-turvy nature of categorisation, the three resettlement prisons are all in category C – closed prisons for higher risk prisoners. The Director of Resettlement has no operational responsibility even for these.

In Victorian times prison places available for resettlement included those in hostels attached to inner-city local prisons such as Exeter, Wandsworth and Wormwood Scrubs. These are no more, which is unfortunate for another reason. The 12 open prisons have one geographical feature in common. All are in the heart of the countryside, miles away from the inner cities from which the majority of prisoners

come and into which they are to be resettled. For example, HMP North Sea Camp, which will no doubt feature in any future book about prisons by Lord Archer, is a hutted establishment built beside 1000 acres of farmland reclaimed from the Wash by Borstal boys shortly before World War II. HMP Hollesley Bay Colony, which will also feature in any Archer book, is beside another 1000 acres of prime farming land in Suffolk. HMP Kirkham in Lancashire, another hutted establishment, is on an old RAF airfield that has been ploughed up for growing vegetables. Thus much of the available work, while helpful for commercial or food-production purposes, does not train prisoners for the kind of jobs likely to be available in their native urban surroundings.

The three resettlement prisons, on the other hand, are located near or inside urban conurbations, have access to urban work, and are fenced. Latchmere House, on the edge of Richmond Park in London, can offer its prisoners a wide variety of external work. The governor of Kirklevington Grange, near Stockton-on-Tees, told me that the fence was there not so much to keep prisoners in as to remind them that they were still prisoners when they returned from outside work. I tell the story of Blantyre House, near Tunbridge Wells, in the next chapter.

To emphasise their importance for the future, sentence plans might be better named resettlement plans. They should be implemented and followed by anyone who has anything to do with returning a prisoner to society during and after the custodial part of any sentence. Currently, however, sentence plans are made only for those with sentences of a year or more, although the recently introduced Detention and Training Orders have set a useful precedent for change. They consist of a set number of months in custody followed by an equal period under supervision in the community up to a maximum of two years. At present these are only arranged for children under the age of 18, and is supervised by youth offender teams, under the control of a local government chief executive. Were there to be similar male and female offender teams for adults, they could ease the current problems facing

an overstretched Probation Service. As with Youth Offender teams, they could be responsible for making and supervising sentence plans and ensuring that treatment begun in prison is continued.

As with so many other aspects of imprisonment, resettlement is not something that the Prison Service can tackle on its own. It can claim fairly that it alone should not be judged on the dreadful re-offending rates, because they are measured over the two years after release over which it has no control. That is very true. But its work to prevent re-offending will be wasted unless it ensures that the treatment it has begun is continued.

To help in this process, Prison and Probation Services have recently adopted a new common assessment form, opened on anyone who is awarded a custodial or community sentence, which should help continuity. However, much more than a common assessment form is needed to overcome a far greater problem, namely the public's lack of confidence in community sentences. This applies to the supervision of both those awarded non-custodial sentences and those released from prison.

There is much talk about the value of restorative justice, or work done in or for the community by offenders, which has the added value of being visible. For example, when I inspected the prison in the Cayman Islands, I was shown a day hospice that had recently been built by prisoners. The result of such a public demonstration of useful co-operation was that the prison received many other offers of work. Such partnerships not only allow prisoners to practise employable skills, but also society to benefit from their employment. The hospice project earned much favourable media comment.

In addition to doing restorative justice work, there is no reason why programmes for those awarded community sentences should not include education, work and social skills training, physical or mental health and/or drugs treatment as in prison. If this became the norm it would make continuity of treatment much easier and treatment programmes more effective, which should influence the re-offending rate, thus increasing public confidence in the system.

It is said that the three things most likely to help prevent an ex-prisoner from re-offending are a home, a stable relationship and a job, all of which are put at risk by imprisonment. Existing jobs may well be lost. Relationships may not survive the strain of separation. Homes can be removed, not least thanks to the 13-week rule introduced by the last Conservative government, which means that council or rent-assisted property can be repossessed if the occupier is absent for more than that time. Considering how long it takes to bring people to trial, this means that many remand prisoners may lose their homes, and all their possessions if they cannot pay for their storage, by the time that they come out of prison. Women, many of them primary carers of children, are particularly affected by this ruling. Housing arrangements, in particular, need to be made well in advance of a release date to ensure that all those leaving have a roof over their heads.

Some prisons, such as Durham and Norwich, have outstanding records of ensuring that released prisoners are housed. So did HMP Buckley Hall when it was an adult male training prison run by Group 4, before being re-roled as a women's prison run by the Prison Service. Two prisoners at Buckley Hall started, and were employed to run, a 'Housing Advice Centre'. All new prisoners were seen as part of the induction process, their housing problems identified, and help given with retaining existing accommodation. Also, the process of finding accommodation prior to their release was begun and, at the same time, plans made to pay off any housing debts. Housing associations all over the country praised the scheme, which was simple, efficient and effective. Had the Prison Service accepted either our recommendation in an inspection report that Housing Advice Centres should be made standard practice, or an immediate proposal from Buckley Hall that similar prisoner-run centres should be set up in a number of other prisons in the north-west, I have no doubt that many would not leave prison without somewhere to live.

Such a centre would have helped Martin, a 17-year-old offender at HMYOI Portland. I was introduced to him one Friday morning during an inspection and told that he was due to be released on

Monday. I asked him where he would live, to which he replied that he did not know.

'Have you got any parents?' I asked.

'Yes,' he said.

'Why can't you go to them?'

'My mother threw me out and my father's in Spain,' he answered.

Becoming concerned, I asked him where he would go.

'To Wales, to my sister,' he replied.

'Will she have you?' I asked.

'She threw me out last time so I don't know,' Martin admitted.

'Does she know that you are coming?' I pressed.

'No,' he said. 'I'll telephone her when I get there.'

I asked him how many times he had been in prison. He replied that this was his fifth sentence. So I returned to the subject of his parents.

'When did your mother throw you out?' I asked.

'When I was twelve,' he replied.

'What happened then?'

'I was in care until I left that.'

'Since then you have been in prison several times, or tried to live with your sister. Where did you live for the rest of the time?'

'Rough.'

At that I turned to the prison officer who was beside me and asked whose responsibility it was to see that the boy had somewhere to go to on release.

'NACRO [the National Association for the Care and Resettlement of Offenders] or the probation officer,' he replied.

'But don't you think that you, as a responsible prison officer, should see that proper arrangements are made for anyone being released, particularly making sure that they have somewhere to live,' I challenged.

'That's probation's job' came his response.

We found that 50 per cent of the children under the age of 18 released from Portland at that time did not know where they were going to spend their first night. Hardly surprising when staff didn't

consider it their responsibility to make any arrangements for them, not even in a Salvation Army hostel, which is where many adults end up. It is no good assuming that all have a home of some kind to go to. In one survey we found that 34 per cent of all those under the age of 18 had been living alone or rough before they entered prison. Without help what hope had they of leading a settled or functional life on release?

Visits are the best way of maintaining relationships, but at present 6000 people are in prisons over 150 miles from their homes, 11,000 over 100 miles away, and the Prison Service has to spend millions of pounds a year on assisted family visits. Relationships are likely to be severely tested in the period immediately after release, as each party adjusts to life with the other. Both prisoner and family must be prepared for this, which is one of the reasons why prisoners should be moved to or held as near as possible to their homes at this time. How wise were those who built hostels in local prisons.

It is impossible to overestimate the importance of visits to a prisoner. Had I been in office for longer I would have conducted a thematic review of visiting arrangements because I was so unhappy with so many aspects of them. I would have recommended the wider adoption of several initiatives that we had seen, beginning with one introduced by the Hertfordshire Association for the Care and Resettlement of Offenders. It publishes leaflets that are handed to the family of everyone committed, telling them how to contact the prison to arrange for a visit. Every prison should also issue a leaflet explaining visiting procedures and how to get to the facility.

Initial visits by families of first-time inmates could include guided tours of a prison. Every prison should have a Visitors' Centre outside the prison itself where visitors can prepare for the visit, and recover from it if it has not gone well before journeying home. Every prison should appoint a staff member to act as Family Contact and Development Officer, a system pioneered in Scotland. He or she, chosen for their personal qualities, would, hopefully, become the confidante of families,

which is bound to improve their communication with the Prison Service.

The administration of visits themselves, including the inevitable searching of visitors, should be humanised. All staff working with visitors must be selected and trained to ensure that no one who makes families feel as if they, too, are prisoners is employed in that role. Arrangements for visiting children must be designed to limit any damage that the experience may do to future generations. Their presence can make or break a visit both for the visitor and the prisoner. Above all, visits must be recognised as having an important part to play in the prevention of re-offending.

In this context no praise can be too high for the work of the voluntary National Association of Prison Visitors, attached to every prison. Distance from home is not the only reason why a number of those inside are not visited. The value of volunteers who visit them is not nearly well enough recognised or encouraged by the Prison Service. The importance of the contact to a prisoner, often maintained after release, is unsung but incalculable and deserves better support. I know that the Association would welcome more younger visitors who could help with unvisited young offenders.

Many different surveys have been carried out of the number of prisoners who were unemployed when sentenced. Results vary between 70 and 80 per cent, according to the age and gender of the prisoner and the part of the country from which they come. Much so-called employment is short term, aimed more at satisfying immediate financial needs than providing a living and without prospects for advancement. The need for prisoners to find long-term employment emphasises the importance of work based on aptitude testing to identify potential, allied to an understanding of local job prospects.

In this coupon-ridden age, it is essential that any skills taught should be professionally assessed so that they mean something to any potential employer, which is why City and Guilds or Non-Vocational Qualifications (NVQs) are so welcome and important. They set syllabi and provide proof of level of achievement. I was always disturbed

when I found that a prison claimed it could not afford to award NVQs because the accreditation process was too expensive. No prison should have to make such a decision. If the Prison Service is serious about resettlement it should ensure that all prisoners have access to qualifications that are likely to lead to a job.

In keeping with its failure to make best use of every assistance available, the Prison Service has, for years, had no machinery for orchestrating the potential represented by the voluntary sector. I am very pleased that a suggestion I made in my second annual report, that Voluntary Sector Contact Officers should be appointed in every prison, in every area office and in Prison Service Headquarters is at last being implemented. I saw their task as being two-fold: first, to make contact with organisations able to provide what help is needed; second, to ensure that any help volunteered is employed to maximum advantage.

An Active Communities Unit in the Home Office is now helping the whole process, working with a Voluntary Sector Contact Officer in Prison Service Headquarters and CLINKS, an organisation that co-ordinates the voluntary contribution. Machinery is there at last but progress is painfully slow. Much initial time and effort has been devoted to designing the minutiae of bureaucratic process. Caution and inertia flavour ministerial and official response to approaches from voluntary organisations. Meanwhile, prisoners are denied access to help that might prevent them from re-offending.

I suspect that the public does not appreciate just how much it owes to the voluntary sector, not least in its work with prisons and prisoners. Aside from the considerable contribution of the Boards of Visitors, or Independent Monitoring Boards as they have recently been renamed, a whole host of voluntary organisations backs them up, covering almost every activity connected with resettlement. The breadth of their contribution is well explained by five examples. New Bridge, started more than 30 years ago by the late Lord Longford, provides advice and practical help in the form of volunteer 'befrienders' who can help bridge the gap between prison and the community. The Foundation Training Company prepares prisoners for release in

Feltham and a number of East Anglian prisons; the Inside Out Trust provides Braille and a number of other purposeful occupations in prisons of all types; Hibiscus looks after the needs of those from ethnic minorities, and Prisoners Abroad tries valiantly to help those returning to this country from prisons abroad, who receive no other form of assistance.

Two other bodies are especially noteworthy as having been set up by ex-prisoners to meet the needs of ex-prisoners. UNLOCK, the brainchild of two long-term prisoners, Mark Leech and Bobby Cummines, finds jobs and homes and provides help with insurance and other financial arrangements. Derek Chisnall, who formed BEAT (Business Education and Training), recognised that many prisoners would have more chance of employment if they started their own business. BEAT organises training in prison and provides trainees with a business mentor whom they can contact for advice and guidance should things begin to go wrong when they are released.

Every prison is involved in resettlement because of what it is required to do with and for any allotted prisoners. In theory, therefore, the two types of prison with a specific resettlement role ought to be at the cutting edge of fulfilling the aim of imprisonment. However, this was not how staff working in open prisons viewed their involvement. They felt that working in such prisons was regarded as a 'soft option' in career terms and that they were seen as lower grade than staff in larger, closed prisons. This was reflected in their promotion prospects, and yet they had to make the most difficult risk assessments of all – determining whether or not prisoners should be released into the community. Also, because such prisons were very short staffed, they had to accept much more responsibility than their colleagues elsewhere.

Theoretically, only long-term prisoners, who need time and careful preparation to help them break free from years of institutionalisation, ought to be sent to open or resettlement prisons. In fact, largely because of the pressures of overcrowding, many short-term prisoners are sent there immediately following sentence. No prisoner ought to

be moved to an open prison until their offending or anti-social behaviour has been assessed and challenged and as much as possible done to treat or correct other identified problems. All ought to earn their transfer, and their suitability for employment in the community must be considered.

When first allowed to take outside employment, prisoners are escorted to work by Prison Service staff, but, once they have proved their reliability, they are allowed to make their own way, sometimes using their own cars. Staff will visit sites where prisoners work to ensure that all is well, but generally they are encouraged to take responsibility for themselves, including checking in and out of the prison. Few abscond because they know that the automatic punishment is return to a closed prison and the loss of considerable privileges.

HMP Kirklevington Grange, a Category C resettlement prison, provides a very good illustration of how a prisoner's time can and should be used constructively. Immediately on arrival, every prisoner is interviewed and a case file opened to which he has access at any time. Personal officers, who act as caseworkers, organise a major case conference six weeks later, attended by everyone within the prison who has contact with the prisoner, together with his family and the probation officer who will supervise him on release. Subjects discussed include the availability of housing, but the conference is also the first step in the process of preparing him for work outside the prison.

After successfully completing an initial assessment period, which includes voluntary testing for substance abuse, prisoners are put through a two-week Prisoner Development Programme, designed to prepare them for the particular work that has been found for them in the community. Many of the job opportunities come from local government and include painting, decorating or gardening for the elderly or disabled, and delivering meals on wheels. Prisoners are taken to and from community work by prison staff; assessment and casework discussion are continued; they receive normal prison wages of £7 per

week. This includes taking part in a most imaginative 'Restorative Prison Project', led by the International Centre for Prison Studies. In this, prisoners from Kirklevington Grange are installing benches and other facilities made by prisoners in nearby HMP Holme House and HMYOI Deerbolt to improve the amenities in a public park in Middlesbrough.

The next stage is to find and apply for paid work outside the prison. I went to see the prisoners at work in a food-processing factory some 30 miles from Kirklevington Grange. The factory management told me how delighted they were with the care that the prison took over the selection of workers, and their performance while on site. They had never had any problems, were visited regularly by the prison staff, and knew that they had only to ask and there would be instant response to any query. The prisoners felt that they were learning transferable skills – rightly so, since this was reflected in the number who obtained gainful employment on release. One prisoner, working in a jeweller's shop, had chased three armed robbers away from the premises, which led to their subsequent arrest. Nothing could have better increased the credibility of the process with potential employers.

Prisoners returned behind the prison fence every night, continued their casework and met regularly with their future probation officer. Such clear and simple processes worked well because everyone involved knew his or her part in them. Judges, magistrates, prison and probation staffs, prisoners and their families, employers and fellow employees, all spoke highly of Kirklevington Grange and supported what it was doing. Furthermore, at £13,500 per head per year – almost half the average – it was the cheapest prison in the system.

The governor, Suzanne Anthony, enjoyed the full confidence of staff and prisoners. She had thought the whole process through and was sensibly cautious about taking risks. Her success was reflected in a re-offending rate that hovered around 20 per cent, way below that of the rest of the Prison Service, but without anyone in Prison Service Headquarters with operational responsibility for resettlement, she had

no one to go to for support or advice other than her area manager. She was fortunate that Ray Mitchell, who had previously been an excellent prison governor in the North East, gave her his unstinting support. However, he would not be there indefinitely and his successor could well adopt a different outlook.

Just how little the hierarchy in Prison Service Headquarters appeared to understand the role of resettlement prisons was starkly illustrated by the Operating Standards Audit Team who, on an inspection immediately before ours, described the Kirklevington Grange regime as 'idiosyncratic'. This meant that they could not measure it against standards in a closed training prison – which it was not. I wondered how the Deputy Director General, to whom these teams reported, explained what this meant to ministers and the Prisons Board.

Contrast this with the experience of HMP Ford, a Category D open prison on a disused naval air station near Shoreham in Sussex, long regarded as a white- rather than blue-collar establishment. Ford's reputation as one of the more decent and less austere prisons in the country was unappreciated by the area manager, Mr Tom Murtagh. He was feared by staff in the prisons for which he was responsible, where he was known to be at variance with the 'diktat' of the Prison Service Staff Care and Welfare Service, which stated unambiguously that 'Victimisation occurs whenever one person unfairly exercises power over another. Victimisation of colleagues is strictly against Prison Service Values.'

When we inspected Ford in September 2000, its governor was a small, pleasant, conscientious ex-army captain called Ken Kan, who had been born in Hong Kong. Ken's previous appointment had been with the Lifer Management Unit in Prison Service Headquarters. This was his first time in charge of a prison.

We found that the area manager had insisted that Kan introduce a number of petty rules and regulations more appropriate for a closed training prison than an open resettlement establishment. For example, prisoners were made to change out of working clothes into prison

uniform for meals, something that was not even demanded in high security prisons. They had to obtain written permission each time they moved anywhere in the prison, which was quite contrary to the ethos of allowing and encouraging them to take more responsibility for themselves. Hardly surprisingly, many prisoners told us that they could not see the point of coming to Ford because there were more restrictions than in the closed prison they had left. Much involvement with the community had been cut, and they were given none of the opportunities to prepare for release, which was the point of a Category D prison. They felt that they had made a backward rather than a forward move.

We discovered one particularly disturbing example of the Prison Service's obsession with targets and performance indicators. For years, one of the jewels in Ford's crown had been its education centre where the very able co-ordinator ran a variety of courses designed to help prisoners either to gain qualifications related to employment, or to begin studies that could be continued outside. This stemmed from his conviction that education has more impact on the prevention of re-offending than any other work done with prisoners.

The co-ordinator told me that he had been forced to reduce the number and variety of courses available because his budget had been drastically reduced, partly to fund other activities in the prison and partly to satisfy the requirements of a particular Key Performance Indicator (KPI). This required him to complete a laid down number of tests at level two, or GCSE, in order to comply with the demands of an overall Prison Service KPI. To achieve this he could count tests of those who might already have degrees. This instruction was contained in a letter from the Head of Education that I quoted in the inspection report, pointing out that it was both cynical and unworthy of the Prison Service. Concentration on such a high level of education ignored the needs of the many prisoners who lacked even the most basic of basic education and those for whom further education could enhance their prospects of employment. Category D Ford, in short, was not helping prisoners to prepare for release. Enforced adoption of

closed prison procedures made a nonsense of its role and purpose. Compared with other similar institutions, nothing demonstrated more clearly the vital importance of having one person responsible and accountable for ensuring consistency.

The Prison Service is faced with a dilemma over the siting of resettlement prisons. The public, understandably, is not keen on having large numbers of convicted criminals such as sex offenders or arsonists living among them in unfenced establishments, yet prisoners *must* be given experience of community life as part of their preparation for return on release. One obvious answer is the use of small hostels, a number of which are already in existence and run by the Probation Service, mainly for those on bail. Unfortunately, Michael Howard closed a number of these when he was Home Secretary because their occupancy was considered to be too low.

Another decision of Michael Howard's has had an even greater negative influence on preparation for release. In line with his drive on 'security, security, security', he tightened rules on the use of what is called Release on Temporary Licence (ROTL), by which governors authorise prisoners to work or spend time outside prison. He did this immediately following public outcry after a murder had been committed by a prisoner who should not have been granted temporary release. As a result governors, having been told in no uncertain terms that they would be held personally responsible for any future ROTL failures, became so nervous about releasing anyone that its use virtually dried up.

Thankfully, one of Jack Straw's first initiatives on taking office was to reverse this trend and encourage governors to make greater use of ROTL. Rightly, he insisted on careful risk assessment, but the damage had already been done. Even now a number of governors are reluctant to risk their careers and ROTL is not used as much as it might be. David Blunkett is now talking about once again using hostels for resettlement. They were an integral part of Victorian thinking on the subject. Wheels really have come full circle!

What is needed, above all, is clear and unequivocal confirmation and direction that resettlement is the purpose of all that is done with and for prisoners throughout their sentence. In order to counter the inevitable cynicism of those who will say that they have heard all that before, ministers and the Prison Service have one important preliminary step to take. They must be seen to repair the damage they did to public perception of their attitude to resettlement by their extraordinary raid on the most successful resettlement prison in the country, Blantyre House, which I describe in the next chapter.

9

THE BLANTYRE HOUSE RAID

'Two other issues have caused us concern in this inquiry and they may be linked. First there are some doubts about the quality of the Prison Service's internal reports. Secondly there have been strong doubts about the accuracy of its statements to the public, press, Board of Visitors and Parliament.'

Para 98 of a report into Blantyre House Prison by the Home Affairs Select Committee of the House of Commons, 9 November 2000

THE 27 DECEMBER 2002 EDITION of *Private Eye* contained the following sentences in a section entitled 'Follow-Ups':

> The Prison Service is being forced to defend in the High Court its misguided raid on one of the country's best performing prisons and its shoddy treatment of the jail's former Governor Eoin Maclennan Murray. Maclennan Murray, who was abruptly removed from his job shortly before the unprecedented raid on Blantyre House, is seeking a judicial review of the Home Office investigation into his complaints about the affair.

HMP Blantyre House is a small, Category C resettlement prison near Tunbridge Wells in Kent. Originally a youth detention centre, it can house up to 120 long-term prisoners, mainly Category D, but

some Category C. These exclude sex-offenders but, unlike the population in other resettlement prisons, include some lifers. In addition to the original old house, the prison site contains a number of new buildings, including an accommodation block and an education centre.

Blantyre's pioneering work in the field of resettlement began in 1987 under a previous governor, Jim Semple. He introduced the idea of assessing prisoner risk and then encouraging and enabling those who were being prepared for release to find work outside the prison. His policy was continued during the short tenure of his successor even though, during his reign, the prison was rocked by a major security scare. Eoin Maclennan Murray was the prison's third governor in its resettlement role.

In 2000, Blantyre House enjoyed a reputation for excellence unrivalled in the Prison Service. Most creditably, only 8 per cent of its population re-offended and were re-arrested within two years, way below the 58 per cent of all adult male prisoners. My predecessor, Sir Stephen Tumim, when he inspected it in 1992, described it as 'an example of all that is best about the Prison Service'.

After our inspection in 1997 I wrote, 'The whole ethos of Blantyre House and the excellence that it represents is that of a resettlement prison, and I strongly recommend that it should be so treated and regarded.'

Martin Narey, Director General of the Prison Service, wrote in 1999, 'Blantyre House performs a valued role as a resettlement prison within the Service. Its general ethos supports its special function and I am committed to protecting this.'

Such were some of the published views on what Blantyre House, under Mr Maclennan Murray, was achieving. But then, as the House of Commons Home Affairs Select Committee reported, following a special inquiry:

> On 5 May 2000, however, the Governor, who had been praised for 'doing an outstanding job' was removed abruptly

from his post. That evening 84 prison officers from other prisons were sent into the prison to conduct a full, overnight search. After it ended, it was reported: 'there were no significant finds'. But the trust which underpinned the resettlement ethos 'has been shattered'.

Why?

Essentially, what underlay the events of 5 May was a personality clash between the governor and his area manager, Mr Tom Murtagh, who has been introduced already in connection with HMP Ford. The Select Committee reported:

> We conclude that the relationship between the area manager and the governor had deteriorated to such an extent that the Prison Service should have addressed it much earlier by moving one of them or altering the chain of command or both.

Most unfortunately, although he was a long-term friend of Eoin Maclennan Murray, Martin Narey, the Director General, failed to recognise, or chose to ignore, what was happening. Eoin Maclennan Murray, a quietly spoken, bespectacled man with a pleasantly open manner, was prepared to take risks, allowing prisoners to work in the community on the clear understanding that any breach of trust would result in immediate return to a closed prison. He believed that prisoners should be encouraged to take as much responsibility for their own lives as possible. He felt that encouraging them to make their own decisions while they were still in custody was the best possible way to help them to do the same when they returned to the community. He was doing neither more nor less than actioning the Statement of Purpose of the Prison Service, namely to help prisoners to live useful and law-abiding lives on their release.

His policy was clearly successful. There had been no escapes from Blantyre House for the past five years. The prison easily exceeded all

the targets set by the Prison Service, even though many were more severe than the average. For example, it was set a target of 4.3 per cent of its population testing positive for drugs against a national average of 14.2 per cent – only 0.7 per cent tested positive. The target of 36 hours of purposeful activity for every prisoner per week well exceeded the average of 23 hours. It achieved an extraordinary 43.6 hours, and no staff were assaulted.

When we inspected the prison in January 2000, it passed the tests of a Healthy Prison with flying colours. Everyone felt safe. Everyone was treated with respect as a fellow human being, and lost no opportunity of telling visitors and others that this was so. Everyone was encouraged to improve himself and given the opportunity of doing so through purposeful activity. All were enabled to maintain contact with their families, and were thoroughly prepared for release. With its low re-offending rate, Blantyre was certainly not failing in its duty of protecting the public.

One of Eoin Maclennan Murray's practices that I particularly liked was that of having prisoners escort visitors around the prison. Once, for example, I was taken round by an ex-corporal who had been discharged from the army and imprisoned after a fight on the night that his regiment returned from a six-month tour in Bosnia. He was an admirable guide and full of praise for the governor and for the staff who, he said, really tried to get to know prisoners and help them. Not only did I learn a great deal about the working of the prison from him, but I also realised, as the governor intended, that the Armed Forces should pay much more attention to the welfare of ex-servicemen after they were discharged from prison if they were not to end up among the homeless. My guide fully justified the confidence of the governor and his staff that prisoners, treated responsibly, were the best advocates of a system in which they believed so strongly.

In the preface to our inspection report I wrote:

> I conclude by praising the consistent, innovative and courageous approach of the Governor and staff at HMP

Blantyre House to their very difficult and challenging task on behalf of the public. It has established a reputation for excellence as a resettlement prison, a most difficult role, in which the recognition and support of the Minister and Director General – and HM Chief Inspector of Prisons – needs to be confirmed not only by official endorsement but early clarification of its future.

This last sentence referred to uncertainties about its future that were affecting the life of the prison. These stemmed from the area manager, who was known to dislike its ethos and disapprove of Mr Maclennan Murray's approach to his task. Despite the lack of escapes or assaults, he ordered the governor to tighten his security arrangements and, as at Ford, made him introduce certain practices that were more appropriate to a closed prison. Mr Maclennan Murray told him that he was perfectly prepared to do this when the full staffing implications had been worked out and satisfied. He pointed out that, at present, he simply did not have enough staff either to study or implement the proposed arrangements. Mr Murtagh declined to help him with either.

The effect of these demands and the manner of their giving so alarmed the Board of Visitors that they wrote to the Director General to complain that, by his bullying, the area manager was making life impossible for the governor. Mr Narey therefore went to the prison to see the situation for himself, and it was after this visit that he wrote the comments quoted above. The Board was understandably encouraged by his public commitment to all that the prison was doing, which message they hoped that he would pass to his area manager.

However, by the time of our inspection, Mr Murtagh had let it be known that the future of Blantyre House was being actively discussed at Prison Service Headquarters. As was his habit, he deliberately excluded the governor from any discussions on the subject, leaving him to find out what was going on through hearsay. The possibilities he was known to be considering included closing Blantyre House or

converting it back into a young offender institution. Quite under-standably, the uncertainty this created led to inevitable rumour and speculation about what Mr Murtagh had in mind. The fact that their governor knew nothing and was unable to tell them what was hap-pening, was particularly unsettling to the prison staff. Because this, in turn, could affect the way in which prisoners might be treated, I drew attention to it in the preface to our report.

What none of us knew was that, quite apart from the future of Blantyre House itself, Mr Murtagh was planning to remove Eoin Maclennan Murray. Having been warned of the consequences of fail-ing to carry out the orders of his area manager, some might think a governor unwise to continue even those successful practices that had been publicly praised by Directors General and Chief Inspectors. It was courageous of Maclennan Murray to stick to his guns, which he did because he felt that what he was doing was right and absolutely in line with the aim of the Criminal Justice System and the Statement of Purpose of the Prison Service.

In March, while Mr Murtagh was hatching his plans, another important player in the story – the House of Commons Home Affairs Select Committee – visited Blantyre House. They too were deeply impressed by the quality of what they saw, but sufficiently concerned about the effects that uncertainty about the future and Mr Murtagh's unknown plans were generating, to write to the Home Secretary on the matter. He replied on 20 April, confirming that Blantyre House would remain a resettlement prison.

Too late. On 18 April Mr Murtagh began to put his plans for removing the governor into operation. These revolved around a detailed search of the prison on a Friday night which, by law, could only be asked for by a governor. Governors hold prisoners in accord-ance with a warrant issued by the Home Secretary, which allows them absolute control over access to their prisons. Mr Murtagh's reason, which, again, he did not share with Eoin Maclennan Murray, was an allegation from the Kent police that illegal items might be found. Eighty-four prison officers were to be used to swamp the tiny

prison, though quite why so many were needed has never been explained. Evenings were a sensible time to search prisons like Blantyre House, because all prisoners would have returned from their outside work, but Friday was an expensive choice because of the cost of extra pay for searchers.

In normal circumstances, if a governor felt that an outside search was needed, he would have to explain his reasoning to his area manager who, alone, was in a position to provide him with the necessary resources. Mr Maclennan Murray knew of no reason why such an extreme step should be taken. If Mr Murtagh wanted to initiate a search, he would have to persuade the governor that it was justified on the evidence, or he would have to find some other way.

Some months earlier, a prisoner in another prison told me that it was possible to buy your way into Blantyre House. I reported this to Martin Narey because, if true, it was something that the Prison Service should investigate. Again, unless he was implicated personally, I would have expected the governor to be involved in any investigation. Mr Maclennan Murray told me that he knew about the allegation and was watching for any evidence, so this rumour did not provide any justification for an expensive 'lock-down' search.

Mr Murtagh's other course was to remove Eoin Maclennan Murray and replace him with someone whom he had primed to ask immediately for a pre-planned full search. He unfolded his plans to the Director General, who approved them on 28 April. The plans included the simultaneous replacement of the deputy governor at Blantyre House.

On 2 May, Mr Murtagh put 84 officers from other prisons in Kent on standby to search Blantyre on the night of Friday 5th. On 3 May he told the nominated new governor in secret of his imminent appointment, and briefed him to ask for the search immediately he had taken over. On 4 May Mr Narey informed Paul Boateng, the Prisons Minister, of the plan. He raised no objection, although, as the minister responsible for Boards of Visitors, he could have been expected to have known of their expressed concern about the state of

the relationship between the governor and the area manager. He would also have known of the concerns expressed to the Home Secretary by the Home Affairs Select Committee.

On the morning of Friday 5 May, Mr Murtagh arrived at Blantyre House and told Mr Maclennan Murray that, in the interests of his career, he was being moved to Swaleside as deputy governor. He was to hand over to his appointed successor at once and immediately leave the prison. Mr Murtagh then remained there so that, the moment Mr Maclennan Murray had left, the new governor could go through the ritual of formally asking him to initiate a search as soon as possible. Any pretence that the request was spontaneous is incredible.

Soon after 10 p.m. that night the 84 officers, in riot gear, arrived at the prison and proceeded to search it. In addition to the main prison and every cell, they searched the chapel, the Health Care Centre and the Education Centre, which were opened by force since the keys were allegedly not available. Smashing down doors and forcing drawers caused over £6000 of damage. Every prisoner was subjected to a mandatory drug test. The Home Affairs Select Committee, in its report, commented that 'the demeanour of the search party created an impression of hostility'. However prisoners, far from being hostile, offered tea and sympathy to the searchers for having their Friday night so disrupted.

And the results?

In the short term the search found a small quantity of cannabis, three ecstasy pills, three unauthorised mobile phones and some un-authorised credit cards. In other words, the 'take' was less than might have been expected of any normal, routine search, carried out by a prison's own search team. No one tested positive for drugs. No prisoners or staff were charged with any disciplinary or criminal offences.

In the medium term the incident set off a chain of events that remain incomplete. The Prison Service commissioned an inquiry into the past management of Blantyre House, which found nothing that could justify the action that had been taken. So it was ordered to look into possible financial irregularities. It could find none.

As far as Blantyre House is concerned more prisoners have since absconded from the prison than at any time over the five years before the raid. There have been a higher percentage of positive drug tests and a number of assaults on staff. Having declined to help Mr Maclennan Murray work out the implications of altering procedures, Mr Murtagh at once made staff available to his successor. A number of organisations that had previously provided outside work for prisoners no longer do so. The prison has fallen back from its previous excellence, not through any fault of its own but because that fall was initiated and driven by those supposed to be responsible for raising standards.

Mr Maclennan Murray sought an investigation into his complaints of bullying by Mr Murtagh. This was conducted internally by two senior civil servants in Prison Service Headquarters, who answer directly to the Director General. The deposed governor's further complaint – the one mentioned in *Private Eye* as being heard in the High Court – was that, in addition to failing in its duty of care to him, a senior employee, the Prison Service investigation had been 'biased, superficial, unfair, flawed by delay and a breach of natural justice'. He also complained that allegations against him by Mr Murtagh were kept secret and that he was given no chance to respond. Hardly comfortable words to describe actions taken by the head of a public service, endorsed by responsible ministers.

The Prison Service also commissioned an inquiry into the manner in which the search had been conducted, which produced a highly critical report. But no action was taken against those who ordered and authorised it or the manner in which it was carried out.

The Home Affairs Select Committee was so troubled by what had happened to a prison on whose excellence they had so recently commented, that it immediately began its own investigation. Twice, Paul Boateng and Martin Narey were called to give oral evidence. They protested that what took place had been wholly justified, claiming that information they would give the Committee in private would fully explain their reasoning. However, even that totally failed to convince

them that the affair had been anything other than a ghastly mistake that should never have been allowed to happen. The Committee did not accept that the search was a proportionate response to the alleged information supplied by the Kent police. It did not believe that the reasons the Director General had given in public justified the exceptional search or the way in which it was carried out.

In particular, the Committee was dissatisfied at what appeared to be deliberate attempts to mislead it and the public over the significance of what was found during the search. On 16 May the Director General spoke of a 'quite frightening amount of contraband material that was found'. Mr Boateng, in a parliamentary answer on 25 May, referred to '98 finds of unauthorised articles'. The Prison Service's own internal inquiry concluded 'there were no significant finds'. Very curiously in view of the date, Mr Boateng had issued a statement on 16 May in which he wrote, 'The undoubtedly valuable work that was and is being performed at Blantyre House . . . is a model for others.'

The inference to be drawn from all this is obvious, as I told Jack Straw on the only occasion that he asked me what I thought about the affair. The raid was bogus and should never have been authorised. The Director General must have realised that a personality clash was distorting relationships between an area manager and a governor, and should have taken steps to eliminate it. Mr Murtagh's attitude towards prisoners was spelled out in a comment he was said to have made to the education co-ordinator at Blantyre House, quoted in the Select Committee report, that '[Prisoners] were not to be trusted because they were beyond redemption.' Mr Murtagh denies he said this.

What was particularly reprehensible was that the Director General allowed a man who held such views to destroy the ethos of a highly praised and extraordinarily successful resettlement prison, to treat a prison governor in such a manner and remain an area manager. Mr Murtagh's retention in post sent all the wrong messages about and around the Prison Service, not least with regard to what I regarded as bullying. How credible was an official anti-bullying policy if it did not include staff as well as prisoners? How could senior managers who

bullied their own staff discipline anyone who bullied prisoners? Could it be that the explanation for senior managers failing to investigate the accusations of bullying of prisoners at Wormwood Scrubs, was that they knew the way they treated their own staff, including governors, made them look hypocritical? Anyone who bullies a subordinate should be removed because such behaviour is not only foreign to the stated ethos of the Prison Service, but also contrary to its own published rules.

However, the damage went far deeper than that. The whole affair, including the roles played by ministers, the Director General, the Deputy Director General, and other senior managers in the Prison Service, casts serious doubts on the sincerity of their views on resettlement. Outwardly, they relished the success of a resettlement prison; inwardly, they sanctioned its destruction. Which more truly reflects their belief?

On top of that there are parliamentary implications. Despite frequent questioning from Lord Mayhew, previously MP for the constituency which includes Blantyre House, Lord Windlesham, Lord Elton and others, the government has not come clean about why the conclusions of the Home Affairs Select Committee were so flagrantly dismissed. Ministers adopted exactly the same attitude towards its report on the raid on Blantyre House as they had to unpleasant prison inspection reports: say nothing and pretend that it did not happen. Failure to respond to such objective criticism must cast doubt on the sincerity of any promises of improvement.

One of the reasons for the reintroduction of an independent Inspectorate of Prisons was that the public had grown suspicious and cynical about a Prison Service that only investigated itself. If it had nothing to hide it need not fear independent investigation and open reporting. If anyone had failed in their duty that, too, would be open, allowing for swift and focussed disciplinary action. I lost count of how often I was questioned about the time it took for anything internally investigated by the Prison Service to be made public. Nobody was held to blame for the murder of Christopher Edwards in HMP

Chelmsford that took nearly four years to investigate. The murder of Mubarrak, a young man in Feltham, was investigated internally and, again, no one was held to blame nor was the report made public. An investigation into racism in Brixton, conducted by the Prison Service's own race relations adviser, was watered down in Prison Service Headquarters and its publication delayed. Why? Surely those concerned were aware of the damage that delay and secrecy did to their own credibility.

Eoin Maclennan Murray has now been seeking an explanation for the events of 5 May 2000 for more than three years. Something is surely very wrong with staff management procedures if senior employees take an organisation to court over their treatment – and Mr Maclennan Murray is not the only governor who is taking this action. Chris Scott, whose treatment at Winson Green was mentioned in Chapter Five, is doing the same. I wonder whether ministers have asked themselves why two such senior members of the Prison Service should feel that they have to resort to litigation to obtain answers to reasonable questions. Pretending that something did not happen will not make it go away, however much that may be the hoped-for solution.

In my opinion, the honourable and sensible thing for Jack Straw to have done would have been to acknowledge publicly that a ghastly mistake had been made. He could at the same time have said that, despite this, he retained full confidence in Martin Narey as Director General. He should have insisted on the instant removal or retirement of Mr Murtagh, as well as a complete and public overhaul of personnel procedures within the Prison Service, to satisfy himself that bullying of subordinates by anyone at any level was never condoned and would be instantly disciplined.

No Home Secretary should feel comfortable that the quotation at the head of this chapter publicly casts doubt on the veracity, and some of the procedures, of an organisation for which he is accountable. What was surprising was that Jack Straw did not use the already available mechanism for avoiding such accusations. HM Inspectorate of

Prisons is required by Act of Parliament to investigate any other matter as the Home Secretary requires. This ruling could certainly have covered the raid on Blantyre House. As the minister responsible, Jack Straw could have been certain that he would be given independent and objective analysis and recommendation, quickly and publicly. Above all, there would have been no attempt to 'spin' to the public, the press, the Board of Visitors or Parliament.

Mr Murtagh has now retired after holding a leaving party in Blantyre House.

The impact of what happened at Blantyre House on 5 May 2000 has not gone away, nor should it be allowed to do so. Eoin Maclennan Murray deserves a public apology and should be recompensed, both for what happened and for all that he has been made to go through subsequently – the charade of the internal inquiries, the time taken to produce neither explanation nor apology, the damage to his career, and the expense of his High Court action.

Then, and only then, can resettlement, in conscience, be said to be at the heart of everything done with and for prisoners and those who genuinely strive for their betterment.

10

THE WERRINGTON EXPERIENCE

'Changing the attitudes and behaviour of many of the young criminals who end up in custody requires tough, challenging regimes run by very skilled staff. But unless they receive individual attention and opportunities to change, their time in custody will make them worse rather than better.'

Preface to Young Prisoners, *a thematic review by HM Chief Inspector of Prisons for England and Wales, Home Office, London, October 1997*

WITH THE WORDS 'THANK GOD you've come', the governor of Werrington Young Offenders Institution, a former industrial training school for boys near Stoke-on-Trent, greeted Rod Jacques and the Alpha team when they arrived to carry out an unannounced inspection in early June 1998. The old main building, built some 120 years ago, had, until a year earlier, held 90 convicted children, aged between 15 and 18, in a number of dormitories. The Prison Service had, however, replaced these with two modern 'quick builds' – prefabricated buildings each designed to hold 60 prisoners in cellular accommodation. Similar buildings were being added to a number of adult prisons around the country to ease the overcrowding problem. In some, two buildings were joined together to form an L; in others, like Werrington, they were in line, with a joint central entrance hall.

Each two-storey building was self-contained, with two landings of cells on each level, washrooms, showers, a food servery, and a number

of other rooms that could be used by staff as offices or for interviews and courses. There were 54 small, single cells and three doubles in each block, all equipped with a lavatory and washbasin. Thus, Werrington was now able to hold 120 boys but it had been ordered to hold up to 190 – 100 in one block and 90 in the other – with a number of cells designed for one having to house two boys.

The physical condition of the old dormitories had left much to be desired, but they did have the advantage of requiring continual staff presence, and therefore supervision, which is particularly important for this volatile and vulnerable age group. There was nothing wrong with the physical condition of the two new blocks. The reason for the governor's outburst, for which he was subsequently castigated by his seniors on the grounds of disloyalty, was that they were quite unsuitable for overcrowding with children. Werrington only had education, work and physical training facilities for 90 boys. Consequently, more than half of the current numbers were unemployed and locked up in their small cells all day. Understandably, the governor believed that this was no way in which to treat children, or to help them towards living useful and law-abiding lives.

It was the same old story: no one in Prison Service Headquarters was responsible or accountable for the custody of children, so there was no one to whom he could appeal for help other than his area manager, who had passed on the order that he take the additional numbers. He knew that the Inspectorate would report the facts as they were, without embellishment. Having read our recently published thematic report *Young Prisoners*, he knew our views on what their treatment and conditions should be. Our inspection report would be based on those views, as would any recommendations for improvement put to ministers as well as Prison Service Headquarters. This was the governor's best hope of persuading the Prison Service to take remedial action.

Talking to staff in the course of the inspection, it became clear that many of those at Werrington were distressed at the enforced overcrowding and its consequences. They had previously operated a very

effective personal officer scheme in the dormitories, with each officer responsible for a number of young prisoners. This was difficult if not impossible to repeat in the overcrowded conditions of the new wings, and the demands of maintaining overall control denied staff time to concentrate on every individual. Dormitory accommodation may not have been ideal, but at least the children were not then locked up in cells all day.

Now officers were faced with confined children, who burst out of their cells with all the exuberance of a puppy being let off a lead whenever they were allowed out. Mass, impulsive, pent-up, adolescent frustration can seem threatening in the confined space of a cellular accommodation block, and a number of incidents had persuaded staff that it was neither safe nor sensible to unlock everyone at the same time. Therefore, to control the numbers who were out of their cells, while giving equal opportunity to all, each child was only allowed two periods of evening association a week. Other than when they were taking part in an activity, this was the only time that they saw anyone other than their cellmate. True, they queued up at the servery to collect their meals, but they had then to take these to their cells to eat. Effectively, these youthful inmates were denied the contact with others that is so essential a part of growing up.

Limited association time also meant limited access to telephones and showers. They were thus denied essential family contact, and their personal hygiene and cleanliness was inhibited. This last was not helped by there being no showers in the gym, to which they went three times per week.

In 1842 the social reforming seventh Earl of Shaftesbury used the following words, in the first report of the Children's Employment Commission, to describe the plight of eight- and nine-year-old boys and girls working in coal mines:

> Although this employment scarcely deserves the name of labour, yet as the children engaged in it are commonly excluded from light and are always without companions, it

179

would, were it not for the passing and repassing of the coal carriages, amount to solitary confinement of the worst order.

Confinement at Werrington in 1998, whether in single or double cells, was also of the worst order. It was completely without either stimulation or challenge. Overcrowding doesn't only mean too many beds crammed into insufficient space. Overcrowded sleeping arrangements can be accepted for a limited period of time, but conditions become unacceptable if prisoners have to spend all day in overcrowded cells. Active programmes are as essential an antidote to overcrowding as they are to preparation for release. The standard of the existing activity places was in fact quite high. Individual sentence planning and risk assessments were well done and all boys went through a three-day course of preparation for release before leaving. This not only confirmed the capability of the staff, but gave hope for the future.

On the other hand, only 30 of the 190 young offenders had access to education. Most of these were under school-leaving age and were required by law to have 15 compulsory hours of education per week. A few worked with a small dairy herd on the farm, or in the car mechanics or computer repair workshops. Other than a limited number of courses in drug awareness and misuse, there were no offending behaviour programmes, although some were planned. Aside from occasional visits to the gym there was no opportunity to burn off surplus energy, either mental or physical. The cells, in which they were forced to eat their meals, were also their lavatories. On top of recreating the chaotic and dysfunctional existence from which so many came, the combination of frustration and idleness created by the conditions was fertile ground for bullying, which was not only rife but began almost as soon as a boy arrived.

Any new arrivals were processed in a small, dilapidated former hospital block near the main building. After their personal details had been recorded, their property removed and their prison clothing issued, children were led to the accommodation blocks at the bottom

of the hill on which the institution was sited. As they approached, they were subjected to a barrage of insults and obscenities shouted from the cell windows, which staff seemed powerless to prevent. Once inside, they were taken into one of the interview rooms and allocated to a cell by the duty officer. There they were left until the following morning. Almost invariably they were moved in with another child whom they had never met. That was the sum of what were called 'first night procedures'.

Every boy had an initial interview with a prison officer the following morning, during which the daily routine was explained. Formal induction was only held on a Thursday, so that anyone arriving on a Thursday or Friday, or too late on a Wednesday to be given an initial interview, had to wait until the following week to be inducted. While they were waiting, their only source of information was their cellmate. In the dormitories, staff had adopted a style with young, frightened and confused new arrivals of 'say it, say it and say it again', whenever they had to pass on information. The demands of trying to maintain control in the new conditions gave them little time to pass on anything even once.

This reception process had been designed for adults, many of whom found difficulty in coping with it. The best description of its impact is contained in a wonderfully brave book called *Inside*, written by John Hoskison, a professional golfer who was sent to prison. Everyone who wishes to understand the impact of imprisonment should read his description of what it is like to be placed in the hands of those whose ethos does not include such notions as 'safety' or 'humanity':

> I had now spent two weeks 'inside' and not one official had spoken to me regarding my future. Not one prison rule had been explained, and I had no idea of my entitlements. It seemed information was deliberately held back. During exercise I had gleaned . . . an accurate picture of what *should* be happening: induction on arrival (for an explanation of the system); sentence planning (what goals you

should try to achieve during the sentence); assessing risk level (what risk level you are); and finally reallocation to a new jail. Rather like the early days of my golf swing: great in theory – lousy in practice.

The way in which prisoners are treated on arrival is a major contributor to the large number of suicides that take place within the first few hours, days and weeks in prison. Sixteen per cent of the total number of prison suicides take place in Young Offender Institutions (YOIs). In 1996 there had been four in quick succession in the Health Care Centre at Glen Parva, a large YOI near Leicester, housing over 800 children and young offenders. An official inquiry into the first suicide recommended that the practice of putting those assessed to be at risk into solitary confinement should cease. It did not. The other three cases were also in solitary confinement when they committed suicide. This prompted us to carry out an unannounced inspection of the Health Care Centre, which disclosed an alarming lack of either common sense, or the duty of care, in what was supposed to be the equivalent of a hospital.

Yet, despite all their hand-wringing and alleged concern about the high incidence of suicide and self-harm, senior management had imposed conditions at Werrington that were bound to lead to distress. We found that 93 children had been formally recognised as being at risk of suicide or self-harm during the year since opening the new accommodation. Many of these were in their first two weeks of imprisonment. This remarkably high figure should surely have rung alarm bells in the heads of anyone with responsibility for the safety and wellbeing of children in prison.

The impact of the arrival and reception process was vividly described to us by B, a nervous 17-year-old, who had arrived – directly from court – shortly after 7 p.m. on the Wednesday evening of our inspection. He told us that before he was arrested he had been living away from home. However, he was on speaking terms with his family, who kept him in touch with his estranged girl friend and his

four-year-old son. He claimed that, right up to the day of his court appearance he had been led to believe that he would not be given a custodial sentence for his part in the robbery with which he and others had been charged. He had never been to prison before. Now, because no member of his family or any of his friends had been in court with him, no one knew that he had been sent to prison, let alone where. After sentencing, he had been left in a cell until the courts closed for the day and a driver, who also acted as a court escort, could bring him to Werrington.

On arrival, B had been given a rub-down search and then, with four other boys who had been in the same cellular van, put into a small, dingy, ill-lit, tiled room, entirely bare even of information posters or reading material. Here they waited until, one at a time, they were taken into an office, strip-searched, and then interviewed. He was asked if he would like to phone home, but declined because he did not know whether anyone would be around to take his call. His family usually went out in the evenings, as he did. He was given a phone card, which he was told he could use on the wing to which he would be allocated, a sheet of writing paper, an envelope and a biro.

After his interview he had been made to sit in a narrow corridor until all new arrivals had been seen. He was then taken to another small room where his own clothes were taken from him, listed, and put into a cardboard box which was sealed in front of him. He was given a prison-issue shirt, trousers, socks and trainers, into which he changed. He also received a towel and what was called a hygiene pack containing shaving soap, toothbrush and soap; razors, he was told, were only issued on the wing.

As B and the others were led down the path to the accommodation blocks, he had been terrified by shouts from the cell windows. He thought that he had been recognised by an older boy, whom he knew was in Werrington and to whom he owed money. He could tell no one of his fears because, other than the officer who left after locking him into his allocated cell, there appeared to be no chance of speaking to anyone in authority. He was not offered the use of a telephone

and was told nothing about what would happen to him the following day.

He soon found out that his older companion was particularly disgruntled and frustrated because he wanted to be in another establishment nearer to his home. In an attempt to achieve this he had smashed the furniture in his previous cell, for which he had been told that it was even less likely that he would be granted a transfer. In a break from venting his unhappiness about this, he told B that he would probably be interviewed the following morning. As far as contacting his family was concerned, he would not get access to a telephone until Saturday, when the wing was next due for association. Even then he was not guaranteed a call, because he would have to join a queue and association could end before his turn came. If his call was urgent he could ask for an application form.

When we saw B early on Thursday morning, his anxiety level was, not surprisingly, extremely high. In addition to coping with his own predicament, he was having to absorb the emotions of a deeply unhappy older cellmate. He was also fearful for his own safety in view of the potential threat from another young prisoner. Because he had arrived so late, no officer on his wing knew anything about him and his name was not on the list of those to go through the induction programme that day. He had not yet been allocated, let alone seen by, a personal officer. No one had approached him to ask if he had any problems; he couldn't know that the attitude of the wing staff was that if he wanted anything he only had to ask.

Had B been sent north from the court where he was sentenced, to Lancaster Farms YOI, instead of south to Werrington, his treatment would have been entirely different. At Lancaster Farms he would have been put into dedicated 'first night' accommodation, where staff remain on duty until they see that a new young offender is settled. They would have insisted that he make contact with someone to tell them where he was. They would have explained the establishment routine over a number of days, giving him time to adjust and ensuring that he knew exactly what he was expected to be doing at all

times. He would not have been allowed to move into the main part of the establishment until deemed ready to do so. The result was less stress and distress. What is more, the all-pervasive anti-bullying ethos, led by the governor, limited the possibility of any verbal or any other assault or threat from other young prisoners. This induction process included identification of problems such as B's debt, and planning their resolution.

It seemed surprising that the Prison Service had not ensured that the Lancaster Farms reception and induction procedures were applied in all YOIs. Quite apart from anything else, they clearly had a potential impact on the high suicide rate that the Director General had announced that he, personally, was determined to reduce. But they had been designed and introduced by an exceptional governor, David Waplington, not by the Prison Service. Also Werrington was in a different geographical area and so under a different area manager, and there was no machinery in operation for spreading good practice across area boundaries.

Bullying is, of course, not confined to prisons. It takes place at home, at school and in the workplace. Unchecked, it can have a pernicious effect on the life of an establishment – particularly one containing children. Dealing with it means dealing with the bully as well as the bullied. There were many examples, up and down the country, of imaginative ways of doing this. In the main, bullies were moved to separate accommodation and made to undergo special courses designed to identify and challenge the causes of their behaviour. Almost invariably, it was found that the majority had themselves been bullied and abused in the past, particularly at home, and were acting out their own experience.

Debt, often allied to bullying, is another major problem in prisons, particularly among those who smoke or use drugs. The intimidation used to coerce those in debt to pay up often extends to the families of debtors, who are pressurised into bringing into prison whatever a debtor is required to provide as interest or repayment. This is bound to cause intense misery to families, particularly those whose limited

finances are already under severe pressure, quite apart from the risk of their being caught.

What is most important is that management should immediately and publicly investigate any suspicion of bullying, leaving no one in any doubt that it will not be tolerated. The worst thing that any member of staff can do – other than themselves bullying prisoners or other staff – is to turn a blind eye to it. However, the most effective antidote, as for so many other problems with imprisonment, is the provision of full, purposeful and active days for all prisoners, particularly young prisoners. Properly conducted and supervised, such activity does not allow time or opportunity for bullying or bullies.

Some of the worst examples of what can happen if bullying is not stamped on were seen at Glen Parva. During our inspection in early 1997, inspectors intervened when they saw prison officers, there to supervise the lunch queue, standing idly by and doing nothing to prevent older boys demanding food just collected by younger ones. They found that the practice had gone unchecked for so long that it was regarded as inevitable.

The last straw for Paul Clarke, our Social Services inspector, was finding an illiterate 15-year-old who had been put on what was called 'basic regime' for six weeks by an officer, for being cheeky. This meant that he was confined in a single cell, without a radio or any means of occupying his time, and denied normal association with others. When Paul saw the boy in mid-March, he had just been given an additional four weeks 'on basic' for a minor misdemeanour. This meant that he would not be able to associate with any of his companions until early June. He was, naturally, considerably distressed, and had no idea as to how he could break out of this cycle. He felt that the officer had picked on him because he was a gypsy.

Prison Officers ought not to be allowed to award unofficial punishments.

These, and countless other examples of unacceptable treatment, encouraged me to challenge the staff who came to the debrief. I asked them if they would be happy for their sons, or the sons of any

of their friends or relations, to be on the receiving end of the regime they were inflicting on those sent to Glen Parva. If so, they should get out of the Prison Service. It did not need staff whose attitude to other human beings, particularly young ones, was so far removed from what is expected in a civilised society. What was so stupid about failing to stamp out such practice was that, far from preventing re-offending, it was highly likely to encourage future criminality.

So concerned were we with what we found at Werrington that I contacted both ministers and the Director General to voice my amazement at the disgraceful treatment of and conditions for children that we had witnessed, and which had been deliberately imposed by senior management. The result was immediate and electric.

Embarrassed senior managers went at once to see for themselves what we had reported. They were suitably shocked, which merely emphasised once again the folly of having no one responsible or accountable for young prisoners, who could have prevented the disaster in the first place. In their embarrassment, the managers at once promised additional financial resources and the provision of more activity places. More importantly, they reduced the numbers at Werrington to the 120 that the new buildings were designed to hold.

When we returned a year later the place had been transformed. Excellent child protection procedures had been designed and introduced by Peter Titley, a very able ex-probation officer, who subsequently joined the Inspectorate. He was encouraged and supported by the Director of Social Services for Staffordshire, Robert Lake, in a profitable partnership that should be repeated in every part of the country in which there is a YOI. Large folding tables had been bought so that everyone had their meals together away from their cells. Everyone had a daily activity programme, and officers felt more confident because they had been trained to look after this age group. Furthermore, parents were involved in their children's casework at the beginning and end of sentence. There was hope that this would become common practice throughout the young prisoner estate.

Sadly, however, governors have changed and my successor has had to report that Werrington has gone backwards since then, an avoidable happening that reinforces the need for consistent direction.

No group of people in custody gave the Inspectorate more cause for concern than those aged between 15 and 21, who present the Prison Service with its greatest challenge in trying to encourage prisoners to join the ranks of tomorrow's responsible citizens. Our reservations about how it was meeting this challenge were spelled out in bad reports on Brinsford, Dover, Feltham (four times), Glen Parva (twice), Hindley, Onley, Portland, Stoke Heath and Werrington, to name but nine establishments that we inspected between 1996 and 2001. It was very pleasing to be able to report later improvements at Brinsford, Portland, Stoke Heath and Werrington. In each case this resulted almost entirely from the drive and initiative of the governor and his or her implementation of Inspectorate recommendations. However, as always, what the governor could do was conditioned by available resources.

The first and most important aspect of a Healthy Prison, particularly one containing children and young prisoners, is that everyone should be – and feel – safe. All too often this was not the case. At Stoke Heath, for example, 50 per cent of the 246 children said that they had not felt safe on their first night, with 33 per cent having had to endure some form of initiation test on arrival. Assault and personal injury fig-ures are a key indicator of safety. In the eight months before our inspection 1080 injury forms had been completed for the 594 children and young prisoners, 268 from assaults and 282 from fights. What was most worrying was that adult control and restraint techniques had been used 232 times by staff, 125 of these in the wings containing children under the age of 18. Their methods had resulted in 95 injuries.

This dreadful catalogue not only gave a clear indication that Stoke Heath was not a safe place for children, or anyone else, but begged the question of why no one in authority had been sufficiently alarmed by

the figures to do something about them. All injuries have to be reported to Prison Service Headquarters. Had no one there thought that such a remarkably high incidence required investigation and remedial action? Because no one had overall responsibility for young prisoners this could only be the area manager, but as he concentrated mainly on budgets, perhaps injuries did not figure in his agenda?

Uniquely, the staff of the juvenile wings at Stoke Heath asked us to inspect them as well. They felt helpless, acknowledging that all was not well but not knowing what to do about it. They had not been trained to look after this age group and, like the governor of Werrington, they could think of no way of bringing this deficiency to official attention other than through inspection.

This draws attention to the difference between the treatment and conditions that young prisoners can expect in the three types of Prison Service Young Offender Institution (YOI).

Those like Werrington, that take only children under the age of 18, are now run on contract to the Youth Justice Board, introduced in 1999. This has laid down standards of treatment and conditions that are subject to sanctions for non-compliance. The Prison Service has responded by providing more facilities, including extra staff. It has also appointed an operational manager for juveniles who can oversee, but not overturn, treatment and conditions.

The second type contains only young prisoners aged between 18 and 21. Area managers manage these in the same way as all other prisons in an area. Some of them, like Aylesbury and Swinfen Hall, hold long-term young prisoners whose sentences will run on into adulthood. Swinfen Hall was the only establishment I reported to be a centre of excellence. Disappointingly, however, when I formally handed over this report at a special ceremony organised by the governor and attended by local mayors, representatives of the Criminal Justice System, and families of both staff and prisoners, nobody from Prison Service Headquarters attended. Again disappointingly, Swinfen Hall's excellent practice has not been transported to any other establishment. But as the Prison Service has not appointed an operational

manager for young prisoners aged between 18 and 21, no one is responsible for doing so.

Finally, there are establishments such as Stoke Heath, known as 'mixed sites', that contain both age groups. Again, area managers manage these, with the operational manager for juveniles given no right of access to or responsibility for their juveniles. Discrepancies between conditions for juveniles and young prisoners are immediately obvious. The Prison Service has to provide minimum staffing levels, education, work and physical education facilities for juveniles, to Youth Justice Board standards. Anything left over from the budget is then made available to young prisoners. Unfortunately, instead of inviting the Youth Justice Board to fund the extra facilities required, the Prison Service, in order to comply with the contract, simply gave priority use of existing facilities to juveniles. This effectively denies them to the older prisoners for most of the working day.

I have mentioned some of the establishments that received bad reports. Over the same period we published good reports on five and commented on good aspects in another seven. The same differences between standards of treatment and conditions were also evident in adult local prisons in which young prisoners were held on remand. Good things in Doncaster, Gloucester, Lewes, Norwich and Woodhill were in stark contrast to the very opposite that we found in Chelmsford, Exeter and Holloway.

Inconsistency arising from the different treatment and conditions available in different prisons, thus making improvement something of a lottery, undoubtedly contributes to re-offending. This is well illustrated in the answer to a parliamentary question on the subject of prison education funding, given by Mr Paul Boateng on 26 October 1999. In listing all prisons, he disclosed extraordinary variations in such funding for young prisoners in different YOIs. At HMYOI Brinsford (mixed), £482 per prisoner per year was made available for education; at Werrington (juvenile), £1598 per prisoner per year, and at Thorn Cross (mixed), £2357 per prisoner per year.

In addition to a job, which took top priority, young prisoners

frequently told us that education was what they most needed to help them in the future. The excellent education co-ordinator at HMYOI Northallerton explained to us how current funding, and direction, frustrated attempts to provide this. She found that, on average, 65–70 per cent of all young prisoners had been excluded from school, either through eviction or truancy. Many had become disaffected from education and developed ways of hiding their inadequacy. She felt that YOIs had the task and the opportunity of encouraging and fostering a return to learning. This required motivating the prisoners to want to learn.

When tested – and she was scornful of the adequacy of the Basic Skills Test currently favoured by the Prison Service – she found that 90 per cent of young offenders were performing at or below level one, or the equivalent of 11-year-olds. Thirty-five per cent were at entry level or below – equivalent to seven-year-olds. The Director General, however, had chosen the number of prisoners who reached level two, or GCSE, as the target for each prison. Average sentence length allowed each young prisoner access to education on 40 working days. To achieve the Prison Service's target, she had to try to achieve in 40 days what took five years at a secondary school.

For this she had £1054 per young prisoner per year. It was not enough. It forced her to choose between doing what was best for those whom she had motivated to want to learn, or sacrificing the basic needs of the majority in order to achieve a ridiculous target. In view of its importance, we could only marvel that no one had done anything to identify, ensure and ringfence adequate and consistent funding for education of every young offender in every YOI. Fortunately, funding is now the responsibility of the Department for Education and Skills.

While we were researching our thematic review *Young Prisoners*, I visited HMYOI Polmont in Scotland. Its excellent governor, Dan Gunn, confirmed the Northallerton co-ordinator's opinion of the inadequacy of current testing. He said that if, by some chance, he had to get rid of all his staff, the last one out of the gate would be his speech therapist. She had found that many young prisoners lacked the

ability to communicate with either their teachers or their peers. This was not due to any speech impediment, but to a lifestyle that had not included normal family conversation, leaving them with neither the confidence nor the ability to express themselves. These were essential prerequisites to learning.

Intrigued, I asked a very experienced speech therapist, Professor Karen Bryan, now of Surrey University but then working in Broadmoor Special Hospital, to come with us on our inspection of Swinfen Hall and interview 10 per cent of the young prisoners. The results confirmed the view that current testing did not unearth some very basic learning difficulties. Fifty per cent were suffering from memory loss induced by substance abuse (most frequently cannabis), 73 per cent were below acceptable grammatical competency, and all had significant difficulties with speech, language and communication, compared with 1 per cent of the general population. My recommendation that this should be studied and speech therapists appointed to all YOIs remains unactioned.

The first Young Offender Institution that I visited was Huntercombe near Oxford. It has long been regarded as a progressive establishment, where a number of distinguished governors, including Colin Allen, had tried hard to point young men in the right direction in life. One of the first places I was taken into was the library, where two boys were carrying books which I asked to see. Much to my surprise, one had a volume of Sir Stephen Runciman's *History of the Crusades* and the other a life of J. S. Bach by Sir Hubert Parry. I looked under the covers to see whether these were the real titles, and not the anarchist's cookbook. They were genuine.

'Did you read books like this at school or at home?' I asked.

'No, Mr X made us,' one replied.

'Who is Mr X?'

'An education instructor.'

'Why? What does he tell you to do?'

'He makes us read certain bits and then discusses them with us.'

'When did you leave school?' was inevitably my next question.

'Can't remember whether it was twelve or thirteen.'

'Why?'

'Can't remember whether it was drugs before boredom or boredom before drugs' was the chilling answer.

Later in my visit I met Mr X, who was invigilating two boys taking entrance exams to the John Moore's University in Liverpool, from which both have now graduated. He explained that one of them was the son of a professor at a well-known university, who had been thrown out of his home at the age of 16, got into bad company, and had ended up in Huntercombe. He was clearly someone of well above average ability, which Mr X was glad to have been able to identify and harness.

During the same visit, I was taken to the carpentry shop where I saw a boy making a wooden lamp, watched by a prison officer. I asked him whether he had ever worked with wood before. He told me that he had not and had never even had a job. I then asked him how old he was and to tell me a bit about himself and life at Huntercombe. He looked at me for a moment and said that he was 19. He then added 'The first time that anyone took any interest in me was when he – [pointing to the officer, whom he described as his personal officer] – made my sentence plan with me. I'd like to do woodwork when I leave.'

Young males are, I believe, in something of a crisis situation. Far too many appear, or consider themselves to be becoming, disconnected from society. Why do so many leave school early? Because they are bored as well as evicted or excluded. Could it be that the way in which they are taught is failing to excite them? Why have they had no work experience since they left school? Yes, work is available, but much of that is unfulfilling and requires no training. Excluded or truanting from school, without a job or supportive home life, many fall prey to those who encourage them to escape from reality with the help of drugs, forming rootless packs or gangs with others in the same boat. Finding no excitement or opportunity to let off adolescent steam, they resort to crime for excitement, to relieve boredom, and to provide money for their needs. In this distorted view of life, fathering

a child is regarded as a personal achievement – often their first and only achievement. An 18-year-old I met in HMYOI Dover reflected this. He was the father of a daughter, born two weeks before, and had fathered another child, due to be born to another girl a week later.

Thus, too many take the law into their own hands, alienated from a society in which there appears to be no place for them, no recognition that they exist, and in which their future seems bleak. Their resulting nihilistic attitude to that society can be summed up as 'no one takes any interest in me, so why should I take any interest in them'.

Appreciating what has to be done to set young prisoners on the right road has to begin with an understanding of what their lives were like before they were received into prison. Sadly – an indictment of us all – the life stories of too many do not suggest any conscious attempt to identify, nurture or develop what Winston Churchill referred to as 'the treasure that is in the heart of every man' by parents, schools or society before they end up in prison. For example, I met a boy in Dover who had been excluded from his playgroup at the age of four and never allowed to attend primary or secondary school. Illiterate and undisciplined, it was hardly surprising that he ended up in prison.

There are those who think that it is a waste of money spending £400 per week on every young offender in prison only for three-quarters of them to re-offend. These fees – the same as those at Eton, Harrow or Winchester – are dwarfed by the £3000 per week it costs to keep someone in local government or Secure Training Centre (STC) accommodation. Not surprisingly, those who have to pay these sums would rather send young offenders to cheap, albeit overcrowded, under-staffed and under-resourced prisons than expensive, lavishly staffed and resourced secure units. The question of which provides better value for money should be answered by re-offending rates. At present this is not possible because the statistics are imperfectly gathered. I suspect that the answer lies in something that does not exist: a compromise between YOI conditions and STC staffing levels.

Many members of the present government, led by the Prime

Minister, have indicated their intention of solving the problem of youth crime. They have introduced a number of important developments, such as the Youth Justice Board, Detention and Training Orders and Youth Offender teams. All these are good, and are having an impact on how those under the age of 18 are treated in prison, but the specific problems and needs of those aged between 18 and 21, called young prisoners by the Prison Service, are being largely ignored.

During my first inspection of a Young Offender Institution, HMYOI Onley, I met an old regimental friend, Senior Officer – formerly Corporal – John Gibbons. He had been a member of my close protection group in Belfast in 1974–5. Now he was responsible for the reception of juveniles, and I asked him to give me the lowdown on what was really going on in the establishment. He at once praised the governor, saying that he was trying to do all he could with insufficient resources, and then gave me an example of the problems that he, personally, faced.

The evening before, he had been warned to expect some new arrivals from Glen Parva, which acted as an exchange point for young prisoners arriving from courts. One arrival was a 15-year-old, who had left his home in Hull early that morning and gone to court, neither accompanied by his mother nor expecting to be given a custodial sentence. In the early afternoon he had been tried and sentenced to nine months imprisonment, after which he had been taken down to the court cells to await transport. Eventually he had been driven to Glen Parva and given a hot meal – his first food of the day – before being transferred. He had arrived at Onley soon after eight o'clock at night, tearful and not knowing where he was. John arranged for a message to be sent to the boy's mother and ensured that the night staff knew that the boy needed care and attention before he himself went off duty – which he should have done when his shift ended some time earlier. He said that this was by no means an isolated incident, adding that each one made him very angry.

'If I had a magic wand, what would you most like me to give you?' I asked.

'Time,' came the immediate and emphatic response. 'Twenty minutes chatting to each of these lads, showing them that you are interested in them as individuals, is worth more than all the programmes. It's probably the first time that they have come across an adult male acting responsibly. I have had masses of cards and letters from boys who have been here, thanking me for being interested and showing them that I cared. It's sad that they should have had to come to prison to get that. But the trouble is that we are rushed off our feet all day and simply do not have time to give them.'

Young people will not unveil the details of their problems unless they have confidence that disclosure will lead to help with putting what may seem pretty hopeless lives in order. It takes time to assess what has prevented them from leading useful and law-abiding lives, and to work out a suitable programme for challenging and rectifying identified deficiencies. It takes time to conduct whatever programmes are designed. Finally, it takes time to prepare them for release. This should include time to pass on all that has been learned about an individual to whoever is to continue the treatment and maintain the momentum of change, otherwise all that has been gained will be lost.

Just as time is needed for young offenders' problems to be adequately assessed at the beginning of their sentence, so must sufficient time be set aside for an ordered process of preparing them for release at the end. First in this process, risk must be re-assessed. Staff at Lancaster Farms told me of their frustration at being unable to convince the authorities outside the establishment that their fears about one young prisoner were justified. He was about to be released but, in their view, represented potential danger. He was not considered sectionable under the Mental Health Act and, five weeks after his release, he murdered someone. Now the prison faced exactly the same problems over the imminent release of another dangerous young man, also not considered sectionable. They were extremely alarmed that no local authorities seemed willing to listen to their fears and wondered what they could do. My immediate response was that this was exactly why there should be someone in overall charge of young prisoners

and some form of contingency machinery to cater for such eventualities. Youth Offender teams, run by the chief executive of a local authority, were responsible for those under the age of 18, but no such link existed for the older age group.

Secondly, young prisoners *must* be resourced if they are to survive without immediately having to resort to crime. I fail to understand why benefits can only be applied for after release, since this inevitably means a delay before they can be collected. Why not use the time in prison to complete all the application forms so that the leaving grant from prison is the first weekly benefit to be drawn? This way, money would be assured for the following week. This of course applies to all prisoners on release.

Once released, young offenders should have someone to report to who is responsible for helping them to resettle. In many cases this will be their family, but what happens to those who have no family, have previously been in care, homeless, or living rough? If they have served long sentences they will have a probation officer; if they are serving a detention and training order they will remain under the same Youth Offender team. For the remainder it could be a social worker, a drug treatment counsellor, a further education official, or a mentor introduced by one of the voluntary organisations, such as Youth at Risk, involved in such work. The point is that all ex-young prisoners need help and support during the first few days and weeks after release, when they are most at risk of re-offending. Finally, they should have a roof over their heads planned for the day of their release. This might have to be a hostel or similar accommodation, but none should be released without having an address to go to.

The dangers of failing to ensure that the right help is available are well put by a young ex-prisoner: 'I'd spent a lot of my young life in prison and for the first time, partly because I had a long sentence, I'd got clean and had a chance to think about my life. At Huntercombe I got skills and came out believing I could go straight. But then I arrived at my hostel and found it was full of people like me who had lived by crime and a lot were straight back on drugs once they got

through the prison gates. There were dealers coming in all the time. I knew I had to get out if I didn't want to get sucked back in. I was lucky I got a job in a bar and earned enough to rent myself a place in the town and that's been great.'

The Prison Service is fanatical about avoiding ministerial embarrassment. Every possible effort is made to prevent escapes, particularly of high-profile and high-risk prisoners. What is so surprising is that neither ministers nor the Prison Service seem embarrassed by inspectors' exposure of unacceptable treatment of young prisoners in places such as Werrington. Set against a considerable amount of good and dedicated work, all reports revealed the same problems that were noted everywhere other than in high security prisons – lack of direction, lack of facilities, lack of trained staff – which compound the problems caused by overcrowding. The results speak for themselves: 88 per cent of those under 18 and 78 per cent of those under 21 re-offend within two years.

Sir Arthur Bryant, in his book *The Search for Justice*, quotes a commentator on the plight of children in coal mines: 'We in England have put ourselves forward in every possible way that could savour of ostentation as champions of the human race: and we are now, on our own showing, exhibited to the world as empty braggarts and shallow pretenders to virtues that we do not possess.'

11

WOMEN IN PRISON:
HMP HOLLOWAY

'Confinement in so dreadful a place was actually a form of torture which could drive people mad.'

Dorothy Speed, psychiatrist and principal medical officer, 1986

WHENEVER WE INSPECTED ANY ONE of the 19 women's prisons I found myself comparing its treatment of and conditions for prisoners with those that we had seen at Holloway in December 1995. Holloway is the largest women's prison in the country. I suspect that it is the only women's prison of which the vast majority has heard.

Immediately following that horrific experience, I determined to produce a thematic report making recommendations for improving treatment and conditions in female institutions. We published *Women in Prison* in July 1997, and in June 2001, shortly before I retired, we published *A Follow-up to Women in Prison*, which contained the following remarks:

> In our view, the general conditions for and treatment of women prisoners in prisons in England and Wales have improved significantly since the publication of *Women in Prison* in 1997. An exception to this is Holloway, where the successful management of the number and complexity of

tasks the prison fulfils continues to defy the best efforts of managers and staff, and where, as a consequence, we continue to have concerns about the treatment of women prisoners. Details of our concerns can be found in the report of an unannounced inspection carried out at the end of the year 2000.

In *Women in Prison* I had called for the appointment of a single director, accountable and responsible for the treatment and conditions of all females in prison in England and Wales. The Prison Service response was to appoint a head of a women's planning group, and, later an operational manager of women's prisons, who was then joined by a second. However, they were not given full operational or financial responsibility. This divided and complex management has not yet succeeded in making common practice of all the improvements noted in separate prisons.

The size of the female prison population, which stood at over 4000 at the time of writing, has increased by 150 per cent in the past ten years. To accommodate this increase, eight male prisons have been re-roled from male to female in the past six years, easing female – but exacerbating male – overcrowding.

Our research for *Women in Prison* in 1996 showed that 28 per cent of all women prisoners come from London, 11 per cent from each of Bristol, Birmingham, Manchester and Leeds, 8 per cent from Liverpool and Essex, and 6 per cent from Newcastle. However, even a cursory glance at the map of where women's prisons are located in England and Wales, will show that it bears no relation to the parts of the country from which prisoners come. All high security women are held in Durham. Many women from Holloway are transferred to Drake Hall in Staffordshire. Women from Lancashire are sent to New Hall in Yorkshire and Low Newton in County Durham, there is no female prison accommodation in Wales, and the Prison Service is building a large new women's facility at Peterborough. The geography inevitably makes visits both expensive and difficult, particularly if

small children are involved. Women visit men in prison. Men tend not to visit women. Particularly in the long-term interest of maintaining relationships with their children, every effort should be made to assist visits to women rather than make it more difficult.

However, despite all the developments that we saw in other places, we kept coming back to the problem of Holloway. All that I knew about it before our inspection in December 1995 was that treatment of and conditions there had deteriorated so sharply over the previous nine months, that the chairman of its Board of Visitors had taken the most unusual step of writing to express her concerns to the Home Secretary. Throughout these nine months, she had pleaded with ministers and prison authorities for urgent remedial action, but none had been taken.

By the time I handed over to Anne Owers in July 2001, we had inspected Holloway three more times. I had come to realise that its story, in many ways, not only encapsulated the problems caused by how women's prisons were managed, but how all prisons were managed. For some reason the Prison Service remained stubbornly resistant to making major change until it was forced upon it. Unless ministers exerted real pressure, or ministerial embarrassment was likely, it would issue a disclaimer making out that all was well and continue business as usual.

This was confirmed when I saw that Martin Narey had said that it was quite wrong of my successor, Anne Owers, 'to suggest that the prison was only galvanised into action by [her] report', following her 2002 inspection. He had used the same words to try to deflect my criticisms in 2000, and after our inspection in 1998. His predecessor had used similar words after our inspection in 1996. And so on and so on.

Surely those responsible must realise that the same criticism about the same undelivered promises, repeated over and over again – with supporting evidence – by successive independent quality assurance inspectors, confirms the stark truth that nothing has been done to address these matters? If officials repeatedly fail to deliver on promises,

they cannot complain if doubt is cast on the veracity of anything else that they say. Martin Narey was aiming at the wrong target. It was not only the prison that needed galvanising. Once again it was ministers, and the Prison Service for which he was responsible, who had failed to provide Holloway with the necessary wherewithal to make promised improvements.

Yet again I found myself wondering what evidence was needed to make ministers realise that something was seriously wrong with a system that was failing, in exactly the same way and in exactly the same prison, as it had done for almost 20 years. They appeared not to want to listen to their own appointed inspectors, neither did they listen to the evidence of countless experienced commentators and observers. As far as Holloway was concerned, this pattern had not begun with my refusal to complete the inspection in 1995.

Over the days and months after that traumatic event, I learned much from Colin Allen about how poor and inappropriate the treatment of women in prisons in general, and Holloway in particular, had been over a number of years. Colin spoke with unique authority because of his own extraordinary experiences while governor of Holloway from 1985 to 1989, followed by eight years as a prison inspector.

Women prisoners and young offenders had been managed as separate groups during the days of the Prison Commission. Later, however, these arrangements were cancelled by the Prison Department. Once there was no longer anyone with overall responsibility for them, less and less attention had been paid, officially, to their treatment and conditions. Colin feared that the stark warning from the Holloway Board of Visitors about what was happening to women prisoners in 1995, so studiously ignored by both ministers and Prison Service Headquarters, could equally well have come from a number of other women's prisons.

Holloway, which had been built originally as the New City Prison in 1852, was re-opened in 1983 following a long and controversial rebuild. In 1984 it received a very critical report from the then Chief

Inspector, Sir James Hennessy, in which he deplored the lack of morale in the prison and the conflict between the operational and medical departments. Staff responsible for discipline were said to be convinced that they were outnumbered, over-worked, and unduly vulnerable to attack in the 'new and bizarre prison that had been wished upon them'. Although the certified normal accommodation of the prison was 253, an overcrowded figure of 350 had been accepted by the Prison Officers Association in view of the numbers of women prisoners who would otherwise be locked out and have to be held in police cells. Even so, up to 25 were held in police cells almost every night. In addition, some of those awaiting trial were temporarily transferred as far away as Low Newton in County Durham.

Within the grossly overcrowded building there was little or nothing for prisoners to do. One remembered that 'doors were locked . . . the sinks smashed, the toilets kicked to bits . . . people were really angry because they were locked up 23 out of 24 hours'.

While conditions in the 'normal' area of the prison were bad, they were far worse on the wing for highly mentally disturbed women, which had moved to the lowest floor of the building, known as C1. It was described as being 'illuminated by slit-like windows that were covered in crazed polycarbonate, claustrophobic and depressing, smelling of urine and excrement, and with a deafening noise of women banging on their cells'.

A psychiatrist who worked there wrote that 'Confinement in so dreadful a place was actually a form of torture which could drive people mad . . . What had gone wrong basically was that there was no proper hospital. There was accommodation for the mentally disturbed, as they called them, on the ground floor level, because it was easier to contain them there. But it was worse because it was dark . . . there was rising damp . . . there were rats . . . and it was infested with cockroaches.'

Sir James Hennessy was very critical of 'the use of disciplinary proceedings against prisoners who appeared to be disturbed or mentally

disordered, many of whom were on extreme medication. It was wrong to discipline them as if they were normal, particularly those suffering from brain damage or mental impairment.' He highlighted that there 'had always been an issue about women and prison and how they behave. Is this mad behaviour or bad behaviour? Are they in control? Should they be on adjudication and dealt with through the disciplinary procedures, or should they be on treatment?'

The inhabitants of C1 were undoubtedly unruly, locked up, drugged up and frequently punished. There were high rates of vandalism, damage, barricading, floodings, arson, and violence against staff and other prisoners. Fifty per cent of the prisoners were said to have suicidal tendencies, and self-harm was alarmingly frequent. There was both tension and conflict between nurses and prison officers as to who should be in charge of those on the wing. Almost invariably the nurses – and appropriate treatment – lost.

Thanks to the few MPs, journalists and penal reformers who were able to enter the prison, this was not unknown to the outside world. In 1983, Chris Tchaikowski, a former Holloway prisoner, formed a charity called Women in Prison with a group of her former colleagues, beginning a fearless fight for the cause of women prisoners that continued until her death in 2002. The group briefed an *Observer* journalist who, in September 1984, wrote an article, 'Holloway Horror Wing', that led to the problems of the prison becoming a national issue. Not for the first or last time in its troubled history Holloway became a centre of media attention. Many newspapers joined in the condemnation. Women in Prison organised demonstrations outside the Home Office and the prison to demand an inquiry into the conditions in C1.

Leon (Lord) Brittan, the Home Secretary, responded by announcing the establishment of a committee to review the function and structure of the prison, and the appointment of a new governor, Colin Allen. The committee's first suggestion was that Holloway should be treated as three separate units. A local prison would be responsible for receiving prisoners on initial committal and ensuring

that they met court commitments. A training prison would hold women with sentences as long as life and as short as a matter of weeks. The third would provide an area for disturbed women and accommodate a hospital. When Colin arrived this contained large numbers of mentally disturbed women from all over the country, because there was nowhere else in the prison system for them to go. It was run by a junior prison governor without clear medical direction.

Colin immediately set about 'opening up the regime of the prison'. He did not accept that women were as potentially dangerous as the worst type of male prisoner, or that they represented the same security threat — escapes and assaults on staff. He was determined that, instead of being locked up the whole time with the consequent damage to their morale and wellbeing, prisoners should be out of their cells from 7.30 in the morning until 7.30 in the evening. During that time, as many as possible should be engaged in a variety of appropriate activities.

His policy was that wings were to be used for sleeping, eating and association only. To help them to live more ordered lives on release, women should be encouraged and enabled to take some responsibility for organising their own lives, rather than sinking into institutionalisation. Therefore unlocked prisoners should make their own way to education, the gym or workshops, at set times during the day. Staff would merely supervise movement.

If staff, led by capable managers who knew what they were doing, operated professionally and were prepared to allow prisoners some responsibility, Colin felt sure that the tension created by their previously confrontational approach would disappear. Proof that he was correct came in a remarkable drop in the numbers of assaults on staff, self-harm and suicide attempts. The level of offending in Holloway by women prisoners fell to well below the female prison average.

He also introduced a clear distinction between the management of the medical section and the other two areas. Women who needed physical or mental health care were considered to be in a hospital, under the supervision of doctors and not discipline staff. Discipline

staff maintained overall security of the prison and supervised all other sentenced and unsentenced prisoners. It seems obvious now but at the time, and compared with previous staff attitudes to control, it was a revolution.

The results were dramatic. Women who showed signs of being disturbed were encouraged to talk instead of being instantly locked up in their cells. Doctors and nurses listened and, having done so, began to appreciate the appalling background from which so many women prisoners came and the impact of the social neglect and sexual and physical abuse that had been their lot since childhood. They realised that many were:

> . . . powerless when in the community, being in social class 4 and 5 and whose families had already broken up etc. They had histories or careers of criminal damage, or breach of the peace, or being drunk and disorderly and then being remanded to Holloway. By the time that they came up against uniformed authority, many of the personality-disordered women were undergoing a catharsis by acting out aggression and violence against others and/or themselves. They had never had the opportunity to resolve all their earlier experiences of loss or abuse . . . over a five-year period we profiled the population on the grounds of virtually everything – serious physical abuse 90%; serious sexual abuse 70%; drugs and alcohol the same.

Many, previously presumed to be mentally ill, were found to be suffering from personality damage resulting from the chaotic and dysfunctional lives that so many of them had experienced in the community.

Colin Allen believed that, rather than operate behind locked doors as it had done for so long, Holloway should be opened to public scrutiny. He saw what had happened following public exposure of the appalling conditions on C1. He knew that, as governor, any further

publicity would put pressure on him to respond. But he hoped that it would also put pressure on those who were responsible for women in prison, to whom he was accountable. It might sting them into recognising that there could be no real improvements without their active intervention.

As the treatment of and conditions for prisoners at Holloway began to improve, and the previous culture to be overturned, the Prison Officers Association (POA) began to feel that its previously powerful position in the prison was being overturned as well. A number of male officers had been brought in to balance the previous preponderance of females, and staff were moved around every so often to prevent them from becoming stale. In order to cut down absence, all cases of alleged sickness were investigated and one officer was dismissed as a result.

And so the POA reverted to its old ways – automatic resistance to any change that appeared to benefit women prisoners. They passed a vote of no confidence in the governor and his open regime. Despite all Colin's careful explanation and discussion of his policy with them, they threatened to take industrial action if there was not what they called 'full and proper negotiation with them' before implementation.

At the time the POA was becoming increasingly militant and confrontational in many prisons up and down the country, opposing the Prime Minister and the Home Secretary who were determined on 'management's right to manage'. The issue the officers chose to fight over in Holloway was the number of staff needed to lock and unlock prisoners. Initially, they insisted that there must always be at least two officers on duty whenever any women were unlocked and out of their cells. They later increased this to three, adding that, if one had to go away for any reason, all prisoners would have to remain locked up.

Colin responded by asking publicly whether the governor of the prison had the authority to say that two officers should unlock up to 32 women, or whether such a decision should be left to the whim of staff. In March 1988 the POA answered by voting not to unlock unless there were three staff. The blue touch-paper for industrial

action was lit soon afterwards when an officer was charged for refusing to unlock because three officers were not available.

The issue was taken up immediately by the National Executive Committee (NEC) of the POA, whose male officials had no idea of what an open regime for women meant or what it had achieved. It was noted that they were in contact with 'a substantial group of staff who appeared only to be comfortable when there was trouble in the prison'.

The NEC said that it wanted to discuss staffing levels. Colin, backed by his regional director, was determined that this was not a national issue, but one internal to the management of the prison and thus non-negotiable. However, the pressure was already beginning to tell on Prison Service Headquarters, which suspended disciplinary action against the officer whom Colin had charged. Colin recorded 'I had naively thought that the Prison Service was serious about introducing the changes at Holloway. It was only when it came to the fore [at a meeting] that I realised that they were actually bringing pressure on me to withdraw.'

The Board of Visitors at once realised the significance of this development. They complained to the Prisons Minister that, by suspending disciplinary action which it had instigated and that the governor had acted upon, 'the Department had undermined the authority of the Governor and his managers in a crucial way. To be seen to hand back power to the POA can only jeopardise the proper running of the prison.'

On 29 July 235 officers walked out of Holloway. However, all governors, nurses and 30 officers stayed at their posts throughout the six weeks of the strike. Colin imported a small number of additional managers and made maximum use of visitors and helpers to maintain the regime, but he knew that he could only continue to run the prison with the co-operation of the prisoners. This he quickly obtained by explaining the situation to them and promising that, whatever else happened, there would be no reduction in the treatment of those who were under medical supervision, nor would any activities be cut.

The second day of the strike was the crucial one. With the exception of escorting prisoners to court, Colin showed that the prison could continue to function. Nothing could have demonstrated more clearly that he was right in his belief that it was possible to maintain an open regime that was peaceable and workable. The POA contention that the prison was a dangerous place, in which no member of staff was safe unless supported by a number of others, had been demonstrably proved to be false.

What in fact Colin had done was to break the power of the POA which, as someone working in the prison at the time said, 'He didn't want to do, and he resisted it for ages. But when [the strike] came, he stood firm . . . Somebody had to take them on because they were just unbearable. Officers in there were just disgusting in the way they behaved.'

It was even said that, in the absence of most discipline officers, the prison was in many ways an easier, more relaxed and less repressive institution.

While it is dangerous to draw too many conclusions from what was an extraordinary response to an extraordinary situation, some lessons stand out. Most prisoners, when treated with respect as human beings, can and will respond. Those who need medical treatment benefit when treated as patients first and prisoners second.

Treating prisoners with respect, regarding them as potentially responsible citizens, is one of the key characteristics of a Healthy Prison. The concept of 'responsible prisoners' was actively pursued by two prison governors. Mike Kirby gave women prisoners in HMP Low Newton as much responsibility for their day to day affairs as possible. This ran totally counter to the traditionally impersonal routine practised in most institutions. However, it was quickly seen to be the best possible preparation for the inevitable release of prisoners, who would have to be responsible not only for themselves but their families.

Stephen Pryor both practised and preached the concept while governing HMP Highpoint, which, at the time, contained both a male and a female prison. I was very glad that he asked to spend the last

eight months of his service with the Inspectorate, because this enabled us to discuss his ideas with him before he published a valuable paper on the subject. In this he wrote that:

> Giving people responsibility, or allowing them to retain it while in prison, means accepting that they are not wholly bad or wholly dangerous, or wholly irresponsible, although that is what the adversarial court process may have shown when finding them wholly guilty. Having the aim of weaning them off prison is a key to rebuilding people, and that demands clear-headed understanding of what imprisonment means and what it does. It also means that prison staff need to treat each prisoner individually, as bad and as dangerous and as irresponsible as they may be, and as good and reliable and responsible as they might be. In the words of a prisoner, 'Being unable to take responsibility because it is denied to you is not the same as being irresponsible.'

Colin Allen treated the women prisoners in Holloway with respect. Finding that, almost ten years after these truths had been exposed, they were once again being ignored at the time of our 1995 inspection, suggested to me that, whatever policies ministers had for imprisonment, they did not include the provision of decent and humane treatment of and conditions for prisoners.

The POA declared the strike over on 9 September. Returning strikers quickly tried to overturn the open regime and return the prison to its former state. Naturally Colin resisted and, once again, the POA's National Executive Committee intervened on the side of a staff member whom he temporarily removed from duty for refusing to unlock without at least two others. This time – as one of the returnees admitted – to confuse management they decided that, instead of withdrawing their labour, they would fight from within.

Unfortunately, as had already become apparent, some in the Home Office and Prison Department had no stomach for further confrontation,

nor were they prepared to show public support for a governor who had dared to step in between the Prison Service and the POA. In November 1988 it was announced that Colin would be relieved of his post in January 1989. The chairman of the Board of Visitors felt that the real reason was to ensure that no one in authority lost face.

Holloway reverted to its former, deeply unsatisfactory methods. The POA remained confident that the authorities lacked the moral courage to back any governor who was brave enough to challenge it, or to discipline any malefactor. No wonder it took years to suspend a number of officers accused of assaulting prisoners and other staff in Holloway. The same applied, as I have described in an earlier chapter, in Wormwood Scrubs.

Lack of ministerial galvanising of the Prison Service to bring about improvements that were both essential and possible was behind what I found at Holloway in 1995, 1996, 1998, 2000, and Anne Owers found in 2002. As well as suggesting that the Inspectorate had not ignited change, Martin Narey added that Anne Owers's criticisms did not reflect 'the significant change in culture that the staff at Holloway have achieved'. She found that this change included showers being denied to women more than twice a week, even to those who were pregnant or had recently given birth. That was worse than I had found in 2000. It was more like the culture complained about by Sir James Hennessy 20 years earlier. Anne also found children under the age of 18 in Holloway, even though Michael Howard had promised their removal in 1996, and the Prison Service frequently thereafter. What evidence is this of high level determination to improve the treatment of and conditions for women in prison?

Since our 1995 inspection report, and in addition to our 1997 thematic report *Women in Prison* and its 2001 follow up, many other organisations and individuals have joined in trying to galvanise ministers and the Prison Service to make improvements. As we reported, and as with every part of the prison system, much good work is done in many prisons around the country, by many dedicated staff. In

addition, very good work is done by a large number of voluntary organisations, such as the Prisoner Advice and Care Trust, formerly the Bourne Trust, who have developed an outstanding programme called 'First Night in Prison'. Volunteers who really understand the problems and worries that they have about their children, their accommodation, dependent relatives and money, interview women arriving in Holloway. This should be done by the Prison Service as a matter of course. Instead, the Prisoner Advice and Care Trust, and many other organisations concerned with the treatment of and conditions for women prisoners, live on a knife-edge, not knowing whether or not their funding will be renewed. If there was a proper overall strategy for the provision of essential services, whether by officialdom or by volunteers, it should include guaranteed funding to ensure consistent provision.

In 1999 the administration of juveniles in the hands of the Criminal Justice System was transformed by the introduction of the Youth Justice Board. This required the Prison Service to conform to laid-down standards appropriate for that age group. In 2000 the Prison Reform Trust published a study entitled *Justice for Women: The Need for Reform,* by Professor Dorothy Wedderburn. One of its most far reaching recommendations was that a similar body, a Women's Justice Board, should be appointed, with similar responsibilities for the conditions and treatment of women who come into the hands of the Criminal Justice System. I could not agree more. It would provide the essential and consistent insistence that the Prison Service conform to laid-down standards of treatment and conditions for women.

The story of the last 20 years at Her Majesty's Prison Holloway is one of obdurate refusal to accept the evidence of past – and continuous – failure as a justification and basis for real and sustained improvement. Only a change of attitude by ministers and the senior management of the Prison Service, and real determination to abolish a consistently failing management style, will ensure that Holloway's future is not as unnecessarily unsatisfactory as its past and its present.

12

LOOKING BACK

'The establishment of an Inspectorate of Prisons, independent of
the Prison Department, and the publication of its reports, are a
vital part of the process of increasing public understanding of the
prison system.'

*Foreword to the first Annual Report of first HM Chief Inspector of
Prisons, 1982, by the Home Secretary, the Rt. Hon. William
Whitelaw*

AS I ENTERED MY LAST two months as HM Chief Inspector, I
began addressing inspection reports to the third Home Secretary in
five and a half years. I also began regular meetings with a fifth Prisons
Minister. None of them appeared to doubt the importance of the role
of imprisonment within the Criminal Justice System. However, while
the treatment of and conditions for prisoners had undoubtedly
improved in some prisons at some times, neither Michael Howard nor
Jack Straw had directed, or produced, the long awaited strategy that so
many people recommended as essential if improvement was to be
robust, consistent and permanent. I wondered whether David
Blunkett, whom I had never met but whose influence as Secretary of
State for Education had been felt in prisons, would listen to and take
account of the evidence.

I also wondered whether any of the new ministerial team would
bother to visit their quality assurance Inspectorate. Michael Howard
once joined us on a training day; Jack Straw never met the inspectors,

but came once to be briefed by the team leaders and me. I corresponded, and had occasional meetings with both, but I realised that, however much more I would have liked to have seen them, Home Secretaries have an impossibly wide responsibility, and their diaries are impossibly full. I did have regular meetings with all Prison Ministers, those with Lord Williams of Mostyn being by far the most rewarding because of his wisdom, courtesy and obvious interest. It was a sad day for prison improvement when he was promoted to Attorney General.

Lord Bassam of Brighton was the only minister to accept my invitation to be briefed. When the team leaders had explained how they went about their task, he said that he wished he had known that two years before. When I asked him whether what he had heard differed from what he had been told about the Inspectorate by officials, he replied that he had to be loyal.

Inspection report after inspection report sent to the Home Secretary after being accepted as correct by the Director General, contained yet more evidence of what needed to be done if the Prison Service was to achieve its own Statement of Purpose. Presumably, the published aim of helping prisoners to live useful and law-abiding lives in prison and on release was fact and not just spin? However, in prison after prison, we continued to find numerous prisoners locked up all day because there were not enough activities to provide this help. The consistently high re-offending rate did not appear to be viewed with any embarrassment. Invariably, every time we identified a failing prison, the same old response was trotted out – 'we do not recognise all that was reported x months ago; significant change is under way'.

In February 2001, prison governors attending the annual Prison Service conference in Nottingham were electrified to hear Martin Narey tell them that he was not prepared to continue apologising for failing prison after failing prison. He said that he had had enough of trying to explain 'the very immorality of our treatment of some prisoners and the degradation of some establishments'.

He bewailed the fact that the Prison Service had more or less accepted that places like Wormwood Scrubs, Birmingham, Leeds,

Wandsworth, Portland and Brixton were terrible and could not be changed. 'Year after year, governor after governor, inspection after inspection, prisons like these have been exposed. Year after year the exposure has led to a flurry of hand-wringing, sometimes a change of governor, a dash of capital investment, but no real or sustained improvement.'

He focussed on Wormwood Scrubs, described as a penal dustbin as long ago as 1982, which had just seen the prosecution, conviction and jailing of a number of prison officers for assaults on prisoners. Very recently he had had to face the press in the light of what he described as my devastating critique of the prison, in which I had captured the atmosphere of neglect and intimidation so starkly.

'But were Sir David's revelations a surprise to us?' he said. They should not have been. 'Four years previously, in 1996, Sir David expressed anxiety about the illegal use of force in the segregation unit.' He went on, 'The point that I am trying to make is that we have to decide, as a Service, whether this litany of failure and moral neglect continues indefinitely, or whether we are going to reform places; whatever the difficulties, whatever the burden of overcrowding, what-ever the resource constraints, whatever the middle management inadequacies'.

These brave words disclosed that Martin Narey realised that the way in which prisons were currently being run was wrong, witnessed by the number of times that their failings were so publicly exposed. However, having demonstrated his own personal honesty and com-mitment to putting things right, he fell into exactly the same trap as all his predecessors. He failed to add that he recognised that the fault did not lie solely with the governors of individual prisons, who could only do what they could, with and for prisoners, with what they had been given. Ultimately the blame for failure in any organisation lies at the door of its management. In the case of prisons, that was not the middle management of the Service – the prison governors to whom he had drawn attention. It was the ministerial and Prison Service senior management, which he was unwilling to criticise in public.

He went on to say that he had the unequivocal support of ministers. What were they supporting? Was it the way in which prisons were managed? If so, they had failed to ask themselves why management methods continued to result in such a catalogue of failure and moral neglect. Was it the appallingly high re-offending rate? If so, it confirmed their lack of understanding of the role of the Prison Service in achieving the aim it had set the Criminal Justice System – to protect the public by preventing crime. Or was it the Director General personally, whose predecessor but one had been made a scapegoat for ministerial failure? If so, it was honourable but of little practical value. This supposed support had led to no amelioration of the competing burdens of unrelieved overcrowding and remorseless resource constraints that combined to make life for him – and the Prison Service – so difficult.

In truth, the Prison Service did not have the ministerial support that the public had the right to expect. Ministers are accountable to Parliament and the electorate for the failure of all or part of any organisation for which they are responsible. The Prison Service was failing the public by its bad management of prisons, but it was being failed by ministers, who were giving it neither the direction nor the resources needed to protect the public from further crimes by those it released from its custody.

Martin Narey also ignored the culpability of Prison Service senior management. He protested that he had the backing of what he described as an 'outstanding, committed and cohesive [Prisons] Board'. I do not doubt that individual Board members are committed to the task they think they have been given. But such a record of failure and neglect can hardly be called outstanding. Did the Board regard the re-offending rate as satisfactory? Did it accept no responsibility for the immorality of the Service's treatment of prisoners? What had it done to identify and eliminate the degradation that he acknowledged continued to blot some establishments? What had it done over the past four years to respond to my concerns about the behaviour of prison officers at Wormwood Scrubs? Could it not see that the way in which it exercised its responsibilities contributed to failure?

The Director General also failed to make clear to his subordinates that he appreciated that the reforms he sought were outside the capability of the Prison Service, in isolation, to deliver. If the re-offending rate was to be used as the measure of success or failure, the Prison Service should concentrate on preparing prisoners for release. What happened after release was the responsibility of the Probation Service and other organisations, such as the Youth Justice Board, that were responsible for supervision and aftercare. Neither he nor the Prison Service could alleviate the pressures generated by overcrowding and resource constraint. Resolution of these is a matter for the Criminal Justice System as a whole. Such resolution requires changes to sentencing policy and the provision of sufficient and satisfactory alternatives to custody. Because it also involves ministries other than the Home Office, it is beyond the capability of the Home Secretary alone. All concerned will have to unite in the 'joined up' government, of which we hear so much, to fight the Treasury for sufficient resources.

Many of the difficulties Martin Narey faced – including lack of adequate selection and training of staff and managers, lack of supervision by management, financial cuts affecting the provision of work and education and poor industrial relations – were of the Prison Service's own making. There was nothing new or surprising about these because they had been highlighted by successive Chief Inspectors in report after report.

Unfortunately, he did not describe what he meant by a failing prison, although he implied that it had to do with immoral and degrading treatment of prisoners. Only a matter of days before, Jack Straw had asked a so-called independent Targeted Performance Improvements Working Group, headed by Lord Laming, a former Chief Inspector of Social Services, to examine why failing prisons were not being identified by the Prison Service before being exposed as such by the Inspectorate. I say 'so-called' independent because two of its five members were the Deputy Director General of the Prison Service and a non-executive member of the Prisons Board.

Had Jack Straw asked me, I could have given him the answer and saved him having to resort to yet another working party producing yet another paper. The Inspectorate and the Prison Service appeared to be working to different agendas. Our parliamentary remit required us to concentrate on the treatment of and conditions for prisoners. Prison Service management concentrated on exact compliance with rules and regulations, and the achievement of a myriad of targets and performance indicators. These were more to do with process in prisons than outcomes for prisoners.

My suspicions that we were working to different agendas were heightened whenever I met with the Home Office Permanent Secretary, Sir David Omand, whom I had known for many years when we worked together in the Ministry of Defence. He never visited the Inspectorate or spoke with any of the inspectors, nor did he appear to like or understand our independence. I often wondered how much he was responsible for ministerial failure to respond to reports or to insist on remedial action. On one occasion Sir David alleged that I was deliberately winding up the tempo of our criticism by the selection of the prisons that we inspected. I pointed out that our formal five-year programme was made known to and published by the Prison Service over a year ahead. I had no control over which prisons were good or bad or why they were failing. That was a matter for the Prison Service to explain. We only knew exactly what the treatment of and conditions for prisoners were like when we inspected.

It was also exemplified by two other experiences. When we inspected HMP Parkhurst on the Isle of Wight in November 2000, I asked the governor what was the aim of his prison. He replied, 'To save £500,000 from my budget in the remainder of the year.'

'That is not what I asked,' I responded. 'Why should a prisoner be sent to Parkhurst in particular and what are you expected to do with and for him?'

'It's all very well for you to ask that question,' he answered, 'but that's what my area manager says.'

Secondly, a comment from an annual report by the chairman of the

Board of Visitors at HMP and YOI Guys Marsh in Dorset, which held a mixture of adult and young offenders, stated:

> A recent Standards Audit rated Throughcare [the word used to describe all work done with prisoners] as 'Good', while Her Majesty's Chief Inspector of Prisons' (HMCIP) inspectors were very critical of it. In the Board's opinion HMCIP's views were and still remain closest to the truth. It is of interest that a senior member of staff has commented that it was as well that the Standards Audit Team focused on procedures and not on outcomes, or the results would have been very different.

My answer should have come as no surprise to Jack Straw if he had read my four annual reports, sent through him to Parliament, in each of which I had drawn attention to the difference. Perhaps he never read any of the reports. Certainly he never acknowledged or commented on them.

What had we been able to achieve over that past five and a half years that had convinced the Director General of the Prison Service that all was not well?

We had conducted 237 prison inspections, 112 of them unannounced, inspecting every prison in England, Wales and Northern Ireland at least once. Some reports received extensive publicity; some, particularly those with a good story to tell, went unreported.

Inspection reports, in addition to numerous and differing recommendations affecting each prison, also recorded over 2800 examples of good practice, covering every aspect of imprisonment. Many recommendations were that a particular prison should adopt an example of good practice found in another. Everything that we recommended was actually happening somewhere. We dealt in fact not theory. Since its management structure was not geared to initiating or supervising common practice, the Prison Service picked up and passed on about

70 of the 2800. Not every example of good practice applied to all categories of prison or prisoner. Senior managers, responsible for each type, could have extracted those that applied to their particular prisons and taken steps to see that good practice somewhere became common everywhere. That is how standards are driven up. With the exception of high security prisons, however, no one type of prison had such a responsible senior manager.

Senior management also appeared to fail to appreciate that every example of good practice stemmed from good work by officers and other members of the Prison Service. Human nature being what it is, people respond when their efforts are noticed and applauded by those in authority. By failing to acknowledge or take advantage of good work, managers were continuing the poor relationships with governors and staff that had drawn the opprobrium of Lord Woolf in his Strangeways report. Some of this work is picked up each year by the excellent Butler Trust award scheme, and the citations of all those who win an award are read out before they are presented by the Princess Royal, at Buckingham Palace, in front of their families and their prison governor. But this is not the same as receiving regular recognition from their own managers.

We also published nine thematic reviews of particular aspects of imprisonment, researched and written up by members of the Inspectorate, which I hoped might instigate improvement. The first, *Patient or Prisoner?*, published in November 1996, recommended that the National Health Service take over responsibility for Prison Service health care. The NHS assumed funding responsibility with effect from April 2003, so this could be said to have succeeded to some extent. The standard of health care provision has not yet reached equivalence with the NHS, but the situation is a great deal better than it was even though progress has taken an inordinate amount of time.

The second review, *Women in Prison*, was published in July 1997 with a follow-up in June 2001. It recommended that, first and foremost, one individual should be made responsible and accountable for the treatment and conditions of all women in prison. The Prison

Service appointed a director of policy, then a separate operational manager, then a second operational manager, but control is still vested in the Deputy Director who controls the managers' budget. Again, progress is painfully slow.

The third publication, *Young Prisoners*, concentrated on those between the ages of 15 and 21. Once more, it recommended that someone be made responsible and accountable for the treatment and conditions of all in this group. It also recommended that no children under the age of 18 should be held in Prison Service custody. The Prison Service is an adult service: holding children in adult conditions risks turning them into adult prisoners. If custody is required, it should be run by a separate organisation. The Youth Justice Board is now that separate organisation, and the Prison Service has recently appointed an operational manager to look after Prison Service establishments in which children alone are held. No one official is responsible or accountable for young offenders between the ages of 18 and 21, and the operational manager for juveniles has no responsibility for children held in establishments that house both age groups. This is a muddle still awaiting a solution.

The report on our unannounced inspection of Campsfield House detention centre, published in April 1998, was also a thematic review of the way in which asylum seekers and immigration detainees were held in Prison Service custody. It recommended that prison rules were inappropriate for those who had not committed or been charged with a crime. Following this, we worked closely with the Immigration Department to produce appropriate detention rules, based on UN rules. These have been published and now apply.

In February 1999 we published *Lifers*, produced jointly with the Probation Inspectorate. There are more life-sentenced prisoners in England and Wales than in the whole of Western Europe added together. Custody of the 4600 lifers then in prison was inconsistently conducted and poorly managed. The Lord Chief Justice complained to the Home Secretary that 60 per cent passed their parole or tariff date by at least a year, which was not to say that all of them should

automatically be released on time. Administrative incompetence was behind much of the expensive delay. The Director General acknowledged that our report enabled him to obtain additional financial resources from the Treasury – a classic example of how independent, objective and constructive reports should be used. The administration of lifers was reorganised, but still leaves much to be desired.

In May 1999 *Suicide is Everyone's Concern* appeared, updating my predecessor's report on the incidence of suicide. This was requested by the Prisons Minister, Joyce Quin, and the Director General, (Sir) Richard Tilt, in the light of an inexorable rise in the number of cases. The record level of suicide reached that year subsided slightly in 2001, but has now been exceeded yet again. No one can pretend that every suicide can be prevented, but it was quite clear that poor management had much to do with the problem. Untrained staff were not supervised and bad practice too often went unchecked. During our research, we learned that the number of suicides in prisons in the USA had been reduced dramatically following the introduction of a system based on the close personal interest of the responsible minister. I recommended its adoption in Britain, beginning with a ringing declaration from the Home Secretary that current numbers were unacceptable. The Director General announced that he would take personal charge of the issue, but proven American methods have not been introduced, managerial oversight has not improved and the numbers continue to rise.

Close Supervision Centres were discussed in Chapter Six. The report was published in February 2000.

The Criminal Justice System (CJS) is made up of a number of different agencies. Once the CJS had been given a common aim, the Chief Inspectors of Prisons, Probation, Social Services, the Constabulary, the Crown Prosecution Service and the Magistrates' Courts Service, began meeting together, unofficially but on a regular basis, to discuss issues that affected more than one. In June 2000 we published a joint thematic report, *Casework Information Needs within the Criminal Justice System*. Our thesis was that every arm of the CJS

needed information from the others in order to function effectively. Each of us listed the information required by the Service we inspected. We then researched whether it was available at all, available with difficulty, or not available. As anticipated, the Prison Service was surprised by the result because it had made no efforts to identify or rectify the common information problems faced by every prison. We hoped that our report, being signed by all six Chief Inspectors, might lead to both action and measurable improvement. However, no doubt because it was an unofficial initiative, lack of ministerial and official interest has led to yet another piece of work, designed to improve performance, gathering dust.

In December 2000 we published *Unjust Deserts*, a survey of the treatment of and conditions for unsentenced prisoners. Again, we were by no means the first to do this. The subject was raised by Lord Woolf after Strangeways, and improving treatment and conditions for this category of prisoner was a priority in the unactioned White Paper, *Custody, Care and Justice*. The National Association for the Care and Resettlement of Offenders (NACRO) published a full and perceptive report on the problem, and the Prison Service published what it called a 'Model Regime' for unsentenced prisoners. Nothing happened – as inspection reports continued to show. Remarkably and uniquely, Jack Straw asked to see me, with the Director General, to discuss the recommendations. He told us that he accepted them, including the suggestion for a two-year study of the problem leading up to an action plan. He told the Director General to prepare a bid for the Comprehensive Spending Review, to ensure that necessary additional funding would be made available. There has so far been no action plan or any extra money.

I planned three other reviews, two of which had to be left to my successor to publish. I temporarily suspended the third because of the opposition of the then Prisons Minister, Mr Paul Boateng.

All work done with and for prisoners amounts to preparation for their release. However, resettlement was inconsistent, uncontrolled,

and without operational supervision. No one ensured that plans were made for every prisoner. No one was responsible for ensuring that sufficient and suitable activities to facilitate preparation for release were present in every prison.

In May 2000, again with the Probation Inspectorate, we embarked on a thematic review of the issue of resettlement, which we called *Through the Prison Gate*. In June of that year members of the Cabinet Office Social Exclusion Unit visited me and told me that the Prime Minister was thinking of tasking them to look at the same subject. I welcomed this, suggesting that we work together – our detailed knowledge and fieldwork could help them, while the signature 'T. Blair' on a document was more likely to have an impact than one signed 'D. Ramsbotham' and 'G. Smith' (the Chief Inspector of Probation). We agreed that co-operation would not mean only one report, because each was writing for a different audience. The admirable Social Exclusion report, *Reducing Re-offending by Ex-prisoners*, published in July 2002, repeats and confirms all the points made by the Inspectorate over the years. *Through the Prison Gate* was published in December 2001. Practical results of the two reports have yet to be seen.

The Youth Justice Board asked us to report on education arrangements for children in Prison Service custody. This we did by inspecting every establishment in which children were held, together with our OFSTED (Office for Standards in Education) inspectors. *A Second Chance*, published in November 2001, went to the Department for Education and Skills, which had assumed responsibility for funding education in prisons in April of that year.

I would have liked to complete a further thematic review called *Inequalities* to address my deep concern about how five separate minority groups were treated in prison. This merited a different kind of study, working in concert with the statutory body responsible for their treatment in society. They would cover the legal and statutory responsibilities of the Prison Service, while we would do the fieldwork in prisons. The report would then be jointly written up. Issues

of race and cultural diversity were to be conducted jointly with the Commission for Racial Equality (CRE), those of gender and sexuality with the Equal Opportunities Commission. The mentally disordered would be studied in partnership with the NHS; the disabled with the Disablement Foundation, and I asked the Social Services to look at the treatment of the elderly. The director concerned, Mervyn Eastwood, produced a comprehensive and constructive report, which would have formed the basis of our recommendations. However, Mr Boateng suddenly announced that he did not want me to include race in the review. Following a murder at Feltham, that would be done by the CRE. In vain, Gurbax Singh, director of the CRE and I tried to convince the minister that the CRE, would have a far better idea about racism in general *after* our review than they would from investigating one racist murder in a prison. To exclude ethnic minorities from a study of the treatment of minority groups was clearly nonsensical, so I suspended the review. Mr Boateng left office in May 2001, but there was no time to resurrect the review before I retired.

There remained possibly the most important publication of all, which became mixed up in the charade surrounding my retirement. We had published the four aspects of the Healthy Prison concept in *Suicide is Everyone's Concern*, but inspectors also needed a guide-book on consistent quality assurance. Therefore, for four years we worked on *Expectations*, which, like so many initiatives, originated from Colin Allen.

When I took over as Chief Inspector I assumed that I would spend much time asking questions of inspectors. However, during my first week, a number of them came to see me separately to ask me *my* opinions about this or that aspect of imprisonment. Eventually I went to see Colin and told him how strange I found this, because I could only offer an uninformed view. At that, Colin smiled his marvellous smile, went to a cupboard, and produced a black folder that he gave me. During the interregnum between Stephen Tumim's departure at the end of September and my arrival, he had taken the inspectors away to

brainstorm what they thought they should look for during inspections. One by one they had been testing me out to see whether or not I was sound on what they had concluded. The conclusions were in the folder.

Gradually, over the next four years and with the help of many experts including experienced members of the Prison Service as well as prisoners and ex-prisoners, we produced a set of 'criteria for assessing the treatment of and conditions for prisoners'. These were listed by subject areas such as Arrival in Custody, Duty of Care, Activities and Resettlement, each of which was broken down into outcomes related to a Healthy Prison and a number of expectations. They could be 'picked and mixed' to suit different types of prison.

We field-trialled the criteria extensively as we developed them, finding them to be an invaluable guide to getting 'under the radar' of the culture of a prison. They were first used together in Wormwood Scrubs in 1999. We were all convinced of their validity, but amazed at how they improved the speed and depth of our ability to understand a prison, which was immediately reflected in our reports. The report on Wormwood Scrubs resulted in the Prime Minister requiring the Home Secretary to stand up in the House of Commons and explain why no action had been taken in connection with our previous recommendations over the past three years. There could have been no more dramatic confirmation of the value that the 'expectations' methodology added to the inspection process.

Naively, I had assumed that ministers and officials responsible for the conduct of imprisonment would welcome such an improvement to its quality assurance. I had mentioned it in annual reports, had briefed members of the European Commission, the Convention on the Prevention of Torture and Inhuman Treatment, and representatives of penal organisations from around the world whom I met at international conferences. All were interested and looked forward, as I did, to publication of our findings.

Colin, the team leaders and I briefed Jack Straw and Paul Boateng on its contents in January 2000. We confirmed that we were working with the Prison Service to ensure that there would be no confusion,

particularly in the minds of prison governors, that there was any difference between required and expected standards. In April 2000 I sent Jack Straw a copy of *Expectations* with a draft foreword that I hoped he would sign, thus adding credibility to the publication of what was a world first.

But, at the time, as it turned out, we were caught up in an elaborate charade. My contract as Chief Inspector was for 'five years in the first instance, extendable to up to eight years by mutual agreement'. On Wednesday, 29 March 2000, Sir David Omand, the Home Office Permanent Secretary, asked to see me. He handed me the draft of a letter from the Home Secretary to the chairman of the Home Affairs Select Committee saying that he had decided to renew my contract until the summer of 2001, while a merger of the posts of Chief Inspectors of Prisons and the Probation Service was under consideration. As there had been no mutual discussion, let alone mutual agreement, I asked to see Jack Straw before agreeing to anything.

On Monday 3 April, Richard Ford, home affairs correspondent of *The Times*, rang me to ask what was happening about my appointment. He said that he had been 'told by officials' that if he rang them last Wednesday, he would hear. However, they now said that they did not know. I at once complained to David Omand that these were his officials and that this was not how such matters were usually conducted. He denied responsibility, saying that he would try to arrange for the meeting that I had planned with Jack Straw to be brought forward to an earlier date than our diaries had shown to be possible.

On Wednesday 12 April, the first day that I was able to see Jack Straw, there was a short article in *The Times* headed 'Prison inspector faces role axe'. Again I remonstrated with David Omand. At our meeting, Jack Straw confirmed that he was thinking about a merger and asked me to give my views to the official nominated to conduct the study and to remain in post until the end of July 2001 when the merger, if agreed, would take place. In answer to my question about what would happen if the merger was not agreed, he said that he

would jump that particular hurdle when he came to it. We did not mention or discuss any three-year extension. He announced my acceptance of his request in the House of Commons on 9 June.

On Tuesday 14 November, while we were inspecting HMP Whitemoor, Jack Straw phoned me from his car. He told me that he had decided against the merger, asked whether I would like to see the announcement that he was going to make in the House that afternoon, and he said he would fax it to the prison. To my surprise, the last paragraph said that the two chief inspectors would be retiring in July, their posts advertised in January, and interviews held in April. I immediately rang his private secretary in the Home Office to say that I was quite happy about the announcement, with the exception of the last paragraph about which there had been no mutual discussion. The private secretary told me that I was too late, because the announcement had already been printed.

I should have expected nothing less because an unmarked envelope had been delivered to my office in June, containing a 'leaked' briefing from the Home Office to the Home Secretary, following the announcement of my extension until July. This said that I was known to be unhappy that I had not been offered a full three-year extension. Legal advice was that the government was under no obligation to give reasons either for extending or not extending the Chief Inspector's term of appointment, and it would be best to avoid doing so rather than offer reasons which could be challenged. Legal advice was also that 'we' should refer throughout to Sir David's 'appointment' rather than his 'contract'. Although, in the opinion of the legal advisers, a court or tribunal would be likely to find that Sir David's appointment was a contract of employment, their advice was that 'we' should not concede the point.

The only reason for this decision that I was able to extract from Jack Straw was that that's what he had decided! It was quite clear that he did not want me to remain in post any longer and there was no reason why he should, but mutual agreement would have been so much more straightforward.

When, by July 2000, I had had no reply to my April letter about *Expectations*, I sent Jack Straw another copy, suggesting that the earlier one might have been lost. He replied that he was waiting for the Prison Service to comment. In April 2001 he said he did not want *Expectations* to be published. When I asked to see him so that I could discuss this, he said that his diary commitments meant that he could not meet me until after the General Election. By law, no official reports may be published during a specified period immediately before a General Election. This meant that my final annual report had to wait until afterwards, by which time David Blunkett had taken over as Home Secretary. There was also a new Permanent Secretary, John Gieve, with whom I had an immensely positive and encouraging first meeting.

When the Inspectorate was originally formed, the Home Secretary wrote a foreword to the annual report. William (Lord) Whitelaw, introducing the first report, said:

> The establishment of an Inspectorate of Prisons, independent of the Prison Department, and the publication of its reports, are a vital part of the process of increasing public understanding of the prison system.
>
> HM Chief Inspector draws attention – quite rightly – to the serious implications of some of the major problems facing the Prison Service such as overcrowding, the poor quality of the regime in local prisons in particular and the maintenance of the prison estate. All are direct consequences of the mismatch between the demands made upon the Prison Service and the resources available to it: a mismatch which the Government has acknowledged and which it is the aim of Government policy to correct.

On the assumption that this was still the perceived view of the importance of the Inspectorate, I decided to publish *Expectations* as an annexe to my annual report. After all, this was a legal requirement of

Parliament, and *Expectations* had been promised to Parliament in previous annual reports. It had also been promised to the House of Commons Home Affairs Select Committee.

On receiving the annual report, David Blunkett at once wrote a most charming and appreciative letter that I immediately passed around the Inspectorate. Everyone was naturally delighted, not only by the recognition of all the hard work that they had put into its presentation and the trialling of *Expectations*, but because they had not been used to official thanks. But more was to come. The new minister, Beverley Hughes, also took the unprecedented step of writing a personal note to the journalists attending the launch of the annual report, commending its content to them.

Before retiring, I asked to see David Blunkett so that I could discuss the conclusions that I had come to from what I had learned over the past five and a half years and to express my hopes for the future. They were exactly the same hopes that I had expressed to his two predecessors. My hope for progress under David Blunkett's leadership was enhanced by what was almost his first act on taking over. He challenged the Director General about our most recent bad report on Feltham – the fourth in five years – asking why no remedial action had been taken for so long. If this was to be his form, the old practice of ignoring reports might at last be dead. Clearly, this Home Secretary was not prepared to preside over preventable failure. I wondered whether this would include paying attention to what had been pointed out by so many for so long.

At the end of our hour's discussion, attended by all his ministers and policy advisers, he said, 'I'm very disappointed.'

'Why?' I asked.

'Because I can find nothing to disagree with in what we have discussed over the past hour.'

Beverley Hughes came with me on my final visit to Feltham. Could this, too, mark a new era? Sadly, September 11th placed many other demands on the Home Office and the momentum of prison reform had to take second place.

There was, however, one other bar to progress, mentioned by Sir Raymond Lygo, that coloured much of what I had seen which also received criticism in the final Feltham report: successful implementation of any improvement strategy would be dependent on a dramatic improvement in industrial relations.

Prison officers top every survey of stressful employment. Equally, I suspect that they would top any list of the most imperfectly understood employment. Why should anyone want to spend their lives locking other people up? What can be purposeful or constructive about such work?

These questions hide a number of misconceptions. Virtually everyone has a prurient interest in crime, particularly violent crime, be it expressed by watching films or TV programmes, reading crime novels or devouring sensational media accounts of crimes, criminals and trials. Although a number of criminals have committed very serious crimes from which the public must be protected, the vast majority of those in our prisons are not violent. Many are themselves victims of economic circumstance, mental disorder, domestic or other violence, or a combination of these. The statistics of their deprivation are horrendous.

Some people have a similarly stereotyped image of a prison officer as an aggressive, stupid, loud-mouthed bully, little better than the prisoners whom he abuses. Again, that is very largely far from the truth. Many are drawn to their work by a desire to work with and for those less fortunate than themselves. The vast majority are caring people, committed to doing a good job on behalf of their fellow men and women. They join the Prison Service for a variety of reasons, including security and family tradition. Many are embarking on a second career after serving in the Armed Forces; some have worked with voluntary services overseas. There is no such thing as a stereotypical prison officer.

Any suspicion that prison officers had any resemblance to those portrayed in the TV series *Porridge* was banished during my very first

visit to a prison – Belmarsh – on my second day in office. While being shown round, I was introduced to a prison officer, who was about to retire after almost 30 years' service.

'What was the most satisfying moment in your career?' I asked.

'Six weeks ago, when we gave that man' (pointing to a prisoner operating an electric floor polisher) 'his certificates for reading and writing, and we taught him.'

Then there was the recipient of a certificate that I saw on the governor's desk during a later visit to the prison. The officer concerned had noticed that a particular prisoner had not joined the lunch queue. He went at once to his cell, where he was able to cut the prisoner down before he hanged himself.

However, these stories are in marked contrast to the attitude of a number – albeit fortunately diminishing – of officers who deliberately set out to disrupt the management of prisons or to inflict their own verbal and physical punishment on prisoners. Much of this was practised by members of the Prison Officers Association (POA), particularly members of its National Executive Committee (NEC).

The POA is often held up as one of the last bastions of unreconstructed Trades Unionism. I found it to be a rather sad organisation because many of the views expressed by its leadership did not represent those of the vast majority of its members. The POA consists of a number of prison committees, whose chairmen should enjoy a special relationship with the governor of their prison. In most cases this is constructive and professional. The governor consults the chairman about change as well as the running of the prison, and the chairman controls the militants by democratic means. However, in some prisons the relationship is confrontational. The fault is by no means always one sided – some governors are equivocal in their dealings with chairmen.

The NEC, which has a permanent secretary but whose chairman and members are elected, is the cause of much of the bad reputation. When I took over, both the chairman and the secretary were reasonable men, with whom I met regularly, and I was able to be quite open

and frank about the inspection process and what I was finding in prisons. However, reasonableness was not to the taste of the militants, who were in the majority on the NEC, and this chairman was voted out. In his place they elected someone with whom one could have a reasonable conversation one minute but who, at the drop of a hat, appeared to me to be able to become more militant than the militant.

In general, most militancy was to be found in old Victorian local prisons and large Young Offender Institutions. Some prison committees, such as those at Feltham, Glen Parva, Wandsworth and Wormwood Scrubs, positively revelled in their reputation for intransigence. The chairman of Feltham for many years boasted openly that he had destroyed governors, and would destroy anyone sent to govern while he was around. His inexcusable resistance to the occupation of the new Health Care Centre denied appropriate care for four years to what my Chief Medical Inspector, John Reed, described as the largest collection of seriously mentally disturbed adolescents that he had come across in his entire professional career.

The fundamental problem with the POA has been that too many members see militancy as the way to the NEC and so to power, whatever that means. Many prison officers joined the rival Prison Service Union (PSU) when the chairman of the Wormwood Scrubs POA committee, asked about his members who had just been charged with assaulting prisoners, declared publicly that 'prisoners were the scum of the earth'. Such sentiments are the antithesis of the Statement of Purpose of the Prison Service.

The election of the recently replaced chairman of the POA read like the death throes of a dying organisation. A militant, whom the Director General had removed from Feltham to enable progress, he was voted in by the narrowest of margins over two other candidates, in an overall turnout of only 30 per cent. The 10 per cent of the total membership that his vote represented fairly reflects the actual strength of the militants. His election was subsequently overturned.

Dealing with the POA has taken up far too much of prison governors' time, already eaten into by the demands of bureaucracy, and the

quality of industrial relations has in too many instances been lamentable. Responsible staff associations – including both the Prison Governors Association (PGA) and the POA – have an important part to play in determining the future. Much depends on the leadership of their chairmen. The public will not thank any of those paid to act in their name who oppose or inhibit measures for their protection.

I had had a fascinating and rewarding five and a half years and a unique opportunity to witness, at first hand, one of the most misunderstood public services in the country. I had grown to admire the professionalism and dedication of the large majority of those who worked in prisons. I had met a very large number of people from all walks of life who took an interest in, or worked in some way with, prisons or with prisoners. I had had the pleasure of working with an exceptional group of people, all of them friends, who had performed their public service with courage, humour and skill. Any frustration I felt was with those, in whose name all this was done, who appeared unable or unwilling to use constructively what was put in their way.

When I handed over to Anne Owers, I knew what needed to be done and had a pretty good idea about how it could be achieved. I hoped that ministers would listen to her. I had no doubt that she would soon be reporting exactly the same shortcomings to which Stephen Tumim and I had drawn attention because, unless there was sudden radical change, they would not have been eliminated. I wished her well and handed over the keys and the team.

Her Majesty the Queen granted her retiring Chief Inspector of Prisons an audience on the day I left office. It was a great pleasure to be able to tell her personally how well she was served by all those who had worked with and for me in her Inspectorate of Prisons.

13

IT HAS BEEN DONE

'It was a model of how a decent and humane prison system might operate.'

Dr Andrew Coyle, Director, International Centre for Prison Studies

DURING THE 1950s, CONCERNED AT adverse publicity about the number of political prisoners, the Polish government allowed groups of students to visit and talk to them in their prisons. One group member, Pawel Moczydlowski, became a professor at Warsaw University, from where he was a loud and persistent critic of prison conditions. So loud and persistent that from 1982 onwards he was banned from entering any prison.

The ban prevailed until April 1990 when the new Solidarity government called his bluff, as it were, by suddenly appointing him Director General of the Polish Prison Service. At the time, in his own words:

> The social and living conditions of prisoners, and conditions affecting their health were poor; cells were overcrowded and often insufficiently heated; prisoners' clothing was largely worn out; food rations were too low and prisoners complained about the quality of food; about

30 per cent of the convict's working time was lost through illness; there were many accidents at work; medical care was inadequate; prisoners' leisure-time was curtailed and many premises meant for education and relaxation were done away with.

In 1981 there had been prisoner protests in 116 of Poland's 146 prisons. There were between 1000 and 1600 escape attempts every year. Prison officers were a highly dissatisfied group, who felt isolated from the public. Staff–prisoner relationships were poor. Discipline was arbitrary and brutality a common feature. Throughout the communist era, the Ministry of Justice ran prisons on military lines.

By the time that he retired in 1996, Pawel had totally transformed the situation. Dr Andrew Coyle, the well-known, highly respected and internationally recognised founder and director of the International Centre for Prison Studies at King's College London and a former governor of Brixton prison, has visited Poland on a number of occasions. Of Pawel's achievements he wrote, 'For a few years during the last decade of the 20th century the Polish prison system shone as a beacon. It was a model of how a decent and humane prison system might operate not only for the countries to its east but also for those in Western Europe.'

What had Pawel Moczydlowski done and how had he done it?

He had a crystal-clear vision of what he wanted to achieve, which he called a culture of 'social re-adaptation' or the preparation of prisoners to return to society and not re-offend. This required prisoners to be treated decently and humanely by staff, and able to maintain and develop links with family and friends. He was entirely confident that this could be done without sacrificing good order in prisons, or endangering public security. The key was to obtain the co-operation of staff and prisoners.

Pawel made arrangements for the early retirement of the many staff who, having grown used to a very different agenda, found it extremely difficult to adapt to the new requirements – only 55 per

cent were still in post by 1992. Those who remained were left in no doubt that refusal to work according to the new direction was not an option. They worked alongside those he recruited and trained.

Furthermore, he reduced the numbers in Headquarters from over 3000 to only 1180 and grouped prisons into 16 geographical regions. The director of the largest was made responsible for allocating prisoners to other prisons in a region. Senior staff, whom he selected and educated, were responsible for laying down what should happen in each prison, prison governors for how it happened.

Every prisoner was treated as an individual, each sentence as an individual case. Separate case managers of about 50 prisoners would meet with psychologists, educationalists and others, to consider individual sentence management issues. An essential element of social re-adaptation was the maintenance of links with families and the outside world. All prisoners who were eligible and whose behaviour was satisfactory were entitled to family and conjugal visits and home leave. Families were encouraged to come into prison to discuss a prisoner's progress. Links between prisons and the wider community included the employment of civilians, who worked alongside prisoners, by firms who brought industries into prisons. He instigated the widespread practice of bringing in theatre and music groups.

When I met Pawel in Warsaw in September 2002, he admitted that he had been fortunate to be given the opportunity of introducing all this at a time of great change in Poland. He had not set out to reduce re-offending but to introduce decent and humane treatment of and conditions for prisoners. Throughout his period in office there were no embarrassing incidents, riots, escapes or scandals, other than initial unrest among some prisoners who had become so used to the old regime that they, like some staff, could not adapt to change. Thanks to the success of his methods, he enjoyed the confidence of government and freedom from media interest.

Regrettably, this welcome regime was not to last. Andrew Coyle has written about what happened after Pawel returned to his old post at Warsaw University after five years:

Sadly, as both it [Pawel's decent and humane prison system] and the country in general have been drawn more into the orbit of Western Europe, the prison system has begun to take on many of the less attractive characteristics of its Western European counterparts. Significant increases in the prison population have led to levels of overcrowding reminiscent of the days of the Warsaw Pact. Western models of centralised prison management have all but obliterated the style of regional management partnerships that existed in the 1990s.

It will take a brave government to appoint a Pawel Moczydlowski to do the same in the United Kingdom, despite Parliament having agreed a similar vision 12 years ago and its advocacy by successive Chief Inspectors of Prisons and many others. Winston Churchill would have rued such woeful lack of national inner strength. He would have appointed a Pawel.

14

LOOKING FORWARD:
IT CAN BE DONE

SHORTLY BEFORE I RETIRED FROM the post of Her Majesty's Chief Inspector of Prisons at the end of July 2001, I was invited by the Prison Reform Trust, chaired by Lord Hurd, to give a farewell lecture in which I could account for my time and outline my hopes for the future.

As I was writing the script my wife, Sue, slapped a piece of paper on my desk on which was written:

> If Prison Worked – there would be work or education for every prisoner.
> If Prison Worked – we would be shutting prisons not opening more.
> If Prison Worked –judges would not be seeing in the dock the same people over and over again.
> If Prison Worked – we would not be imprisoning more people than any other European country except Turkey.
> If Prison Worked – less children would be in care and less mothers in prison.

If Prison Worked – we would be saving billions of pounds
with less prisons, less care homes and fewer court cases.

She is absolutely right.

Alas, as the previous pages will have indicated, prison is not working as well as it could and should do. It is not working in its own right,
nor is it working as a part of the Criminal Justice System. That is not
to say that much good work is not going on in prisons, or that there
are not a large number of people dedicated to doing all they can with
and for prisoners. But the high re-offending rate reflects the failure of
the prison system.

Some people will always believe that harsh punishment deters
crime. Others will maintain that cruelty and harshness only breeds
cruelty and harshness. They will argue that criminals may be deterred
from further crime by being given the means by which to make an
honest living; and sufficient self-esteem to convince them that they
can do so. The majority will remain neutral until something drives
them into either camp. Few people who have worked with prisoners
believe that, however unpleasant the conditions and however harsh the
treatment, prison deters those who are determined on crime.
Deterrence is more of a pious hope in the minds of those who live
reasonably pleasant day-to-day lives than a practical reality. Fear of
imprisonment may deter those who have a job, a home and a family,
but not those who have no hope of achieving or retaining them.

Almost all prisoners will come out of prison. How they then
behave will depend on how successfully they are rehabilitated back
into society. Imprisonment, as currently conducted, is failing both its
prisoners and the public that it is required to protect. Rehabilitation
protects the public; re-offending does not.

In the previous chapters I have tried to describe some of the reasons
why imprisonment, as currently conducted, is not working, in an
attempt to answer at least some of the question 'why?' The inevitable
supplementary is 'So What?' Should those responsible wring their
hands, say it is all too difficult and do nothing? Should they go on as

at present, merely tinkering at the edges of what is wrong? Or should they refuse to accept the situation and determine to make it work? That would be my course of action if I were in their position. How could it be done?

Anyone publicly recommending reform – or improvement in performance – should be certain that it can be achieved. Certainty requires that a number of preconditions be satisfied. Any recommendation must be in line with the operational purpose of the organisation. The organisation must have a management structure that is capable of directing and monitoring the improvements. Sufficient human, physical and financial resources must be available. Above all there must be a will to match the need for reform.

To date there is no clearly laid-down operational purpose. The present management structure has proved that it is not capable of directing or monitoring major and consistent improvement. Human and physical resources are insufficient. There is so much waste in prison organisation that it is impossible to know whether or not adequate financial resources are available. The will to reform imprisonment appeared to be lacking.

In putting forward a vision of how imprisonment might be better conducted in this country, I have one overwhelming advantage. My inspectors and I saw everything that I think should be happening with and for prisoners actually working now, in a prison, somewhere in the United Kingdom. The tragedy – indeed the principal indictment of the current system – is that it is not working everywhere all the time.

Achievement of my vision for the future requires, first of all, an explanation from Prime Minister Blair. What exactly did he mean when he pledged to be 'tough on crime and tough on the causes of crime'. He cannot have been uttering a rallying call to the Criminal Justice System to be more efficient, because that has no control over the causes of crime. Was it therefore a rallying call to society? If so, then society has every right to expect the Criminal Justice System to be tough on crime while it tackles the causes.

The aim of the Criminal Justice System – to protect the public by preventing crime – is also a rallying call to society. The factors that contribute to crime – poverty, unemployment and social neglect – are easier to talk about than to address. Their resolution, or at least amelioration, are also essential factors in society's ability to prevent crime. The Criminal Justice System ought, in the way that it punishes criminals and administers punishment, aim to prevent their next crime. Or, as put so succinctly in the motto of Her Majesty's Young Offender Institution Lancaster Farms, 'Prevent the next Victim'.

Based on that aim, it is very easy for those responsible for the Criminal Justice System to give the various parts of the system, separately and collectively, clear direction on their contribution to its achievement. Her Majesty's Prison and National Probation Services, the two organisations most concerned with the treatment of those sentenced by the courts, should be given the same aim – to protect the public by preventing re-offending. Each will then have to work out their strategy for achieving the aim. This will require them to carry out the sort of appreciation I outlined in Chapter Four.

The aim decided, the first factor to be considered in a military appreciation is ground. In the case of prisons that is prisoners. Prisons exist to hold prisoners. The Prison Service has a duty to help prisoners live useful and law-abiding lives in prison and on release. In doing so it must ensure that prisoners do not escape from custody for the period ordered by the courts. All prisoners must be treated with humanity. That is what the Prison Service Statement of Purpose lays down.

Some of the other factors affecting the aim are in the gift of the Prison Service, some are not. It has no control over the numbers of people sent to prison, or the crimes that they have committed. It does, however, have total control over the determination and delivery of what treatment they need and the conditions in which they are held while in prison. It has no control over how much money it is given to carry out its task. But it *is* responsible for informing ministers how much it needs to carry out the aim. It is also responsible for

telling ministers what it cannot do if sufficient funding is not made available.

The Prison Service requires sufficient prisons to hold all the different categories and types of prisoner given to their charge. It also requires enough staff to keep them securely, assess them, and provide what treatment they need to prevent them from re-offending and to manage imprisonment. Governors are the key people in this. They, too, need direction and appropriate resources for treating the prisoners for whom they are responsible. They must be carefully selected and trained for their task.

Imprisonment requires a Headquarters that is designed to help governors govern their prisons, providing them with clear and consistent direction and adequate resources. Each type of prison – local, high security, training, resettlement, women's and young offenders – has a different task and needs separate direction. Each needs a director – a senior manager responsible and accountable for overseeing the work of each type. Directors ought to be responsible for providing governors with direction that includes budgetary provision, supervision of treatment and conditions of prisoners, including availability of courses, selection and training of staff, circulation of good practice and, above all, ensuring consistency of provision for prisoners in each prison. Each will need suitable supporting staff, including training and monitoring teams to ensure that standards are not allowed to slip. All directors ought to be accountable to one responsible Prisons Board member.

In implementing this, the opportunity ought to be taken to examine the fault line that has existed since 1877, when the treatment of unsentenced and short-term prisoners was nationalised with that of long-term, under the Prison Commission. Prison administrations in Canada and the United States keep long-term prisoners in federal prisons; the remainder in state, province, county or city prisons. Attempts to compromise over the satisfaction of their separate needs have been the root cause of much of the failure of the prison system since 1877. What has happened in the intervening 126 years should be

regarded as a learning experience. There is no reason why the two types of prisoner should not be looked after differently. The managerial arrangements I suggest would allow this to happen.

Geographically, prisons ought to be grouped into community clusters as advocated by Lord Woolf, with each cluster including sufficient prison places to hold all types of prisoner in their own Criminal Justice area. High security prisons would remain the one exception. There are not enough high-risk prisoners to justify more than a small number of those.

Each Criminal Justice area should have its own Prison Service area manager, responsible for ensuring that every prison in the area is provided with the facilities it needs to carry out its role. Facilities include health care, education, work for prisoners, drug treatment programmes, resettlement programmes, liaison with the voluntary sector, links with other Criminal Justice System agencies, and staff recruitment. These ought to come from local providers to ensure that they are appropriate for the geographical area. All area managers ought to be accountable to a senior manager with a seat on the Prisons Board.

This management structure would look like a matrix, with prisons in the centre. All prison governors would be accountable upwards, to a director responsible for their type of prison, and responsible downwards for the treatment of and conditions for all prisoners in their establishment. Governors would be able to call on an accountable geographical area manager, responsible for ensuring that appropriate support is provided to their prison.

Ministers have to fight for resources. In order to know what resources are needed, they must be able to measure the success or failure of whatever they are responsible for so as to identify shortfalls. If the aim of the Prison Service is to prevent re-offending, the reasons why prisoners re-offend must be identified. Did a prisoner attend an offending behaviour course? If so, when and where? Was it followed up by a booster or relapse prevention course? If so, when and where? Was the prisoner prepared for release? What happened after release? These, and many other questions, can only be answered with the help

and co-operation of all Criminal Justice agencies. Unless strenuous and sustained efforts are made to gather and analyse such information, re-offending will remain as it is now – the vital factor that is imperfectly understood. Prison will continue not to work.

Such a system does not require a totally new approach. All the information and all the advice is there already, spelled out in reports that ministers have called for, inspection reports, reports of numerous penal reformers, and consistent observation by many experienced, caring and interested people. The one thing all of them have in common is that little or nothing has been done to put their recommendations into effect. That is why prisons continue to fail.

Without a framework within which prison can be made to work, and a vision of how it should work, expensive, avoidable muddle will continue to be the best description of the administration of imprisonment. This is as true now as it was when the reports, mentioned earlier, were written.

Examination of how to make prison work ought to begin by ignoring all the tinkering of the past 12 years and returning to the impetus for change, begun after the worst riots in prison history in 1990, as follows:

1. Resurrect *Custody, Care and Justice*, already agreed to by all political parties in Parliament as the way ahead for the Prison Service in the twenty-first century. Action the ten hitherto ignored priorities.

2. Resurrect the report on management written by Sir Raymond Lygo, accepted by a previous Home Secretary. Action the recommendations.

3. Examine the comments and recommendations made in 18 annual reports and countless inspection reports and thematic reviews, by successive Chief Inspectors of Prisons. Extract best practice for each type of prison and make it common. Eliminate poor management practice.

4. Make the Prison Service a true agency, accountable to the Home Office but not subject to the minutiae of day-to-day interference. Ministerial direction can be passed down through the Corrections Board.

5. Regard prisons as operational units that require operational leadership and adjust management style accordingly. Abandon the cult of managerialism, set meaningful targets and release governors from 'the confetti of instructions'.

All the players are in place. All the evidence is there. All that is lacking is the political will to make it happen.

The Criminal Justice System is currently on the receiving end of a confetti of initiatives. In themselves, they are designed to improve the performance of one or other of its agencies, but their impact on other agencies, particularly the Prison Service, is frequently ignored. The inexorable rise in prisoner numbers is as much due to sentencing and policing initiatives as any factor other than the crime rate.

Prison is expensive but so is crime caused by released prisoners who re-offend. This begs the question of affordability. Can the country afford the cost of imprisonment? It has to afford the cost of keeping in prison those sentenced by the courts. But can it afford not to ensure that offending and anti-social behaviour is identified and challenged and prisoners helped to lead useful and law-abiding lives?

Alternatives to custody in the form of community sentences are not working either. They are frequently held up as being more suitable for many of those now in prison but, at present, public confidence in them is sadly lacking. Their re-offending rates are almost exactly the same as those of more expensive imprisonment. Community sentences ought to improve if due attention is paid to recommendations that will be put forward in the report following an admirable initiative of the Esmee Fairbairn Foundation, entitled *Rethinking Crime and Punishment.*

My vision is completed by two other recommended changes.

The time has now come to appoint a Minister of Justice, responsible for co-ordinating the administration of justice. Too many

different ministers are responsible for different aspects of the administration of imprisonment. Inevitably, cracks exist between their responsibilities, through which too many problems fall. In the interests of simplicity, responsibility and accountability one person ought to be in charge.

Secondly, we should see the reinstatement of a former practice, currently used only in Western Australia, where the responsible minister is required to produce a written response to every report of the Chief Inspector of Prisons. This should include comment on the report as a whole and description of the action that is to be taken, which would be subject to regular review and update. This would mark a return to the Home Secretary's practice when HM Inspectorate of Prisons was first formed.

Society has a right to expect prison to work. I do not pretend that the solutions I advocate will be easy to achieve. But they will enable prison to be made to work as well as possible for those for whom it is deemed an appropriate punishment.

It *can* be done.

NOTES

CHAPTER 3: HM INSPECTORATE OF PRISONS

49 Act Elizabeth II, c.52 s.5A(5), 1952.

51 John Howard, *The State of the Prisons in England and Wales*, Wm Eyres, Warrington, 1777.

52 5&6 William IV c.38, 1835.

52 *House of Lords Report of Select Committee on Gaols*, Parliamentary Papers 1863, Vol. 56.

53 *Report of the Departmental Committee on Prisons*, Parliamentary Papers 1895, Vol. 56.

54 *House of Commons 15th Report from the Expenditure Committee, Reduction of Pressure on the Prison System*, Vol. 1, HMSO, London, 1978

54 *Report of the Committee of Inquiry into the United Kingdom Prison Services* (Chairman Mr Justice May), Cmnd 7673, HMSO, London, 1979.

54 *Ibid.*

55 Eric Stockdale, 'A Short History of Prison Inspection in England', *British Journal of Criminology*, Vol. 23, No. 3, July 1983.

66 *House of Commons Official Report*, 20 July 1910, Column 1354.

CHAPTER 4: THE CONDUCT OF IMPRISONMENT

74 *Report of the Committee of Inquiry into Prison Disturbances April 1990*, Cmnd 1456, HMSO, London, February 1991.

75 *Report of the Committee of Inquiry into the United Kingdom Prison Services*, 1979.

77 Sir Raymond Lygo, *Prison Service Management Review*, HMSO, London, December 1991.

78–9 *Custody, Care and Justice: The Way Ahead for the Prison Service in England and Wales*, Cmnd 1647, HMSO, London, September 1991.

CHAPTER 8: RESETTLEMENT PRISONS

147 *Report by the Controller and Auditor General on Reducing Prisoner Re-offending*, HC 548 Session 2001-02, The Stationery Office, London, 31 January 2002.

147 *Report by the Social Exclusion Unit on 'Reducing Re-offending by ex-Prisoners'*, London, July 2002.

CHAPTER 9: THE BLANTYRE HOUSE RAID

163 *Private Eye*, 27 December 2002.

164 Sir Stephen Tumin, quoted in *House of Commons Home Affairs Select Committee, 4th Report, Session 1999–2000*, The Stationery Office, London, 9 November 2000.

164 *Report of an Unannounced Inspection of HMP Blantyre House, 3–4 March 1997*, by HM Chief Inspector of Prisons for England and Wales, Home Office, London, 14 October 1997.

164 Martin Narey, quoted in *House of Commons Home Affairs Select Committee* 9 November 2000.

164–5 *Report of an Unannounced Inspection of HMP Blantyne House*, 14 October 1997.

166 *Report on HMP Blantyre House*, by HM Chief Inspector of Prisons for England and Wales, Home Office, London, January 2000.

170 *Quoted in House of Commons Home Affairs Select Committee, 4th Report, Session 1999–2000*.

172 *Ibid.*

CHAPTER 10: THE WERRINGTON EXPERIENCE

179 *House of Commons 1st Report of the Children's Employment Commission*, 1842.

181 John Hoskisson, *Inside: One Man's Experience of Prison*, John Murray, 1998.

198 Arthur Bryant, *The Search for Justice*, Vol. 3 of *A History of Britain and the British Empire*, Collins, 1990.

CHAPTER 11: WOMEN IN PRISONS

199–200 *A Follow-up to Women in Prison: A Thematic Review* by HM Chief Inspector of Prisons for England and Wales, Home Office, London, June 2001.

203 Paul Rock, *Reconstructing a Women's Prison: The Holloway Redevelopment Project 1968–88*, Clarendon Studies in Criminology, Oxford 1996.

203–04 *Report on HM Prison Holloway*, by HM Chief Inspector of Prisons for England and Wales, Home Office, London, 1984.

206 Rock, *Reconstructing a Women's Prison*.

210 Stephen Pryor, *The Responsible Prisoner: An Exploration of the Extent to which Imprisonment Removes Responsibility Unnecessarily*, Home Office, London, 2001.

CHAPTER 12: LOOKING BACK

214–15 Martin Narey, Address to Prison Service Conference 2001, *HMP Review*, London, Spring 2001.

219 *Annual Report of Chairman of Board of Visitors of HMP and YOI Guys Marsh, 1999–2000*, Home Office, London, 2000.

CHAPTER 13: IT HAS BEEN DONE

235–36 Pawel Moczydlowski, *The Hidden Life of Polish Prisons*, Indiana University Press, Bloomington and Indianapolis, 1992.

236 Andrew Coyle, *Managing Prisons in a Time of Change*, International Centre for Prison Studies, London, 2002.

238 *Ibid.*

BIBLIOGRAPHY

Brodie, Allan; Jane Croom and James O'Davies, *Behind Bars: The Hidden Architecture of England's Prisons,* English Heritage, Swindon, 1999.

Bryan, Shane and David Wilson, 'Prison Governors, Theory and Practice', *Prison Service Journal,* 1999.

Bryan, Shane; Clive Martin and Roma Walker eds. *A Bridge into the Community: Prisons and the Voluntary Sector,* Waterside Press, Winchester, 2002.

Carlen, Pat, ed. *Women and Punishment,* Willan, Cullompton, Devon, 2002.

Church House Publishing, *Prisons: A Study in Vulnerability,* London 2000.

Coyle, Andrew, *The Prisons We Deserve,* Harper Collins, London, 1994.
Managing Prisons in a Time of Change, International Centre for Prison Studies, London, 2003.

Creesey, Richard, W.F. Bynum, and J. Bean, eds. *The Health of Prisoners,* Wellcome Trust, London, 1995.

Devlin, Angela and Bob Turney, *Going Straight,* Waterside Press, Winchester, 1999.

Dunbar, Ian and Anthony Langdon, *Tough Justice: Sentencing and Penal Policies in the 1990s,* Blackstone Press, London, 1998.

Fairweather, Leslie and Sean McConville, eds. *Prison Architecture, Policy Design and Experience,* Architectural Press, Oxford, 2000.

Faulkner, David, *Crime, State and Citizen,* Waterside Press, Winchester, 2001.

Flynn, Nick, *Introduction to Prisons and Imprisonment*, Waterside Press, Winchester, 1998.

Genders, E and E. Player, *Grendon: A Study of a Therapeutic Prison*, Clarendon Studies in Criminology, Oxford, 1995.

Gordon, Winston, Philip Cuddy, and Jonathan Black, *Introduction to Youth Justice*, Waterside Press, Winchester, 1999.

Graef, Roger, *Living Dangerously*, HarperCollins, London, 1993.
Why Restorative Justice?, Calouste Gulbenkian Foundation, London, 2002.

Gravett, Steve, *Coping with Prison*, Cassels, London, 1997.

Howard, John, *The State of the Prisons in England and Wales*, Wm. Eyres, Warrington, 1777.

Ireland, Jane L., *Bullying Among Prisoners*, Brunner-Routledge, Hove, 2002.

Harding, Richard, *Private Prisons and Public Accountability*, Open University Press, Birmingham, 1997.

Hibbert, Christopher, *The Roots of Evil*, Wiedenfeld and Nicolson, 1983.

Hoskison, John, *Inside*, John Murray, London, 1998.

Jones, Christopher and Peter Sedgwick, eds. *The Future of Criminal Justice*, SPCK, London 2002.

Liebling, Alison and David Price, *Prison Officer*, Prison Service Journal, 2001.

Liebling, Alison, ed. *Deaths of Offenders*, Waterside Press, Winchester, 1998.

Martin, Carl and Elaine Player, *Drug Treatment in Prisons*, Waterside Press, Winchester 2000.

Mathieson, Thomas, *Prison on Trial*, (2nd edition), Waterside Press, Winchester, 2000.

Medlicott, Diana, *Surviving the Prison Place: Narratives of Suicidal Prisoners*, Ashgate, Aldershot, 2001.

Mocydlowski, Pawel, *The Hidden Life of Polish Prisons*, Indiana University Press, 1992.

Morris, Norval and David J. Rothman, eds. *The Oxford History of the Prison*, Oxford University Press, 1995.

Murray, Charles, *Does Prison Work?*, Institute of Economic Affairs Health and Welfare Unit, 1997.

Newell, Tim, *Forgiving Justice*, Quaker Home Service, 2000.

Neustatter, Angela, *Locked In, Locked Out*, Calouste Gulbenkian Foundation, London, 2002.

Reynolds, Jack and Ursula Smartt, eds. *Prison Policy and Practice*, Prison Service Journal, 1996.

Roberts, Julian and Mike Hough, eds. *Changing Attitudes to Punishment: Public Opinion, Crime and Justice*, Willan Publishing, Devon 2002.

Rock, Paul, *Reconstructing a Women's Prison*, Clarendon Studies in Criminology, Oxford, 1996.

Rose, Jim, *Working with Young People in Secure Accommodation: From Chaos to Culture*, Brunner-Routledge, Hove, 2002.

Rutherford, Andrew, *Transforming Criminal Policy*, Waterside Press, Winchester, 1996.

Shannon, Tom and Christopher Morgan, *Invisible Crying Tree*, Doubleday, London, 1996.

Smartt, Ursula, *Grendon Tales*, Waterside Press, Winchester, 2001.

Stern, Vivien, *Bricks of Shame*, Penguin, 1987.

Stockdale, Eric, 'A Short History of Prison Inspection in England', *British Journal of Criminology*, Vol 23, No 3, 1983.

Towl, Graham, Louisa Snow, and Martin McHugh, eds. *Suicide in Prisons*, The British Psychological Society, Leicester, 2000.

West, Tessa, *Prisons of Promise*, Waterside Press, Winchester, 1997.

Williams, Jessica, ed. *Life Within Hidden Worlds: Psychotherapy in Prisons*, Karnac Books, London and New York, 2001.

Wilson, David and Anne Reuss, *Prisoner Education*, Waterside Press, Winchester, 2000.

Windlesham, Lord, *Responses to Crime, Volume 2*, Oxford University Press, 1993.

Reports from HMSO, London

Report of the Committee of Inquiry into the United Kingdom Prison Services, Report Chairman Mr Justice May, Cmnd 7673, 1979.

Report of the Committee of Inquiry into Prison Disturbances April 1990, by Lord Justice Woolf and Judge Stephen Tumim, Cmnd 1456, February 1991.

Custody, Care and Justice, the Way Ahead for the Prison Service in England and Wales, Cmnd 1647, September 1991.

Prison Service Management Review by Sir Raymond Lygo, December 1991.

Review of Prison Service Security and the Escape from Parkhurst Prison, by General Sir John Learmont, Cmnd 3020, October 1995.

Report by the Controller and Auditor General on Reducing Prisoner Re-offending, 31 January 2002.

Report by the Social Exclusion Unit on Reducing Re-offending by Ex-prisoners, July 2002.

House of Commons Home Affairs Committee, 4th Report Session 1999-2000, 9 November 2000.

Reports from HM Inspectorate of Prisons

Reports of announced or unannounced inspections of all prisons in England, Wales and Northern Ireland, December 1995 – July 2001.

Annual Report to Parliament, April 1995 – March 1996, 13 November 1996.

Annual Report to Parliament April 1996 – November 1997, 23 June 1998.

Annual Report to Parliament December 1997 – November 1998, 13 April 1999.

Annual Report to Parliament December 1998 – November 1999, 13 June 2000.

Annual Report to Parliament December 1999 – December 2000, 17 July 2001.

Patient or Prisoner? A new strategy for health care in prisons. Discussion Paper. 25 October 1995.

Women in Prison: A Thematic Review, 17 July 1997.

Young Prisoners: A Thematic Review, October 1997.

Suicide is Everyone's Concern: A Thematic Review, May 1999.

Inspection of Close Supervision Centres, August-September 1999, 22 March 2000.

Lifers, A Joint Thematic Review by Her Majesty's Inspectorates of Prisons and Probation, 1999.

HM Inspectorate of Prisons Strategic Plan, Balancing the Interests of Prisoners and the Public, 1999-2002.

Casework Information Needs within the Criminal Justice System, A Review by HM Inspectorates of Constabulary, the Crown Prosecution Service, Magistrates Courts Service, Prisons, Probation Service and Social Services, June 2000.

Unjust Deserts, A Thematic Review of the Treatment and Conditions for Unsentenced Prisoners in England and Wales. December 2000.

Follow-up to Women in Prison, A Thematic Review, July 2001.

A Second Chance: A Joint Review of the Education of Juveniles with the Office of Standards in Education, November 2001

Through the Prison Gate: A Joint Thematic Review by HM Inspectorates of Prisons and Probation, December 2001.

INDEX